Three Russian Tales of the Eighteenth Century

Three Russian Tales

of the EIGHTEENTH CENTURY

The Comely Cook, Vanka Kain, and "Poor Liza"

Mikhail Chulkov, Matvei Komarov, and Nikolai Karamzin

TRANSLATED AND WITH AN INTRODUCTION

BY DAVID GASPERETTI

NIU PRESS

DeKalb, IL

Published by the Northern Illinois University Press, DeKalb, Illinois 60115
Manufactured in the United States using acid-free paper
All Rights Reserved
Design by Shaun Allshouse

Jacket illustration courtesy of the Lilly Library, Indiana University,
Bloomington, Indiana

Library of Congress Cataloging-in-Publication Data
Three Russian tales of the eighteenth century : The Comely Cook,
Vanka Kain, and "Poor Liza" / Mikhail Chulkov, Matvei Komarov, and Nikolai
Karamzin ; translated and with an introduction by David Gasperetti.
pages ; cm
Includes bibliographical references.
ISBN 978-0-87580-674-7 (paperback : alkaline paper) — ISBN 978-1-
60909-031-9 (e-book)
I. Gasperetti, David Wayne, 1952–, translator, writer of added commentary.
II. 880-01 Chulkov, Mikhail Dmitrievich, 1740–1793. Prigozhaia povarikha.
English. III. 880-02 M. K. (Matvei Komarov). Obstoiatel'noe i viernoe opisan-
ie dobrykh i zlykh diel Rossiiskago moshennika, vora, razboinika i byvshago
Moskovskago syshchika Van'ki Kaina. English. IV. 880-03 Karamzin, Nikolai
Mikhailovich, 1766–1826. Bednaia Liza. English. 2012.
PG3213.T47 2012   891.73'208—dc23
2011047289

CONTENTS

Notes on the Text   vii

Acknowledgments   xi

INTRODUCTION

Mikhail Chulkov, Matvei Komarov, Nikolai Karamzin,
and Eighteenth-Century Russian Literary Culture

by David Gasperetti   3

THE COMELY COOK (1770)

by Mikhail Chulkov   54

VANKA KAIN (1779)

by Matvei Komarov   109

"POOR LIZA" (1792)

by Nikolai Karamzin   179

Appendix A

Michurin's Map of the City of Moscow, 1739   197

Appendix B

Monetary Values in Eighteenth-Century Russia   199

Notes   201

Works Cited   233

NOTES ON THE TEXT

The Source Texts

The three works in this collection have been translated from the first edition of each tale in order to keep the English version as close to the author's original intent as possible. Since *The Comely Cook* was issued just once in the eighteenth century, selecting an edition for this work became a moot point. With some modification, the same could be said about *Vanka Kain*, even though it went through numerous printings in the late 1700s. Given all the resources available to me—three eighteenth-century editions of the novel and various scholarly commentaries—it appears that Komarov did not revise his original text, so, as with *The Comely Cook*, there was no need to select one version over another. In the end, legibility became the paramount concern. The first two printings of *Vanka Kain* were issued in 1779: both contained identical prefaces and narratives of Kain's life, but they had different titles reflecting the extra material—forty-seven songs as well as another translator's version of the adventures of the French outlaw Cartouche (Louis Dominique Bourguignon)—appended to the second printing. Since there is no compelling reason to incorporate into this collection either the songs (which have virtually no bearing on Kain's story) or the tale of Cartouche (which is itself a Russian translation of a German translation of the original French), I have used the title and confined myself to the content of the first printing of *Vanka Kain*. The second printing, however, served as my source text, since it provided a far more legible copy of Komarov's novel than the first one, which was available only in a severely water-damaged version.

"Poor Liza" is different from the other two texts in this collection in that Karamzin did make slight changes to it during his lifetime. I have chosen, however, to translate the original version for two reasons.

First, the 1792 printing presents the tale exactly as it was when it became a literary and cultural sensation in Russia and helped to catapult Karamzin into the first rank of Russian writers. Second, in later editions, some of the hallmarks of Karamzin's Sentimentalist style (for instance, exclamation points and italics) were slightly reduced (Hammarberg xii). Since one goal of this project is to capture the defining features of each text and the period in which it was written, I have chosen to translate the most overtly Sentimentalist version of the story.

Formatting/Style

A guiding principle of this collection is to retain both the look and style of the three Russian texts as much as possible without sacrificing clarity and readability. Perhaps the most striking divergence between contemporary norms of formatting and the look of the three eighteenth-century Russian tales in this collection concerns the structuring of paragraphs. Many of them, especially in *Vanka Kain*, cover pages at a time, and dialogue is generally not set off from the narrative context by discrete paragraph breaks. Although reproducing these traits has created what would now be considered overly long blocks of text, readers should be able to follow the twists and turns of the story and the give and take of dialogue without difficulty. Such protracted paragraphs are generally the result of quite lengthy and, in some cases, run-on sentences. For this reason, to facilitate comprehension in *Vanka Kain* and *The Comely Cook*, independent clauses joined by a coordinating conjunction, semicolon, or even a comma have frequently been divided into two separate sentences. Lastly, Komarov's trademark of building phrases around verbal adverbs ("*having arrived* at the monastery," "*praising* his plan") has been replicated even though this technique sounds heavy to the modern ear. It is hoped that what is lost in stylistic gracefulness by taking this approach will be counterbalanced by the faithfulness of the translation to the original text.

Punctuation/Spelling

Wherever necessary, quotation marks have been added to delineate dialogue, and the use of commas, semicolons, and colons has been brought into alignment with the norms of modern English. No attempt has been made to reproduce the non-contemporary spelling of words in *The Comely Cook* and *Vanka Kain*.

Transliteration

Transliteration of Russian words follows the Library of Congress system with the exception that first names, last names, and place names have frequently been simplified or rendered in a way that lends itself to a more intuitive pronunciation for English speakers. For example, soft signs are omitted (Tver rather than Tver'), the –ий and –ый endings of Russian names have been shortened to *y* (Grigory rather than Grigorii), and the Russian character я has been rendered as *ya* rather than *ia* when it begins a word (Yakov rather than Iakov).

Monetary Values

For an explanation of the value of money references in this collection, see Appendix B.

ACKNOWLEDGMENTS

I would like to thank Marcia Morris and Marcus Levitt for their insightful reading of the entire manuscript. Their numerous comments have significantly improved the final version of this collection. I am also indebted to several colleagues and friends at Notre Dame, namely, Alyssa Gillespie and Alexander Martin for their help with several particularly vexing questions, Maria Rogacheva for the hours she spent working through difficult areas of the original stories with me, Linda Lange and Chantelle Snyder for their time and talent in setting up Michurin's map of Moscow, and Kenneth Kinslow for his skill in finding me working copies of centuries-old texts. Last of all, I would like to express my appreciation to the wonderful staff at Northern Illinois University Press. From the beginning of the process to the end, their efficiency and expertise have been greatly appreciated. I, of course, accept full responsibility for any mistakes and shortcomings that still exist in this work.

This book is dedicated to my children, Claire and Matthew. More than anyone, they have taught me, and continually remind me, why the humanities are so important.

Three Russian Tales of the Eighteenth Century

INTRODUCTION

Mikhail Chulkov, Matvei Komarov,
Nikolai Karamzin, and Eighteenth-Century
Russian Literary Culture

THE AUTHORS IN THIS COLLECTION have much
that distinguishes them from one another, from their social status
to their level of literary sophistication and intellectual depth. The
most gifted of the three, Nikolai Karamzin, was a nobleman born
into the type of privilege that allowed him to befriend and work
with the social and cultural elite of late-eighteenth-century Russia.
By the end of his rather short-lived literary career, he was the most
celebrated Russian writer of his age, justly praised for the graceful
style, emotional intensity, and aesthetic refinement that define his
work. In the last two decades of his life, Karamzin's reputation and
connections reached such proportions that when he decided to abandon belles-lettres to concentrate on writing a history of Russia, Tsar
Alexander I supported his project by appointing him official court
historiographer. On the other end of the spectrum stands Matvei Komarov. An enslaved servant or serf, he belonged to the largest, and
most downtrodden, social class in eighteenth-century Russia—some
of whose members Karamzin's family, though far from rich, would
have owned. As a house servant, his life was immeasurably easier

than the lot of those serfs toiling in the fields, which not only explains his ability to read and write but also his familiarity with the commonplaces of Enlightenment philosophy and Russian Neoclassical literature. Melding this knowledge with the irreverent wit and wisdom of the lower classes, Komarov parlayed his modest talents into becoming the most popular Russian writer of the eighteenth century. Residing socially somewhere between these polar opposites, Mikhail Chulkov was born into the thin layer that passed for the middle class in eighteenth-century Russia. Although from a relatively modest background, Chulkov acquired an education that equipped him to do battle with the best-known writers of his day. In his verse, journalism, and prose fiction, he fully engaged in the literary debates of the late 1760s, displaying both an encyclopedic knowledge of the norms of Russian Neoclassicism and a savvy command of the same subcultural resources, especially folklore, that Komarov exploited.

Despite substantial differences in their backgrounds and abilities, Chulkov, Komarov, and Karamzin share one important trait: they all produced seminal texts expressing the major literary, social, or philosophical concerns of late-eighteenth-century Russia. The first of the three to enter the world of belles-lettres, Chulkov utilized a light-hearted sense of humor to deflate the literary pretensions of his age. In his finest work, *The Comely Cook* (1770), a rollicking description of the bawdy misadventures of the prostitute heroine Martona serves to lampoon the devices, philosophy, and grave sense of mission underpinning the reigning literary aesthetic of Neoclassicism while also subverting the excesses of the early stirrings of Sentimentalism in Russia. Beginning his career two decades later, Karamzin came of age as well-established trends in West European Sentimentalism were taking ever deeper root in Russian soil. From the time he began publishing his first major literary work, *Letters of a Russian Traveler* (1791), he not only observed the many facets of the literary etiquette of Sentimentalism but also did more than any other author to define their use in Russia. This is especially true of "Poor Liza" (1792), in which Karamzin creates a template for the movement by concisely laying out its major themes, introducing an archetypal heroine of increased psychological complexity, and recounting her story in an elegant language whose vocabulary and syntax were modeled on the speech of Karamzin's noble peers. Though far less skilled than Karamzin or even Chulkov, Komarov nevertheless touched even more readers than they did, both during his lifetime and after it. His adaptation of the popular legend surrounding the eponymous outlaw-protagonist of *Vanka Kain* (1779) became Russia's first best seller, which he followed up just three years later with yet another wildly successful novel, *The Tale of the Adventures of the English Milord George and the Brandenburg Margravine Friderika Louisa*. Taken together, these two works secured Komarov's popularity with a large segment of the Russian reading public for well over 125 years.

The Rise of Russian Prose Fiction

Although Chulkov, Komarov, and Karamzin can be considered pioneers of modern prose fiction in Russia, they were comparatively late arrivals on the European scene. By the mid-eighteenth century, the British could count to their credit the publication of Defoe's *Robinson Crusoe* (1719), Swift's *Gulliver's Travels* (1726), Richardson's *Pamela* (1740) and *Clarissa* (1748), and Fielding's *Joseph Andrews* (1742) and *Tom Jones* (1749), yet the Russians were still two decades away from making their first original contribution to the genre of the modern novel, much less coming close to matching the British lead in literary mastery and universal appeal. The reason for Russia's backwardness can in large part be attributed to the long-term effects of missing the secularizing influence of the Renaissance. While a renewed interest in Classical literature and history was radiating out of northern Italy, the Russians were still reeling from the aftereffects of the Mongol invasions, which had begun in 1237.[1] As a new Russian state coalesced around Moscow in the fourteenth through sixteenth centuries, a variety of factors—including Russia's great distance from the epicenter of the Renaissance, the fall of Constantinople, and the ability of the Orthodox Church to maintain a medieval-like prominence in the life of the country—combined to insulate Russia from the West and delay the development of a secular culture (Riasanovsky and

Steinberg 88–122, 131–60). During this period, the Russians made out-standing contributions in the areas of icon painting and church archi-tecture, but even by the end of the seventeenth century their progress toward creating a secular literary tradition was meager at best. The West wind of change that would allow Russia to move in the same direction as the most enlightened countries in Europe was to build slowly throughout the 1600s before finally reaching gale force during the reign of Peter the Great (1682–1725). As Marc Raeff describes the process: "Conscious assimilation of European culture dates from the reign of Peter the Great in the sense that from this time on the Russian elites endeavored to re-shape Russia in the image of the West, rather than merely to use foreign inventions without transforming the traditional Muscovite pattern, as had been the case in the seventeenth century" (28).

In the more than forty years of his reign, Peter instituted many sub-stantial and at times even history-altering changes by recasting every-thing from the organization of the government, the church, and the military to the way Russians dressed, spoke, and acted according to Western models. Cracraft summarizes the grand scope of what he calls Peter's "cultural revolution," writing that "new ways of dress, deport-ment, communication, navigation, building, gardening, gunnery, drawing, computing, measuring, sculpting, writing, visualizing, in-deed of thinking had to be adopted along with the new vocabularies needed for naming these activities and all the new weapons, tools, and devices associated with them" (*Revolution of Peter the Great* 75).[2] In the arts, and in literature in particular, however, the situa-tion was more nuanced. On the one hand, the Petrine period encom-passed a crucial transition in Russian culture, in which "the previous structure of literature changed and what was laid down in its place has been preserved in its basic features up until our day" (Nikolaev 7). For example, during Peter's reign there was an upsurge in the printing of various types of secular stories, both native and foreign, that had already been circulating in Russia and the West for decades and even centuries. Chapbooks based on the cheap one-page prints known as *lubki*, literary miscellanies, and a wealth of translated lit-erature offered readers, among other things, an assortment of chivalric romances, rogues' tales, prose satires, and folktales.[3] On the other hand, originality was not a hallmark of these years, at least not in the domain of prose fiction.[4] Except for a few anonymous adventure stories known collectively as the Petrine Tales, in which bold heroes make their way in the world owing to their abilities rather than the accident of birth (Brown, *18th Century* 17–21; Moiseeva and Serman 41–45), they produced little that was new.

Although Peter's rule facilitated the dissemination of a large amount of literary raw material that would influence readers and writers alike as the century unfolded, it did not immediately inspire the creation of a new literature reflecting the latest achievements in the West. The advent of this stage in the development of modern Russian culture would have to wait until the reigns of Peter's daughter Elizabeth (1741–62) and, to an even greater extent, of Catherine the Great (1762–96), whose own literary output fills twelve volumes of her collected works (Brown, *18th Century* 215).[5] With the encouragement of these two relatively enlightened monarchs, fledgling authors sought to build a modern Russian literature from the foundation up by compressing what had been a hundred years of organic growth in the West into the shortest time possible. In just three decades, from roughly 1745 to 1775, they succeeded by absorbing the theory and praxis of various foreign literatures as templates for their work.[6] Although these models were culled from a variety of times and places, including the Baroque and Greek and Roman Classicism (Segel, "Classicism" 49–50, 55–63), the single greatest source of inspiration and guidance was found in the work of French Neoclassicists.

In 1747 Alexander Sumarokov (1717–77), "the most influential representative of classicism in Russia during his age and the revered master of . . . other classicists" (Brown, *18th Century* 113), read his theoretical work "Two Epistles" before members of the Academy of Sciences in St. Petersburg. In the second epistle, entitled "On Poetry," he boldly advanced his program for the development of a new Russian literature based on Western norms (Brown, *18th Century* 119–22). Taking his inspiration from the codification of French Neoclassical literature contained in Nicolas Boileau's *Art poétique* (1674), Sumarokov instructed

Russian writers on the suitability, advantages, and limitations of a variety of genres.[7] Commenting on everything from the grand genres of the tragedy, epic, and ode to smaller ones like the epigram, ballad, and song, he closes his epistle with the names of those authors whom Russian writers would do well to emulate, a list that includes Boileau, Molière, Pindar, Virgil, and Homer.[8] Nowhere, however, does Sumarokov touch upon any prose genre, much less the novel or adventure tale. When he did take the time to address prose fiction elsewhere, Sumarokov generally appraised it with typical Neoclassical condescension. In his "Letter on the Reading of Novels" (1759), he dismisses the entire genre for "taking up much time but having little use," and adds that such works, "which are written by ignoramuses, teach readers an artificial and deformed view of the world and lead them away from what is natural, which alone is important and pleasing" (350). From Sumarokov's perspective, prose fiction was essentially a suspect enterprise because it generally failed to emphasize the hallmarks of the Neoclassical worldview, which comprised, among other things, an "emphasis on restraint, the rule of reason over the emotions, the unquestioned acceptance of hierarchic distinctions in art as in social life, [and] the transcendence of civic duty" (Brown, *18th Century* 182). In short, Sumarokov found that most writers of novels and stories failed to heed his final exhortation in "On Poetry"; that is, to "present nothing but enlightenment to the mind" (126).

Mikhail Lomonosov (1711–65), the second great arbiter of literary taste in mid-eighteenth-century Russia, assessed the impact of prose fiction in virtually the same terms that Sumarokov did. In his *Brief Introduction to Rhetoric*, he derides "French fairy tales, which they call novels . . . because they contain no morality, . . . and there is such dross in them which has been invented by people who spend their time in vain that they only lead to the corruption of morals and to stagnation in luxury and passions of the flesh" (223). Like Sumarokov, Lomonosov generally considered prose fiction to be unworthy of his notice. For example, disdainful neglect of the entire enterprise is clearly revealed in his approach to the language question. In order to create a modern literature based on West European norms, the Russians first had to forge a literary language capable of expressing the new themes, tropes, and genres. Beginning in the mid-1700s, they struggled with this task for the greater part of a century, and a suitably expressive, universally accepted literary language would not be a fait accompli until roughly 1825. Lomonosov's great contribution to this debate was his "Forward on the Utility of Ecclesiastical Books in the Russian Language" (1757), in which he advanced a hierarchy of five levels of the Russian language and then distributed them among three styles of usage. The highest style was to be employed for "'heroic poems, odes, and prose orations on important matters;'" the middle for "'theatrical productions . . . friendly epistles in verse, satires, eclogues and elegies [as well as] descriptions of memorable events [i.e., histories] and noble instructions;'" and the lowest should be reserved for "'comedies, humorous epigrams, songs, and . . . prose letters to friends and descriptions of ordinary doings'" (Brown, *18th Century* 79–80). As with Sumarokov's treatment of genres, any form of prose fiction is, at least from a modern perspective, conspicuously absent from this list.

Despite their inherent mistrust, even the most scathing critics of prose fiction did approve of a select subset of works whose didactic value met their stringent requirements. For example, in the same piece in which Lomonosov censures novels for being responsible for the corruption of morals, he pointedly exempts *Gulliver's Travels* from his critique, cataloguing it instead with other works of pure imagination that were "created for moral instruction," a list that includes such titles as Aesop's fables, Petronius's *Satyricon*, and the *Colloquies* of Erasmus (1518) (*Rhetoric* 222). Explaining a related motivation behind Lomonosov's reaction, Ronald LeBlanc writes that in general, "the English novel's claim to greater verisimilitude helped it to escape the strong condemnation of those Russian Classicist critics, who, when speaking of the dangers inherent in reading *romany* [novels], would ridicule the impossible feats of implausible heroes who travel in purely imaginary worlds" (29). For his part, although Sumarokov generally derided novels for "weighing a lot but having little value" (350), even he was not above praising what he termed such "good" and "worthy" examples of the genre as Fénelon's pseudo-historical prose romance *Télé-*

maque (1699) and Cervantes' *Don Quixote* (1605, 1615) (350–51). The former work was held in such esteem, in fact, that Vasily Trediakovsky, who along with Lomonosov and Sumarokov formed the literary triumvirate of mid-eighteenth-century Russia, rendered it in a verse translation that came to 16,000 lines of hexameter (Brown, *18th Century* 65). John Barclay's allegoric defense of absolute monarchy *Argenis* (1621), which Trediakovsky translated from Latin in 1751, was yet one more novel that was deemed to be of a sufficiently serious and instructive nature to merit an educated reader's attention (Brown, *18th Century* 64).

In spite of strenuous resistance or, at best, condescending neglect from the literary elite, prose fiction quickly began to sink its roots into the virgin soil of eighteenth-century Russian literary culture. In addition to Sumarokov, Lomonosov, and others of their mind-set who could at most be moved to recommend a small number of novels based on their didactic merit, there were others who tried to meet such lofty standards through their own creations. In an article about one of the works in this collection, Komarov's *Vanka Kain*, I. R. Titunik explains the impulse among some of Russia's first writers of prose fiction to claim the moral high ground. Though it was

> a target of Classicist condemnation and ridicule, the new prose culture wanted to claim for itself precisely the functions which Classicist canons had established as the prime functions of art and to ground itself, in precisely the Classicist way, on authority. . . . This Classicist prose was a reaction to the dominant trend and an effort to establish a countertrend that would redirect Russian prose fiction into what was, from the Classicist point of view, its proper channel. ("*Van'ka Kain*" 352)

The person to achieve the most noteworthy success, at least ideologically if not commercially, in producing works that could be placed under the rubric of a Neoclassical prose fiction was Mikhail Kheraskov (1733–1807). In a long and storied career, Kheraskov was in many ways the quintessential Enlightenment figure. Among his many accomplishments, he wrote ten epic poems—including the Russian national epic the *Rossiada* (1779)—nine tragedies, two comedies, a comic opera, many genres of the lyric poem (odes, sonnets, fables, epigrams), and three novels: *Numa, or Flourishing Rome* (1768), *Cadmus and Harmonia* (1789), and *Polydorus, the Son of Cadmus and Harmonia* (1792) (Baehr, "Kheraskov" 222).[9] As their titles imply, Kheraskov's novels "all use classical themes (taken especially from Plutarch's *Lives* and Ovid's *Metamorphoses*) as an allegorical focus for discussing both Russia specifically and the human condition in general" (Baehr, "Kheraskov" 222). A representative example of the didactic values motivating these works is clearly expressed in the ending to *Cadmus and Harmonia*. Writing for the educated elites who no doubt made up virtually his entire reading public and also with one eye glancing in the direction of Catherine the Great herself, the author concludes that "'the mortal who masters his feelings, who reins in the turbulence of his passions, who regulates according to the rules of reason his spiritual qualities, is a mighty king on earth. Many wearers of crowns have not merited this title'" (Brown, *18th Century* 255–56). In these two pithy lines, Kheraskov managed to summarize what is perhaps the central tenet of the Age of Enlightenment.

Although singing the praises of reason was commonplace in the higher genres of eighteenth-century Russian literature, the tenor of Kheraskov's comments was still something of an anomaly in the world of prose fiction. Beginning around 1760, the number of prose works available to Russian readers increased dramatically, and, certain rare exceptions notwithstanding, for the most part they fell well outside the bounds of Classicist norms. As David Budgen puts it so colorfully:

> Prose in Russia throughout the eighteenth century . . . was a bastard, outlawed and orphaned literary type, and the novel which constituted its greater part was more often than not written precisely by bastards, outlaws and orphans—sometimes, as in the case of the first Russian novelist,[10] by men who were all three. And this despite the fact that from 1750 onwards the Russian Parnassus begins to groan under a welter of prose works, both original and translated.[11] (65)

Of the 1,175 editions of novels printed in the eighteenth century, both original and translated (Goodliffe 126), more than 1,000 were issued during the reign of Catherine the Great (1762–96) (Garrard, *Čulkov* 41). For example, only five novels were published in Russia between 1730 and 1754, and although this number rose to thirty-one for the years 1755 through 1759, it hardly qualifies as a tidal wave of output. In 1763 alone, however, thirty-two novels were brought to market, with this number rising to eighty-one in 1764; by the end of the century, in some years over one hundred and twenty-five novels were being published (Goodliffe 126). From a weak beginning in the first half of the century and after having to struggle against the strident criticism of Russia's celebrated literati, by the 1760s the outlaw genres of narrative prose fiction were "transformed from being persecuted into the standard setter of the book market" (Moiseeva and Serman 52).

The rise of prose fiction, and in particular of the novel with its many subgenres (moralistic, sentimental, historical, magical-adventure, political), was spurred on by a transformation in Russian intellectual life and institutions. More specifically, advances in the production and distribution of books in the last half of the eighteenth century were essential in ensuring that the growing demand for the new type of literature could be met. For example, between 1752 and 1774 eight new government-approved institutional presses opened their doors, including one at Moscow University in 1756 (Marker 76–77), and with the attendant increase in publishing activity that was at least partially responsive to consumer demand, the number of literary and general-interest books rose significantly to account for more than 50 percent of all published titles (Marker 71). Moreover, the process of producing more books was greatly facilitated by the government's gradual release of its control over publishing. After granting a handful of exceptions to the state monopoly in the 1770s, Catherine authorized the "Free Press" Law of 1783, which allowed private individuals to own and run presses (Marker 103–5). Collectively, the private enterprises "published over two-thirds of all Russian books in the last quarter of the century," which is a sizable figure given that the almost 8,000 titles issued in Russia during that period amounted to "over three times what had been produced in the previous two centuries" (Marker 105). With more presses turning out more books, the number of sales outlets also grew. In Moscow and St. Petersburg, the ranks of booksellers increased from six to fifteen between 1759 and the 1770s, and outlets began to open up in the provinces. Beginning in 1768, the Academy of Sciences sent books to thirty-six locations outside the two capitals, and by the 1780s the provincial centers of Arkhangelsk, Nizhny Novgorod, Kursk, Orel, and Kiev could each lay claim to several bookstores (Marker 177–79). Combined with the advent of lending libraries in the early 1770s, the dramatic expansion of printing facilities and distribution centers established the necessary framework for Russia's reading public to satisfy its interest in the new literature, especially prose fiction.

Improving the ways in which printed material was produced and distributed allowed more works to get into the hands of more people than ever before in Russia, yet the reading public was still quite meager in the last quarter of the eighteenth century, perhaps as slight as just 3 percent of the population (Schaarschmidt 425). While such a low level of literacy severely limited the dissemination of the elevated ideas promulgated in the highbrow literature of the Enlightenment, it was not as debilitating to the various genres of prose fiction. If stories were simple enough, adventurous enough, or risqué enough, they warranted being read aloud to those who could not read themselves. It was this very principle that led to the explosion in the eighteenth century of what is known in Russia as *lubok* literature. Originally, *lubok* referred to a genre of cheap, colorful, one-page prints that encompassed everything from practical, serious, and religious subjects to topics appealing to a taste for something humorous, satirical, and even bawdy.[12] With the ability to produce printed material rapidly expanding, however, there arose the phenomenon of *lubok* literature, in which publishers turned out multi-page stories and even entire novels, but like the prints from which they took their name, these works were produced on cheap paper and were also designed to catch the reader's attention with a lurid picture on the cover or the promise of adventure, intrigue, and love in their titles (Marker 119–20). In addition to being inexpensive to produce and catering directly to a wide variety of tastes, *lubok* literature was able to build a broad readership because it did not rely solely on established shops to reach its audience but was also "sold in the streets of Moscow and distributed widely in villages, fairs, and bazaars by wandering booksellers" (Schaarschmidt 427). Starting as early as the 1760s, works that had been brought out by more reputable publishers were also offered in *lubok* editions. Such was the case with Sumarokov's fables[13] and then later in the century with Komarov's second, wildly successful novel *The Adventures of the English Milord George* (Schaarschmidt 432–35). Although *lubok* printing houses were selective in their publication of titles and often issued works in ways that altered and frequently simplified their content, *lubok* literature offered yet one more way in which prose fiction in general and the novel in particular could leave its imprint on the consciousness of the eighteenth-century Russian reading public.

Supported by an increase in publishing facilities and booksellers and catalyzed by the explosion of relatively cheap copies of *lubok* editions, prose fiction became the unrivaled leader among the genres of Russia's new, Western-inspired literature. At first, though, readers could indulge their appetites almost solely through translations. For example, the first Russian-language version of Lesage's *Gil Blas* (1715–35) was published in 1754 and 1755, the first six parts of Prevost's *Memoirs of a Man of Quality* (1728–31) were issued in Russian translation between 1756 and 1765, and Defoe's *Robinson Crusoe* (1719) first appeared in Russian between 1762 and 1764 (*Svodnyi katalog* 5: 14–15, 20). Before long, however, Russian authors also began trying their hand at satisfying public demand. Although the title of the first Russian novel is in dispute, it is safe to say that it reached the marketplace sometime between 1763 and 1770. The soundest claim to this honor would belong to Chulkov's *The Comely Cook* (1770), which is undeniably Russian and original. On the other hand, some critics regard Fyodor Emin (1735?–70) as Russia's first novelist, although the originality of every one of his efforts in the genre could be called into question.[14] Between 1763 and 1766 Emin churned out six novels, several of them multi-volume works, ranging in subtype from the adventure romance (for example, *Inconstant Fate, or The Adventures of Miramond*, 1763) to the philosophical novel (*The Adventures of Themistocles*, 1763) to a Russian version of Rousseau's *The New Heloise* (1761) that ranks as the first epistolary novel in Russian literature (*The Letters of Ernest and Doravra*, 1766). Although Emin's fiction would fall out of favor with the rise of Karamzin and his peers some twenty-five years later, all but one of his novels went through multiple printings before the century was out.[15] Whether he was simply aping a host of foreign-inspired conventions or was a true pioneer in the field of Russian letters, Emin has earned his place in literary history as the first Russian writer to achieve celebrity status through his efforts in the genre of the novel.

If Emin was the first star of the Russian novel, the title of its first best seller goes to Matvei Komarov. Not only did Komarov sell more copies of his work than any other writer in Russia's emerging literary culture, in most instances he left them far behind. Print runs of eighteenth-century literary texts were not large, typically ranging between 400 and 1,200 copies. Even at these levels, however, it was hard to sell out the works of some of the most prominent names of the day. Marker notes "Novikov's lamentation that he could not sell 200 copies of Sumarokov's plays in ten years" and that "in a statement prepared in the late 1760s, the Academy [of Sciences] revealed that most of Sumarokov's plays had gone unsold" (205). In the 1760s and 1770s, a spate of satiric literary journals came onto the market, including one led by Catherine the Great herself. The high-water mark of the genre belongs to Nikolai Novikov's *The Drone*, which sold roughly 2,000 copies of Enlightenment wit and wisdom per issue, yet there seems to be no doubt that Komarov reached far more readers than even this centerpiece of the new literary culture. With his first novel, *Vanka Kain* (1779), Komarov struck exactly the right chord with the reading public. In this oftentimes humorous narration of the escapades of a thief, robber, and police spy, Komarov satisfied what critics have recognized as the primary demand of eighteenth-century Russian readers in their leisure-time books: adventure, bold heroes (or in this case an anti-establishment anti-hero), and a little love intrigue. Komarov was able to capitalize on this formula, and *Vanka Kain* enjoyed seven printings before the end of the century (*Svodnyi katalog* 2: 56–57). His second work, *Milord George* (1782), fared almost as well, with a total of six print runs in the first eighteen years after its initial publication (*Svodnyi katalog* 2: 435–36).

As impressive as these credentials are, perhaps the highest form of praise has come in the past twenty-five years not just for Komarov, whose works were forcibly removed from the market by the Communist authorities right after the 1917 Revolution, but also for Chulkov, whose *Comely Cook* enjoyed only one printing in the eighteenth century. *The Comely Cook, Vanka Kain,* and *Milord George* have all been reprinted multiple times since 1987 by both Soviet and post-Soviet publishing houses, with several editions coming out in the last decade.[16] While some of these texts would pass for the equivalent of *lubok* literature today, with their cheap paper and lurid covers, others give these works their due. More recent editions are accompanied by a lengthy introductory article detailing the life of the author or the culture of eighteenth-century Russian prose fiction, and one printing of *Vanka Kain* (St. Petersburg, 2000) includes over twenty pages of footnotes, in which the editor defines obsolete words; describes eighteenth-century persons, customs, and institutions; and compares Komarov's tale with the historical record surrounding the real-life Vanka Kain. Given this renewed interest among contemporary readers, it is clear that the works in this collection continue to strike the right chord in Russian society more than 200 years after their initial release.

The Authors

Mikhail Dmitrievich Chulkov (1743?–92)

As a pioneer of Russian prose fiction, Chulkov may not have been a bastard, outlaw, or orphan, but his biography is full of the sorts of twists and turns that naturally led him to challenge, rather than loyally follow, the norms of the literature of Enlightenment. Much of Chulkov's background is unknown, but he did acknowledge late in life that he had studied at the gymnasium for *raznochintsy* attached to Moscow University (14).[17] Although the term *raznochintsy* ("people of various ranks") had more than one meaning in the eighteenth century, when it was applied in the area of education, it was synonymous with a person belonging to any class other than the nobility (Becker 66–67). In the 1755 charter for Moscow University, the empress Elizabeth established two gymnasiums: one for the nobility and one for *raznochintsy* other than serfs. Since Chulkov studied at the latter, he most likely came from a clerical or merchant family (15). This biographical fact, virtually the earliest we have of Chulkov, can be used as a template in analyzing his life. Given his social status, he was privileged enough to receive an education, only not sitting side by side with the sons of the nobility. As he made his way in life after his time at the gymnasium, which he attended without completing his studies from 1756 until at least May 1758, Chulkov always strove to be accepted into the highest levels of society. This desire would be frustrated, however, in the positions he managed to attain from the late 1750s through the mid-1760s as well as in his foray into literature in the late 1760s. It would not be until later in life, after a long and successful career in the civil service, that Chulkov finally attained his goal of joining the ranks of the nobility himself.

After Chulkov left Moscow University, the next reference point we have in his life places him as an actor in the court theater in St. Petersburg (16–17). Although the historical record is not completely clear, he may have begun his work with the troupe in the capacity of a wig dresser or barber (18–19), but however his career started, it did in fact culminate with Chulkov being on stage. From the scanty sources available, it appears Chulkov acted in plays by Sumarokov, Destouches, and Molière, among others, but that he was unable to claim the limelight, instead specializing "in supporting roles, and even walk-on parts in the case of *Richard III* " (20). Whether he felt his career as an actor would not bring him the fame and fortune he had hoped, or perhaps because he had gotten married (his son Vladimir was born in 1766 [20–21]), Chulkov asked for his release from the court theater in January of 1765. His request "met with a prompt and favorable reply and in the following month we find him officially registered as a court lackey . . . with a salary of forty rubles a year," a position he held until sometime in 1766 (23–24). From the information at our disposal, the first eight years or so of Chulkov's entry into society went well enough, but there was always something lacking. Just as with his education, he drew up to the margins of polite society but was unable to press on to its very center. His position as a court lackey brought him a steady job and the opportunity to be closer to a world of wealth and power, yet as Chulkov's hasty exit from this post strongly implies, it was not the niche he was struggling to find. Chulkov apparently continued to work at court and as late as February of 1767 held the position of quartermaster (24), but by 1766 he was already determined to try a different approach to making his way in the world: writing.

In just over twenty-five years, Chulkov produced an impressive array of publications.[18] From 1770 on, his work consists almost entirely of nonfiction with a heavy emphasis on commerce and law. For example, he published *A Historical Account of Russian Commerce* (7 vols., 1781–88), *A Brief History of Russian Trade* (1788), *A Dictionary of Fairs Established in Russia Published for Those Engaged in Trade There* (1788), and *A Dictionary of Jurisprudence* (1792–96). Chulkov's later work also shows a continuing interest in mythology and folklore, a focus that had first come to light in his *Brief Mythological Lexicon* (1767) and four-part *Collection of Various Songs* (1770–74). Publications in this vein include *A Dictionary of Russian Superstitions* (1782) and *The A, B, Cs of Russian Superstition* (1786). In the realm of literature, Chulkov's oeuvre comprises two novels, *The Mocker, or Slavic Tales* (1766–68, 1789) and *The Comely Cook, or The Adventures of a Debauched Woman* (1770); and two literary journals, *Both This and That* (1769) and *The Trinket Shop of Parnassus* (1770).[19] As with so much of Chulkov's fiction, the very titles of these works are self-referential and laden with commentary on his approach to the art of writing. The reference to a trinket shop in the title of his second journal hints at the commercial motif running throughout Chulkov's original work, which is almost certainly an expression of his inability to find a wealthy patron willing to guarantee his financial security. More importantly, the title of *The Mocker* reveals Chulkov's fundamentally parodic attitude toward the reigning literary aesthetics of his day (Neoclassicism and early Sentimentalism), a mind-set that is echoed in the playful phrase *Both This and That*, itself a teasing commentary on the title of Catherine the Great's *All Sorts and Sundries*, the enterprise that initiated the fashion for satiric journals in the 1760s and 1770s.

Perhaps it was the result of Chulkov's status as an outsider who could claim neither noble birth nor the privileges that went with it, or, perhaps, it was the natural consequence of his cast of mind, but from his creative work and his comments about literature, it is clear that he reveled in the role of the merry mocker. In both his prose and verse, Chulkov generally eschewed vitriol and the rapier's edge of satire and instead relied on a playful jesting that could just as easily be aimed at himself as at others.[20] What Chulkov simply could not abide were those authors who took themselves too seriously, and his ridicule is chiefly directed at what he considered the bombast and misplaced utilitarian zeal so common in Russian literature of the 1760s. As opposed to one of the core values of the literary and philosophical worldview of the Russian Enlightenment, Chulkov's sense of humor was anchored in his firm belief that literature was incapable of reforming people. As he states in his preface to *The Mocker*: "In this book there is little or even nothing at all that is important or didactic. It is not suited, it seems to me, to correcting coarse morals, but then there is nothing in it that could increase them either" (1: ii). There is no greater proof of Chulkov's opposition to the Neoclassical dictum that literature needed to be morally useful than the image of author he creates in his fiction. Time and again in the prefaces to his two novels, Chulkov describes himself as simply not up to the heady task of teaching others. This motif is so central to his philosophy that it appears in the very first paragraph of his very first literary creation, where he warns readers in the preface that he is no truth-seeker but rather someone of whom they should be wary. While admitting that he has no intention of lying to them upon first acquaintance, he adds that "after we have gotten to know each other rather well, that would be another matter" (*The Mocker* 1: i).

Building on his admission that he is partial to stretching the truth, Chulkov consistently sounds two refrains in support of his contention that readers should not look to him for moral instruction. The first of these concerns his inability to play the role of expert. In the preface to *The Mocker*, Chulkov explains that "as this is my first work, I didn't dare take up important subjects because I couldn't immediately become skilled in everything," and he views his initial literary effort as a test case that will allow him to identify his shortcomings and not introduce them into "a quality work" (1: ii). Four years later, his opinion of his abilities, or lack thereof, had not changed, for in the second, verse preface to *The Comely Cook* he proclaims: "Errors are normal for us, weaknesses acceptable, / And all mortals are accustomed to making mistakes." After positing this general description of the human condition, Chulkov makes it quite clear that he is as fallible as the next person, entreating readers not to judge his shortcomings harshly, for he, too, is "quite capable of committing a blunder" (62). Chulkov's confession that his works are flawed leads naturally into the related refrain of his far-from-exalted view of his place in the world. In the preface to *The Mocker*, Chulkov calls himself a "puny teller of tales" (1: iv–v), "a person of little importance who at times is lighter than a feather" (1: vi), and he admits that his readers would be hard pressed to identify him if they ran into him on the street. In his typically unassuming manner, he states: "My status in society is just as low as my understanding is narrow, and you would almost not notice me at all among a crowd of renowned citizens" (1: iv). Although Chulkov does not intone this idea specifically in his introductory comments to *The Comely Cook*, there is no doubt that the teller of this tale, the alluring prostitute and first-person narrator Martona, embodies a similarly self-deprecating image of herself. While Martona's desire to flaunt her good looks always does get her noticed in a crowd, she is the first to acknowledge that she lacks any number of virtues, including modesty, gratitude, and loyalty. Contrary to the exalted representation of the author common in the Age of Neoclassicism,[21] literary creators in Chulkov's universe harbor all the vices of the common person on the street.

From global aspects of novel writing such as authorial image down to individual devices like the metaphor, Chulkov's view of his craft was driven by the dominant concept of laughter. It is no coincidence that he titled his first work of fiction *The Mocker* and in it openly and unapologetically spelled out his comic understanding of both life and literature. In the preface he writes that his interests lie not in the realm of the didactic but rather in creating beauty and, even more importantly, reflecting the fundamentally humorous nature of the world around him.

> I ought to apologize that there are several foreign words in the simple style of my writing. Sometimes I put them there because they sound more pleasing, and sometimes I do it in order to laugh at others, or even for the reason that others will laugh at me. Man, as they say, is an amusing and jesting animal, one who mocks and is mocked, for we are all subject to being laughed at, and we all laugh at others. (1: iii)

However much this attitude was the result of Chulkov's personal inclination, it was reinforced by two powerful currents in the culture of his time. One of them was the Neoclassical literary aesthetic, which despite its primary goal of educating readers did sanction large doses of laughter. Both in theoretical works, such as Sumarokov's epistle, and in practice Russian Neoclassicists supported humorous genres like the satire, comedy, and mock epic. Generally, the type of humor encountered in such works was more cutting and didactic than what Chulkov would have used, but at least Neoclassicism acknowledged his approach as legitimate. Providing Chulkov with even greater inspiration and assistance, however, was a rich subculture of laughter and mockery that stood mostly outside the bounds of respectable literature. Consisting in large part of *lubok* broadsides and tales, translated adventure romances, and folklore, its most potent symbol was the Russian carnival, from which it took both its view of the world as well as several specific devices.

In his pathbreaking work *Rabelais and His World*, Mikhail Bakhtin illustrates in detail how the author of *Gargantua and Pantagruel* marshaled the forms and spirit of the carnival to subvert what Bakhtin terms the official culture of church and state. For most of the inhabitants of medieval Europe, especially the lower classes, life was bounded by laws and religious strictures that gave the individual few opportunities for self-expression and empowerment. The great exception to this rule, according to Bakhtin, was the celebration of carnival, which provided a place where the normal hierarchies of life were, at least for a time, turned upside down.[22] Mocking the established power structure of society, carnival-goers placed the lowest members of their temporary world at their head, proclaiming a beggar or idiot their king and elevating a prostitute to the role of queen. Under the aegis of such benign monarchs, the attendees of the carnival indulged in one outlandish behavior after another, which during almost any other time of the year would result in their censure if not arrest. Cursing, drinking, eating, and sexual activity were taken to extreme levels; people regularly changed and even challenged standard notions of identity by wearing masks and cross-dressing; thieves and pickpockets ran through the crowds with immunity; and the plays, performances, and other humorous forms of entertainment that anchored the carnival mercilessly ridiculed the highborn and their world. Throughout this topsy-turvy universe there reigned a particular type of humor that bound carnival-goers together. As Bakhtin describes it, carnival laughter is universal, it is the laughter of all the people and "is directed at all and everyone, including the carnival's participants" (11). As opposed to satire, the preferred vehicle of Russia's enlighteners in their attempts to improve society, carnival laughter does not stand above or outside the target of its humor in a posture of condemnation but rather "expresses the point of view of the whole world; he who is laughing also belongs to it" (12).

Bakhtin's conception of a carnivalized subculture epitomized and symbolized by the carnival itself applies extremely well to the society Chulkov found himself in as he embarked on his career as a novel writer.[23] By the second half of the eighteenth century, the carnival had sunk deep roots in Russian society that stretched back at least 300 years. Moscow had over twenty sites for carnivals, including the Moscow River near the Kremlin and Maidens' Field, and in St. Petersburg such choice locations as Admiralty Square, Palace Square, and the frozen Neva River opposite the Winter Palace were given over to these antiauthoritarian spectacles of release, chaos, and mockery (Kuznetsov,

Iz proshlogo 35–38). No matter where it was staged, the grounds of the carnival would be crowded with revelers who gathered to listen to the jokes and humorous doggerel of wandering comics or strolled among the booths to watch performances by singers, dancers, musicians, jugglers, acrobats, and charmers, among others. Attendees were fueled by copious amounts of food and drink, and as one foreign observer noted, "They drink as though they were never to drink more. Some drink *aquavitae* four times distill'd until it fire in their mouths and kindle a flame not unlike that of *Bocca di inferno*, which issues at their throats; if they have not milk given them to drink, they presently die" (Collins 22). In winter, the centerpiece of the carnival was the high, sloping toboggan runs known as ice mountains; in summer, it was the gently turning arc of the swings, a primitive type of Ferris wheel. And in the midst of all this chaos stood the most important representative of carnival humor, the *karusel'nyi ded* (carousel granddad).

Perched on top of a carousel or booth, the *ded* functioned as the comic catalyst of the carnival, as he entertained the crowd between breaks in the action and encouraged people to patronize the various performances. Dressed in ragged clothes and wearing a fake beard of combed string and ribbons, he looked like one of life's down-and-outers, but as was the norm in the carnival, being on the bottom of a hierarchy was simply the justification for turning the world upside down. Although the *ded* appeared to be a pauper (he claimed to have been dismissed from his position as a servant in a wealthy household), in reality he was the unrivaled high prince of the carnival grounds who utilized a nonstop comic chatter and any number of frenetic ploys to keep his rowdy subjects' attention riveted squarely on him. In addition to his monologue, in which he irreverently commented on important issues of the day, he might have tried to auction off an imaginary teapot that was just a handle without a top or bottom, spice up his routine with obscene double entendre, or dance with beautiful women or even a trained bear. In Bakhtin's conception of the carnival, the *ded* was the embodiment of a sense of humor in which "the high are laid low and the 'merry' truths of excess, fecundity, and pleasure supersede the lifeless platitudes and exhortations of officialdom" (Gasperetti 31).

From a narrow perspective, the Russian carnival provided forms (jokes and comic patter) and a relationship toward verbal expression (an emphasis on the process of storytelling over didactic conclusions) that would be welcomed by a writer with Chulkov's inclination for mocking the established order of things. Taking a broader view, however, the carnival also lends its name to an entire subculture of artistic expression that Chulkov, and Komarov as well, exploited to create the foundation of their work. More specifically, the important characteristics that constitute the carnivalesque mentality—excess, bawdiness, irreverence, rapid movement, role playing, shifting identities, and the overcoming of barriers between high and low—were also found in *lubok* broadsides and tales, translated adventure stories, and Russian folklore. For example, some of the best-selling *lubok* prints included such carnivalesque subjects as "buffoons and jesters modeled after Callo's Punchinello, . . . carnival fistfights, representations of grotesque and extraordinary happenings, and, in a fittingly Rabelaisian touch, the 'famous glutton and merry drunkard' Gargantua" (Gasperetti 39). Publishers of *lubok* prose helped to popularize the frenetically paced, foreign-derived adventure romances "Bova Korolevich," "Eruslan Lazarevich," and "Peter of the Golden Keys" (Ovsianikov 20–24), and via the intermediary languages of French, German, and Polish even more translated fiction made its way into Russia. Indicative of the carnivalesque tastes that dominated in this area of the subculture is the Russian translation in 1680 of the medieval compilation entitled *Facetiae*. This eclectic blend of stories, which was designed "to entertain and amuse readers but by no means educate them," was issued at least twenty-five times in the eighteenth century (Kukushkina 180, 181–82). As for folklore, Martona, the prostitute heroine of *The Comely Cook*, spouts one suggestive proverb after another to excuse and even justify her far-from-virtuous conduct (Morris 94), and each of Komarov's three often morally ambiguous novels—*Vanka Kain*, *Milord George*, and *Nevidimka*—is indebted to folk culture for its very inspiration (Gasperetti 48). With an abundance of models to choose from, including a rich tradition of carnivalesque laughter that was ideal for lampooning the gravity and didacticism of Enlightenment society,

Chulkov had at his disposal all the raw materials he needed to make his mark not only as a pioneer of Russian prose fiction but also as the most insightful—and humorous—critic of the new Russian literature.

While disagreeing on the exact significance of *The Comely Cook*, scholars generally do acknowledge its landmark status. Brown considers it the first Russian picaresque (*18th Century* 544–45), and Garrard views it not only as the first autobiographical novel in Russian literature (*Čulkov* 143) but also as the first modern Russian novel of any type (*Čulkov* 118). Serman also gives *The Comely Cook* high praise when he writes that "depicting life 'as it is,' Chulkov, like Defoe (*Moll Flanders*) and Lesage (*Gil Blas*), is the creator of the Russian novel of everyday life" (Moiseeva and Serman 59).[24] *The Comely Cook* warrants each of these titles, but to uncover its true significance in the history of Russian letters, another comparison springs to mind: it is the Russian *Tristram Shandy*. Sterne was a much better writer than Chulkov, and his wit and abilities as a wordsmith far surpass Chulkov's accomplishments in these areas. If one looks at how each author's chef d'oeuvre functions in its respective national literature, however, one overriding similarity shines forth: both works are the ultimate parodic novel of their time and place. Like *Tristram Shandy*, *The Comely Cook* is a thoroughgoing, unrelenting parody of the literary practice of its day. By the time Chulkov is finished, virtually no device of the reigning literary aesthetic of Neoclassicism and the nascent movement of Sentimentalism remains unscathed.

Chulkov signals his intention to undermine the values of Russia's highbrow literary culture of the 1760s starting with the very title of his novel. Short and to the point, *The Comely Cook, or The Adventures of a Debauched Woman* appears to be luring readers into its fictional world by enticing them to have a peek at the seamier side of reality. Once Martona begins the narrative of her life, it soon becomes clear that this is precisely Chulkov's goal. Rather than trying to improve or even educate readers, Chulkov aims only to entertain them with tales of sex and intrigue, for as Martona says: "It's worth giving yourself up to vice, for it will always seem sweeter and more pleasing than virtue" (83).[25] If readers do not sense the mischief lurking in the title of the novel, they should soon divine Chulkov's plan in his two prefaces. As Alexander Levitsky notes, Chulkov uses them to parody a number of established literary practices of his day, including the "bombastic seriousness" of dedications, "the then current and spreading sentimental sensibility," the "baroque theme of *vanitas*," Sumarokov's "Epistle" of 1748 (103), and "the modesty *topos* practiced by Kheraskov and Emin" (104).[26] Most of all, however, the authorial persona in the prefaces emphasizes that readers should not expect too much from him—or, for that matter, any author. As opposed to the lofty goal of transforming society espoused by many writers of the period, Chulkov admits that he does not know the value of what he has written (57). He foresees that *The Comely Cook* will garner its share of "controversy, criticism, indignation, and abuse" along with a "trifling" amount of praise and then will eventually "be transformed into dust, just as the person who praised or defamed it" (59). Given Chulkov's background and literary cast of mind, there can be little doubt that these words are also aimed at deflating the air of self-importance surrounding the epics, odes, and tragedies of his more high-minded contemporaries.

Chulkov continues his assault on the literary aesthetic of his day by investing *The Comely Cook* with the ethos of the carnival, a strategy that insinuates itself into virtually every step his heroine Martona takes. From the very beginning of her tale, when she laments becoming a widow at the tender age of nineteen, Martona recounts the vicissitudes of her life to the accompaniment of an undulating, carnivalesque rhythm. After her husband, a sergeant in the army, is killed at the Battle of Poltava, Chulkov's heroine admits that she was left without any means of subsistence and immediately found herself among the legions of the poor. Essential to Chulkov's design, Martona's personal tragedy and her short-lived descent to the bottom of the social hierarchy have been brought about by officialdom, for her husband's death at Poltava was the direct result of the expansionist worldview and actions of the supreme authoritarian figure of eighteenth-century Russia, Peter the Great. Based on this first biographical fact, the pattern of Martona's story is set, with the machinations of official culture continually casting her down into the depths until she eventually rises

back up again, just as though the plot of *The Comely Cook* were following the gently turning arc of a carnival Ferris wheel. Unlike a Moll
Flanders, for whom an incident such as this would be fraught with
the threat of homelessness and starvation, the carnivalesque heroine
Martona shrugs off her ill fortune, becomes a prostitute, and soon has
enough wealth to hire a servant, whom she orders about to do her bidding. When she is later expelled from the home of a Muscovite official
with nothing but the clothes on her back and a procurer arranges for
her to become the mistress of a doddering seventy-year-old retired
colonel, it would seem that Chulkov's heroine has landed in a most un-
enviable situation, that her freedom and life prospects are virtually nil.
For a less resilient character this might be the case, but for Martona,
whose tale is informed by the lustiness and mutability of the carnival,
setbacks are only the occasion to attain even brighter prospects than
before. As Martona herself describes it, in no time she has carried the
day against the former military man: "In one hour I took control in the
house and had the entire estate in my hands, and not much more than
two hours after that I had command of the master as well" (75). And
so it goes straight through to the end of the novel, as Martona swings
between the antipodes of ruin and riches until at last the former widow,
prostitute, and kept woman inherits the property of a dying nobleman
to become the queen of all she surveys.[27]

Like the *karusel'nyi ded* of the carnival, Martona stands amid the
crowd, commenting on the chaos swirling all around her and engaging
the audience with a bawdy sense of humor designed to cut the high and
mighty down to size. The guiding principle of her narrative is to turn
the discourse of official society against itself by inverting the significance of character types, themes, and devices common in the literature
of Enlightenment. To begin with, given her earthy, relatively rounded
character and flexible attitude toward virtue and vice, Martona is herself a challenge to the kind of heroine common at the time. In this vein
Garrard interprets her as a parody of "the flat, anemic virgins" popu-
lating the adventure romances of Fyodor Emin ("Narrative Technique"
556), the author who bolted onto the Russian literary scene by churn-
ing out six novels in the mid-1760s. In the telling of her tale, Martona

stays true to her subversive nature by tearing down the façade of near reverence surrounding many of the commonplaces of the official literary culture of the time (Levitsky 104). In other words, where others find virtue, Martona finds vice—or at least a good laugh. At one point, she reveals that a literary salon run by her friend is in fact a brothel, where all the would-be poets vie for the favors of its mistress; at another, she creates a burlesque of Classical mythology, calling herself Helen of Troy while naming one of her lovers Adonis and another a gray-haired Cupid; and on yet another occasion, she punctures the aura of self-importance surrounding highbrow literature when she recounts how the clerks in a government office could not make heads or tails out of one of Lomonosov's odes and find him, contrary to the Neoclassicists' insistent rationale for their work, to be utterly impractical. No matter how hallowed the subject, Martona can make it the object of our laughter by refracting it through the gently warped prism of her carnivalesque view of the world.

Chulkov's playful sense of humor permeates not just the larger building blocks of literary creation but virtually everything it touches, right down to the level of individual words. For example, one of Martona's favorite devices is the proverb, which she frequently employs to deflate the pretensions and sense of propriety of those in charge of things, even if that includes her. Early in the story, when she turns to a life of prostitution to support herself, Martona is at first quite unsettled by her change in circumstances, but within two days' time her feelings experience a complete turnabout. As an attractive woman, she salaciously concludes that no matter what polite society might demand in the realm of personal conduct, human nature will work in her favor, for *"the bee always flies to a pretty flower"* (63). Before long, Martona has a lover and is even able to hire a servant for herself, whom she, imitating the behavior of the wealthy and powerful, berates and even beats. In an excellent example of what Bakhtin would call an inclusive type of humor indicative of the carnival mentality, Martona does not spare even herself from her mocking wit. Sizing up her insensitive behavior with another proverb, she proclaims that *"you get nothing but misfortune when a fool has his way"* (64). Given Martona's plain beginnings, it is understandable that she is well-versed in folk wisdom, but it comes as somewhat of a surprise (and this is part of Chulkov's burlesque of Russian Neoclassicism) that she is also adept at using such tropes and figures as the metaphor, maxim, and philosophical monologue. Rather than fostering an Enlightenment view of the world, however, in Martona's hands these devices undermine it. By merrily referring to herself as captured "booty," "inherited wealth," and a "fortress" that has been successfully stormed, she subverts the image of maidenly purity espoused by the Neoclassicists and a proto-Sentimentalist like Emin, and when she philosophically discourses on the cyclical nature of the natural world, proclaiming that the seasons change four times a year and the sea ebbs and rises (79), her monologue is in defense of a decidedly unvirtuous end: her inherent need to replace a current lover with one who is younger and more handsome. No matter which device or theme Martona plunders from the world of official culture, she is always sure to deflate it with a type of ribald, self-effacing laughter infused with the spirit of the Russian carnival.

Matvei Komarov (ca. 1730–1812)

Although two of Komarov's novels were the first best sellers in Russian literature, his life is far from an open book. What little we do know of it has been compiled by the Russian scholar Viktor Shklovsky using information gleaned from the prefaces and dedications in Komarov's works, stray comments in the texts themselves, and advertisements for them.[28] According to Shklovsky's investigations, Komarov was a serf belonging to the Russian noblewoman Anna Loginovna Eikhler (20). The exact date of his birth is unknown, and the first mention we have of him is in his preface to *Vanka Kain*, where he reports that in 1755 he heard Kain recite his story in the Department of Criminal Investigations in Moscow (21). As a serf, Komarov would almost certainly have had a minimal education at best, and as he himself admits in the preface to his fantasy tale *Nevidimka*, "being among that number of people of low condition, I am untaught in any kind of learning other than Russian grammar" (ii). Just one page later, Komarov also mentions, however, that "from my youth I have been practiced in the reading of books, at first religious and then also secular ones" (iii), and he was skilled enough to begin his career as a writer by composing a poem to his owner's brother-in-law. Entitled "A Letter to Prince Khovansky" (1771), this work shows both the strengths and limitations of Komarov's knowledge and literary abilities. On the one hand, no doubt influenced by certain Enlightenment clichés in the air at the time, he praises Khovansky's rational approach to combating the effects of the plague that was then ravishing Russia and also cites as authorities such renowned figures as Aristotle and Copernicus. On the other hand, Komarov's language is conversational in style, and unrhythmical lines interrupt the generally iambic pattern of his verses (22–24). Eikhler died in 1785, and by 1787 Komarov was most likely given his emancipation. In that year he began signing the dedication to his works with the word "servant" rather than "slave" and also advertised to find a patron. At first, freedom apparently meant straightened economic circumstances, for Komarov resorted to selling some of his works himself, as well as a dog that was most likely willed to him by Eikhler, as a way of meeting expenses (27–28). Soon his fortunes took a turn for the better, however, as *Vanka Kain* and *Milord George* rolled off the presses in printing after printing. The last time we hear his voice is in the dedication of his miscellany *Various Written Materials*, which he published in 1791. Although a popular legend has it that Komarov died in 1812 in Moscow at the hands of the French, there is no reliable information to confirm such a claim.

As difficult as it is to paint a portrait of Komarov the man, it is much easier to assess the character of Komarov the literary figure. In the span of just twelve years, he published a wide array of works, both fiction and nonfiction. To the latter category belong *An Account of Thirteen Ancient Weddings* (1785), *Ancient Letters of the Chinese Emperor to the Russian Sovereign* (1789), and, at least partly, the miscellany *Various Written Materials* (1791). More specifically, *Ancient Letters* comprises five missives full of complaints about the violence and license of Russians who kidnap, rob, and trespass in Chinese lands, and *Thirteen Ancient Weddings* describes the weddings of various monarchs, mostly Russian princes and tsars, beginning with Grand Prince Vasily Ivanovich (reigned 1505–33) and ending with Aleksei Mikhailovich Romanov (1645–76), Peter the Great's father (145–47; 134, 138–39). With the publication of this type of historical material, Komarov was following a trend of the time (134), and *Thirteen Ancient Weddings* in particular shows that he could be in step with even such a leading figure of the Enlightenment as Novikov, who offered an account of the very same unions in his *Old Russian Library* (1775) (139–44). The last title in the category containing Komarov's nonfiction, *Various Written Materials*, demonstrates quite clearly that he was more than just a would-be imitator of the leading lights of his day. On the one hand, it does contain odes, sonnets, and idylls—to name just a few of the genres represented—by some of Russia's most celebrated enlighteners, therefore confirming Komarov's familiarity with high culture of the late-eighteenth century. On the other hand, some of the material that fills out this miscellany, such as folk remedies for preserving fruit and eradicating cockroaches and mice, also underscores that their compiler was at the same time very much a son of the subculture.

Komarov's nonfiction titles and miscellany all appear to have sold well, but it is of course with his novels—*Vanka Kain* (1779), *Milord George* (1782), and *Nevidimka* (1789)—that he built his reputation. Although it is the least well known of the three, *Nevidimka* most clearly reveals the strategy Komarov employed to become the first best-selling writer in Russian literary history. In order to target the widest audience possible, *Nevidimka* was issued in large type with only two-thirds the number of lines per page as in *Vanka Kain* and *Milord George*, and as Komarov himself puts it in the preface, it was written "in a simple Russian style which uses no kind of rhetorical eloquence so that people of any station can profit by the reading . . . of such simple tales" (iv, v). As successful as *Nevidimka* certainly was by eighteenth-century standards (a second printing was issued in 1790 [*Svodnyi katalog* 2: 56]), its popularity was dwarfed by Komarov's first two efforts in the genre. Not only were these works runaway best sellers in their own century—between them they were issued more

than a dozen times before 1800 (*Svodnyi katalog* 2: 56–58, 435–36)
—but they remained so into the nineteenth and even the twentieth century. Shklovsky has calculated that Komarov's individual works were
published a minimum of thirty times with his first two novels making up the bulk of this total (*Komarov* 16), yet even this figure fails
to account for what must have been a high number of unauthorized
versions. As Shklovsky notes, after Komarov's lifetime no printing of
Milord George bore his name, and anyone who wanted to could pub-
lish it (*Komarov* 77, 122).

In his analysis of Komarov's place in the history of Russian letters,
Titunik categorizes him as something less than a full-fledged author.
Summarizing Komarov's accomplishments, he labels him a "literary
professional 'adaptor,' [someone who prepared] materials for printed
publication, often supplying prefaces and notes and sometimes revis-
ing or completely rewriting the material itself" ("*Van'ka Kain*" 353).
Even though Komarov was not the author of a single work he could
completely call his own, Titunik argues that scholars still have a lot
to learn from him. He writes that "Komarov's sophistication may not
have been markedly above the level of the material with which he
dealt, but he had the appropriate pretensions; and in this case the pretensions are far more important for literary history than the quality of
the actual results" (353). Of all Komarov's publications, no individual
work illuminates his pretensions—and abilities—as an adaptor better
than *Vanka Kain*. As his treatment of the Kain legend bears out, Komarov was a man who was at home in the literature of the subculture
but who also had a good ear for the ideas and standards of the Russian
Enlightenment. Kain was a historical figure who operated in Moscow
and central Russia in the 1730s and 1740s. An escaped serf who turned
to a life of crime and became a thief, robber, and arsonist, he won
his freedom when he agreed to turn police informer, yet even then he
continued to work both sides of the law by using his official position
to cover his activities as a crime lord in Moscow. In the 1770s, at least
two first-person accounts of Kain's life were published, which it is believed were either written or more likely dictated by Kain himself. As
Komarov mentions in his preface, he adapted one of these accounts to

form the core of his third-person retelling of the Kain tale. In addition
to switching the voice of the narration, Komarov made other significant changes to his first-person source, and, to paraphrase Titunik, it
is the nature of these alterations that offers an insight into Komarov's
importance in Russian literature.

Komarov's chief modification to the first-person account of Kain's
life was to insert into his version of the story a moralizing presence
that reflects an Enlightenment view of the world. He begins the process
in just the second sentence of his preface by defending the primacy of
reason in life and denouncing the obscurantism of the church: "It is
well known to many, I would say, that the reading of books, which
enlightens the mind, has become a common occurrence in our country, and that time which was darkened by the shadow of ignorance,
in which those who read the writings of Aristotle and various other
books were anathematized, has already passed" (111). Komarov then
expands the focus of his Enlightenment perspective by endorsing the
spreading tendency among people of the lower and middle classes to
engage in reading (111); flatly declaring that "nature brings all people
into the world equally" (111); and offering his tale of Kain to the good
will of his readers in the hope they will find it "worthy of some note"
(113). On more than one occasion in his brief preface, Komarov emphasizes the Enlightenment conviction that writing, especially on a
historical topic like the legend of Vanka Kain, is akin to a civic duty,
and he closes this section by asserting that despite the difficulties he
confronted in finding source material on Kain, he has decided to push
on with his project in order to be of use to society, unlike "the lazy servant of the Gospel who hid his master's money in the ground" (113).

As soon as Komarov starts recounting his version of Kain's adventures, he immediately resumes the didactic, authoritative voice he
established in the preface. After opening the novel with a one-sentence
statement defining Kain's social class and place and date of birth, the
narrator enters into a monologue on his subject's upbringing and the
impact it had on his adult life. Comparing human reason to a stream,
he maintains, on the authority of "wise people," that the purity of its
water will be determined by its course: "should it go through sand

and stone, [it] will emerge as the purest, crystal-clear source, but if its course goes through slime, swamps, and unclean places, then its water will be cloudy and not good for anything" (115). No doubt with the limited education of his readership in mind, Komarov explains his metaphor by directly stating that if children are brought up in the company of less-than-reputable people, they themselves will become depraved (115). Before bringing this brief opening monologue to a close, Komarov bolsters his authoritative credentials by paraphrasing the words of Pascal and Aristotle regarding an individual's susceptibility to the social environment. Although he mentions neither philosopher by name, referring instead to "learned people," the categorical way the narrator proclaims these ideas leaves little doubt that Komarov views them as unassailable truths. By the time he has finished explicating the central metaphor of the stream, Komarov has established a moral framework for analyzing Kain's adventures and even gives us his authoritative assessment of them. As his final thought on the subject, he concludes that Kain was unable to escape the malignant influence of the society he kept, which led him to a life of crime and, eventually, to "irrevocable ruin" (116).

After this opening salvo of overt moralizing, the narrator continues to intersperse his account of Kain's life with didactic commentary all the way to the close of the novel. It is interesting to note, however, that even though his interjections leave no doubt as to his interpretation of an event, they are rather few and far between and often stated almost in passing. For instance, after a lengthy description of an incident in which Kain is released from police custody only through the machinations of a duplicitous clerk, the narrator quickly exclaims: "However, Dear Reader, we shall leave these civil servants to rattle their bones, we shall leave them in peace and let them, as is their wont, practice their insidious, slanderous deceits, for this pertains to us not in the least; only may God grant that we never have anything to do with them" (135). As strong as this condemnation and warning are, the total space allotted to them in comparison to the description of Kain's (and the clerk's) transgressions is quite brief. The same could also be said about the didactic conclusion of the novel. Toward the end of the lengthy recounting of numerous episodes in Kain's criminal career, the narrator unambiguously states: "But now we shall direct ourselves to the end of Kain's deeds, to which a just fate is preparing worthy retribution and his destiny is drawing nigh, for it is not possible to evade the hand of fate" (175). Again, the message is clear, but it is squeezed in between accounts of two of Kain's many criminal acts, and the promised description just one page later of his eventual arrest, conviction, and sentencing to hard labor is treated so factually and dispassionately that it is hard to see which side the narrator is on. Clearly, despite the effort Komarov has invested into framing the first-person account of Kain's adventures with a moralizing presence, it would seem that his sole intent is not to make Kain an example of a life gone wrong.[29]

The element of the Kain tale that Komarov could not, or would not, totally efface from his novel was the carnivalesque spirit that runs throughout his source material. Shklovsky writes that "both in Komarov's account and in the anonymous [first-person] version [of the story], the orientation is not on Kain's crime but rather on his adventures" (*Komarov* 63). Taking such an approach to Kain's life no doubt increased its audience appeal, but doing so paints a decidedly different picture of the brigand than the historical record would seem to justify. For example, in reality, the flesh-and-blood Kain so terrorized Moscow with the fires he set that many of its unnerved inhabitants fled to St. Petersburg to escape the threat he posed (Shklovskii, *Komarov* 56). In the version of events that Komarov presents to us, however, only one passing mention is made of Kain the arsonist, and even then it is recounted as something of a joke. Besides adding a moralizing presence to his novel, Komarov made several other revisions to the first-person account he adapted,[30] but just as important as these changes was the core idea that he borrowed mostly intact: the image of Kain as more of a merry prankster than a dangerous criminal and urban terrorist. Throughout the novel, Kain's transgressions are described in great detail and at times even denounced, yet when they are judged against the conduct of the criminal element surrounding him, he looks rather good by comparison. In Komarov's version of his life, not only does

Kain never kill anyone,[31] but the actions he undertakes in his dual roles
of police spy and kingpin of the Moscow underworld, most of which
end up working against the interests of officialdom, are often recorded
with at least a dash of humor.

Ingrained with a carnivalesque view of life, Kain frequently suc-
ceeds in temporarily turning the world upside down by coming to the
rescue of those, including himself, who are oppressed by the official
order of society. No sooner are we introduced to Kain, than we find
him plotting to save himself from "the yoke of slavery" (116) by es-
caping from his master after stealing whatever valuables he can carry
off. Despite the seriousness of such behavior, which he knows will be
met with the cruelest of consequences if he is caught, Kain encapsu-
lates the experience with the following mocking piece of doggerel that
he tacks to his master's gate as he leaves the premises:

> Drink water like a goose, eat bread like a swine,
> but let the devil work for you, not I. (118)

Like the self-proclaimed carnival king of Moscow, Kain enjoys tweak-
ing official culture whenever the opportunity arises, and if the incident
can be capped off with a wink and a nod, so much the better. In another
episode, Kain tells a general's servant that he intends to rob his master.
Rather than saying this in so many words, however, he uses a coded
phrase, proclaiming: "'Is it not so your general always goes around in
a fur coat, and that is why he is nicknamed Shubin [in Russian *shuba*
means "fur coat"]? Well, tell him we'll send some tailors for the sewing of his summer clothes'" (141). For Komarov's Russian readers,
the humor in Kain's reference to the general's name is immediately
apparent, and the grinning bandit's wit helps to deflate some of the
menace lurking in his threat. On another occasion, Kain makes use
of a humorous play on words when he frees a peasant who was being
forcibly conscripted into the army. Before concluding this escapade,
he throws a bucket of tar over the head of the peasant's former captor,
saying: "'Your archimandrite is a fool: it's long past time you became
a monk'" (162). Once again, Komarov's eighteenth-century readers

would no doubt have chuckled over Kain's pun on the Russian root meaning "black," which not only describes the color of tar but also forms the basis of the Russian word for "monk."

Many of Kain's adventures end with a joke or at least with a wry description designed to elicit a smile, but the incident that shows him at his insolent best involves his machinations in the service of love. In this episode, Kain is entreated by an acquaintance to free his wife, a nun who had run off to marry him only to be captured by the authorities and sequestered in a convent. For a price, Kain will do anything, and in short order he impersonates an emissary of a high governmental office, gets the nun placed into his custody, and then returns her to her husband. With this briskly executed ruse, Kain not only manages to line his own pockets but also ends up thwarting the efforts of the powers that be, in this case the church. This is not a bad day's work for any rogue, but for a carnivalesque hero the moment needs to be punctuated with a humorous lesson. As the grateful husband gives Kain his reward, the jester replies: "'If they gave me one hundred rubles for every nun, then I would drag all of them out of the Ascension Convent'" (167). With a personality infused with the spirit of the carnival, Kain would no doubt even do this for free—or perhaps for a hearty measure of vodka.

Nikolai Mikhailovich Karamzin (1766–1826)

Nikolai Karamzin, "the foremost Russian Sentimentalist writer and thinker" (Hammarberg 14), was born the year Chulkov published volumes one and two of his first literary work, *The Mocker*. The son of a "relatively poor" retired army captain (Kochetkova, *Karamzin* 18), he spent the first ten years of his life on the family's small estate near Simbirsk (present-day Ulyanovsk), which is located on the Volga River approximately 550 miles east of Moscow. While at home in these early years, Karamzin learned German from a local doctor and French from the wife of a neighboring landowner (Cross 1), and he also indulged a healthy appetite for reading, being "especially drawn to the popular moral tales and novels of heroic adventure which were available to him" (Anderson vii). In 1777 he was sent to Moscow, where he entered the boarding school of Matthias Schaden, a professor of moral philosophy at Moscow University (Cross 1; Kochetkova, *Karamzin* 18). During the four years he spent there, Karamzin honed his love for languages, was introduced to German literature, and became an admirer of England, which he called "'the country most attractive to my heart'" (Cross 2). The young Karamzin must have been a promising student, for he was permitted to attend lectures at the university (Anderson viii), and in general he acquired a sound education based on the firm bedrock of "the mainstream Germano-masonic pedagogy, with its pronounced moral and religious basis, which dominated Moscow University and its *pensions* in the 1780s and 1790s" (Cross 2).

In 1785, after spending some time in St. Petersburg as a member of the Preobrazhensky Guards as well as back home in Simbirsk, where he entered the local Masonic lodge, Karamzin returned to Moscow. According to his close friend the poet Ivan Dmitriev, it was here that Karamzin was transformed into "'a pious student of wisdom, with a burning eagerness for self perfection'" and that his "'education began, not only literary but moral'" (Cross 4). In the company of some of the most distinguished Masons and Enlightenment figures of late-eighteenth-century Russia, he began to make his mark in literary history with his guiding star the ideal of "the individual's obligation to live by a transcendent creed of moral awareness" (Anderson viii). Karamzin quickly joined two of the most prominent ventures of the day, both sponsored by Nikolai Novikov: the Friendly Learned Society and the journal *Children's Reading for Heart and Mind* (Cross 4, 21–22). The common denominator of Karamzin's contributions to these two undertakings, and indeed their very raison d'être, was an emphasis on the moral and spiritual improvement of the masses. For the Learned Society, he translated, among other works, Haller's *On the Origin of Evil* (1786), Shakespeare's *Julius Caesar* (1787), and Lessing's play *Emilia Galotti* (1788) (Cross 11–21), and his efforts for the journal, which he co-edited from 1787–89, included translations of moral tales by Mme. de Genlis, Thomson's *The Seasons*, and Gessner's idylls (Page, "Karamzin" 215). Moreover, the pages of *Children's Reading* also contain Karamzin's first original work, including the tale "Evgeny and Julia" (1789), where "with a simple, graceful prose style [he] tempered the story's Masonic-religious theme of submission to the will of God" (Page, "Karamzin" 215). By 1789, after four years of apprenticing with the leading figures of the Russian Enlightenment, Karamzin had become a new man. As Cross sums it up:

> Karamzin's reading had made him familiar with many of the leading writers of the eighteenth century; he was fluent in French and German, translated proficiently from English, knew a little Italian and Greek. In general, he received the literary education of a cosmopolitan in the approving eighteenth-century sense of a man equipped to take his place in a brotherhood of enlightened minds, rising above nationalistic squabbles and imbued with a love of humanity and true enlightenment. (34)

In May 1789, aided by the efforts of his influential Masonic friends, Karamzin left Moscow for a European tour. When he returned in July of 1790, he resumed his literary career in earnest, and by 1803, when he abandoned literature to concentrate on the writing of his epic *History of the Russian State* (12 volumes, 1818–26),[32] he had risen to become the most celebrated Russian writer of his time. Given the relatively brief span of his literary activity, Karamzin's list of accomplishments is extraordinary. He was Russia's first professional author (Hammarberg 10), the first Russian to write classic works in prose (Page, "Karamzin" 216), and "the leading representative of sentimentalism in Russia," "the first to express it fully in his work and to exemplify its main tenets in his poetry and prose" (Nebel 7). More specifically, in the realm of prose fiction, Karamzin can also lay claim to having pioneered Russian efforts in the genres of the Gothic tale ("Bornholm Island," 1794), the *Bildungsroman* (*A Knight of Our Time*, 1802), and the historical tale ("Martha the Mayoress," 1803) (Anderson 19). Karamzin's impact on Russian belles-lettres also resulted in part from his broad range of interests and activities. In addition to being the foremost Russian prose writer of the last decade of the eighteenth century, he was also a poet, an essayist, the editor of four literary journals and almanacs, and a critic of Rus-

sian and foreign literature (Kochetkova, *Karamzin* 34–38). Through his
wide-ranging efforts in prose, verse, and criticism; his development of
a simple, expressive, and elegant writing style; and his ability to incorporate the most fashionable forms and ideas of West European literature
seamlessly into his work, Karamzin did more than anyone in eighteenth-
century Russia to create a modern Russian literary language and mold a
sophisticated reading public (Hammarberg 11–12).[33]

The philosophy, forms, and language of Russian Sentimentalism,
which were "most fully and richly expressed in Karamzin's works"
(Kochetkova, *Karamzin* 7), were not an indigenous inspiration. Like
the aesthetic of Neoclassicism in the middle of the century, they were
imported into Russia after "decades of maturation in the West. England
contributed its Sterne, Richardson, Thomson, Gray and Macpherson.
France made its offering through Rousseau, Marivaux and Prevost.
Germany had its Goethe, Kant (in his late moralist writings), Gessner,
Herder and Lavater. The full impact of their combined thought and
work made itself known in Russia almost as a monolithic force. Its
influence was irresistible" (Anderson 33–34).[34] In drama and poetry
and in novels such as Richardson's *Pamela* (1740), *Clarissa* (1748),
and *Sir Charles Grandison* (1754); Rousseau's *Julie, or The New Heloise* (1761); Sterne's *Tristram Shandy* (1759–67) and *A Sentimental
Journey* (1768); and Goethe's *The Sorrows of Young Werther* (1774),
Sentimentalist writers replaced the rationalist, objective view of the
world that served as the touchstone of the Neoclassical movement
with a "cult of feelings," in which "the artist's chief requisite was that
he must have an open and feeling heart" (Anderson 31). Emotion now
takes precedence over reason as both "the characterizing element in
human nature and as the chief guarantor of virtue. . . . The abstract and
generalized figures of classical fiction are replaced by living, actual,
flesh-and-blood men and women located in a perfectly concrete place
and time," and fictional characters frequently belong to the middle
class, as did their authors (Brown, *18th Century* 546).[35] Other traits
of the movement include a preference for the country over the city,
an appreciation for the beauty of nature, and an emphasis on the individual and the local rather than on society and the world (Anderson

30–31). It is during the period of Sentimentalism, for instance, that an avid interest in national history, language, folklore, and architecture begins to replace a universal preoccupation with the wonders of classical Greece and Rome (Pumpianskii 433–35).

When Karamzin embarked on a full-time literary career in the early 1790s, there was little for him to build on in the way of Sentimentalist prose fiction in his native language. Although the roots of Russian Sentimentalism stretch back at least into the late 1750s, they mostly tapped the genres of drama and verse. One of the oldest original Russian works to incorporate the sensibility of the new movement came from the pen of Mikhail Kheraskov. During his lengthy career, Kheraskov was best known for producing epics, tragedies, and odes within the framework of the Neoclassical aesthetic, but in 1758 he issued *The Nun of Venice*, a work that was the first in a long list of sentimental dramas written by Russian playwrights over the next two decades (Page, "Sentimentalism" 395–96). In the 1770s and 1780s, the sentimental drama was wedded to music to launch the genre of the comic opera, and this period marks the beginning of sentimental verse in Russia as well (Page, "Sentimentalism" 396).[36] As for a Sentimentalist prose fiction, however, there are few highlights before Karamzin comes on the scene. Fyodor Emin, the constant target of Chulkov's mockery, led the way with his *Letters of Ernest and Doravra* (1766) (Segel, "Classicism" 52), which was itself modeled on Rousseau's *The New Heloise*,[37] but it failed to start a trend. In the next twenty-three years, there are only a handful of major works that could be placed under the same rubric as this pioneering effort, including two by Emin's son Nikolai and Pavel Lvov's *A Russian Pamela, or The History of Maria, a Virtuous Peasant Girl* (1789), which, as the title implies, is an imitation of Richardson's novel (Nebel 72–75, Tosi 194–95).[38] It would be up to Karamzin through the publication of his *Letters of a Russian Traveler*, which he began issuing serially in 1791 in his *Moscow Journal*, to set the standards for the still emerging genre.[39]

In answer to the question he poses with the title of his famous essay "What Does an Author Need?" Karamzin responds that "he must have a good heart if he wants to be a friend and favorite of our soul, if he wants his talents to shine like an unwavering light" (60). Art "should concern itself only with *the beautiful*, depict beauty and harmony, and disseminate pleasant impressions in *the realm of feeling*" (61). With these two brief passages, Karamzin expresses what Gitta Hammarberg has identified as the three guiding principles of the Sentimentalist view of the world: solipsism, sympathy, and pleasure. In the first of these, an emphasis on "the poet's mission as an official intellectual leader and teacher," which was essential in the Age of Neoclassicism, gives way to an appreciation of his "subjective aesthetic experience" (4–5). Thus Karamzin sees an author as someone who wishes to touch readers by "paint[ing] a portrait of his soul and heart" for them ("Author" 61). The author's solipsism was to be tempered by the principle of sympathy, which posited that people were "able by nature to sympathize with each other, to identify in some way with the experiences of their fellow humans" (Hammarberg 6). In other words, an author can serve as a light for others, as the "friend and favorite of their soul," because he can understand their plight, and they his. As Karamzin instructs us later in his essay: "You wish to be an author: read the history of the misfortunes of the human race — and if your heart does not bleed, drop your pen" (61). From this dictum would come the torrent of tears that stains the pages of virtually every work of Sentimentalist literature. Karamzin's insistence that art be concerned with the beautiful underscores Hammarberg's third principle, pleasure. It is based on "the recognition of one's goodness," that the "divine spark" of God is in each person. Sentimentalists presupposed that "since man is naturally inclined towards his own pleasure and towards avoiding pain, it follows that he is also naturally inclined toward goodness and beauty" (Hammarberg 7–8). It is on the basis of this belief that Karamzin could find pleasure not only in the overt virtues of this world but even in a fundamentally tragic story—if through his affective narration of it, he was able to touch the hearts of his readers.[40]

"Poor Liza" is an iconic text in the history of Russian literature. Not only is it Karamzin's most famous work, but it also serves as a model of the sentimental tale in Russia.[41] For example, Karamzin's account of a simple peasant girl who falls in love with and is eventually betrayed by the nobleman Erast satisfies the Sentimentalist preference for creating believable characters anchored in a concrete time and place. In an advertisement for the separate edition of *Poor Liza* published in 1796, the story was described as "'a moving and sensitive historical tale'" (Kochetkova, *Karamzin* 39), an idea reinforced in the text itself when the narrator laments that he has written a history rather than a novel (195). Apparently a significant number of readers accepted "Poor Liza" as a page torn from the book of life, for after its publication people made frequent pilgrimages to the site of the story, where they carved their names and sentimental inscriptions on a nearby oak tree and wept over the fate of the trusting, unfortunate, and to them quite real heroine (Kochetkova, *Karamzin* 38; Nebel 122).[42] Focusing on a virtuous young woman from the peasant class also enabled Karamzin to indulge in any other number of clichés of the Sentimentalist worldview.[43] Liza resides with her mother in the near-perfect world of the countryside, where it is still possible to lead a virtuous life. They are devoted to each other and to the golden memory of Liza's departed father, revel in the peacefulness and beauty of nature, and earn a meager but honest living from Liza's weaving and knitting and the flowers she sells in nearby Moscow. Unbeknownst to her, her first encounter with Erast on one such trip to the capital marks the beginning of the end of her country idyll. Good-natured but weak and infected with the vices of upper-class society, Erast is enchanted by Liza, tracks her to her humble cottage in the countryside, and eventually wins her over, body and soul. Full of such Sentimental commonplaces as breathless oaths of eternal devotion, copious tears, and numerous declarations of friendship, their love affair is itself a standard plot line of the movement.

In his essay "On the Book Trade," Karamzin warns that "as soon as there is a distance between author and reader, the former cannot strongly influence the latter no matter how intelligent he may be" (119). To facilitate a sense of intimacy with the readers of "Poor Liza," Karamzin creates a narrator who knows how to use his knowledge and sensitivity to become a trusted "friend and favorite" of our hearts. He begins the tale by underscoring his credentials: "Perhaps no one living in Moscow knows the environs of the capital as well as I do, for no one is more often in the countryside than I, no one roams about on foot more than I. . . . Each summer I find pleasant new settings or discover new charms in familiar ones" (181). The narrator knows the ground Liza walked some thirty years before as well as anyone, and, even more important, he confides at the end of his tale that he has learned of her story from an authentic source: none other than Erast himself. In addition to positing the veracity of his "melancholy history," the narrator quickly moves to impress us with his sensitivity. Echoing the dictum in "What Does an Author Need?" that one's heart needs to bleed over the misfortunes of humanity, the narrator introduces Liza's tale with the lament: "Oh! How I love those subjects that touch my heart and compel me to shed tears of tender sorrow!" (182). And of course, it is Karamzin's intention that we shed those very same tears along with his narrator, an intention he actively and openly pursues at every turn in the text. From the moment he begins telling Liza's story, the narrator makes no secret of how this tale has affected him and where his sympathies lie. Liza's unjust fate is "lamentable" (182), she is "beautiful in soul and body" (196) as opposed to the "rash young man" Erast (190), and as Erast leaves Liza behind to go off to war, the narrator says of the scene: "What a touching picture!" (193) Later in the story, when Erast tells Liza he is abandoning her to marry another woman, the narrator unashamedly registers the impact this news has on him by exclaiming: "My tongue does not move—I gaze toward heaven, and a tear rolls down my face" (195). More than two hundred years after Karamzin first wrote these words, it is clear that he has realized his literary credo, for as Toporov sums it up: the introduction of "a narrator who is present and telling the tale right here and now, as opposed to some abstract author who existed in another time and place, creates the indispensable effect of a direct interaction with this narrator or, if you prefer, of a spontaneous intimacy of relations between the reader and narrator" (88).

In addition to the narrator's explicit cues, Karamzin employs a host of more subtle ploys to prompt a sympathetic response from readers. For example, the numerous exclamation points and dashes strewn throughout "Poor Liza" often impart a racing, breathless quality to the speech of both the narrator and the characters, thereby intensifying the reader's experience of the tale.[44] Hammarberg points out that "the epithets used to describe Liza are of an emotive and positively evaluative nature, rather than strictly descriptive (*poor, beautiful, tender, complaisant, timid, sweet, wan, abandoned, sorrowful*)," and are frequently doubled and even tripled, thus underscoring the narrator's emotional involvement with his heroine (144). Other devices used to heighten the affective coloring of the text include interjections, repetitions of Liza's name, italics, ellipses, diminutives, anaphora, and rhythm, intonation, and sound (Hammarberg 144, 152). Regarding the last of these, Karamzin employs sound symbolism to aid in setting the mood for the sad story his narrator is about to recount. While surveying the gloomy ruins of the Simonov Monastery, the narrator envisions its former inhabitants: here a gray-haired monk prays for "swift delivery from his earthly fetters," there a young one sheds bitter tears as he contemplates the freedom of the natural world outside his cell (182). As an accompaniment to this melancholy scene, the wind wails and moans, as do the narrator's words with their "suggestive repetition of back vowels" (Anderson 78–79). Karamzin returns to this technique—the narrator's language "an accumulation of back vowels and suggestive sibilants"—as he begins the story of his heroine with a description of the deserted country cottage where Liza and her mother, now both deceased, once lived (Anderson 80). From the level of sound to the direct exhortations of the narrator, Karamzin employs a variety of means to attain the Sentimentalist goal of moving readers to a "full co-experience of artistic creation" (Hammarberg 151).

"Poor Liza" is a "melancholy history," but it was not meant to leave readers despairing. On the contrary, on at least three levels there is reason for them to find comfort. First, according to the tenets of Sentimentalism, there is joy in tears, for they are indicative of the "good and tender heart" Karamzin spoke of in "What Does an Author Need?" (60). As Liza forcefully reminds Erast when he tells her not to cry over him as he goes off to war: "'Cruel man! You wish to deprive me of even this comfort! No! After we have parted, I will cease to cry only when my heart has dried up'" (192–93). Second, although Erast's crass conduct toward Liza, his seduction and subsequent abandonment of her, brings the narrator to the verge of cursing him, he restrains himself. As much as Erast's actions have led to Liza's tragic end, such a benign approach is justified, for it is Erast himself who has recounted this story to the narrator, and he has not tried to spare himself in the telling of it. By expressing his regret over his role in Liza's death, Erast shows that he "has acquired a conscience and sincerely repents his past conduct. Although this cannot bring Liza back, virtue has triumphed, and the libertine streak in Erast is reformed. By telling his story, he is in essence making a confession and is entitled to forgiveness" (Hammarberg 142). Lastly, "Poor Liza" "can be seen as a picture of a rather hedonistic narrator, who revels in his own aesthetic sensitivity, which, according to Sentimentalist poetics, is tantamount to his own virtue. Therefore the fact that he can find the most intense pleasure in remembering what, objectively speaking, is a tragic story is not as paradoxical as it may first seem" (Hammarberg 145). According to the aesthetic of Karamzin's age, the one that he did more than any other person to establish in Russia, an author was to be a sensitive soul, someone who could find pleasure in goodness, describe the pain caused by evil, and then transmit these sensations to his readers in a touching and elegant manner. Judging "Poor Liza" against this standard of measure not only provides solace to its readers but also qualifies Karamzin's tale as the quintessential work of Russian Sentimentalism.

The Legacy

Each of the writers in this collection influenced the further development of Russian literature in his own distinctive way. At the time the three were active, in the last half of the eighteenth century, Russian literati had two immense tasks before them: creating a secularized literature on a Western model and forging a standardized literary language capable of expressing the themes, emotions, and devices of such a literature. When the field of focus is narrowed to the second question, there is no doubt that Karamzin stands head and shoulders above not just Chulkov and Komarov but any writer of the period. Although a detailed analysis of the lengthy struggle to fashion a literary language is beyond the scope of this essay, a brief overview of the stylistic merits of the three texts in this collection will give a good idea of how significant Karamzin's achievements were.[45] As a serf who had attained a limited education at best, Komarov was able to couch his account of *Vanka Kain* in what passed for the standard literary expression of his time (Titunik, *Van'ka Kain* 357), but his prose is generally wooden and often confusing. For example, his rendition of the tale is marked by a rather limited vocabulary, pronouns that are often cut adrift from their referents, the inconsistent use of punctuation, and convoluted and at times quite lengthy sentences, the longest of them stretching across fifty lines of text. Chulkov certainly had a more sophisticated command of Russian than Komarov did—including a larger and more expressive vocabulary, a generally far less cumbersome sentence structure, and the ability to establish a comic cadence in his prose when the situation called for it—yet his writing is uneven and at times plodding. On the other hand, "by modeling the literary idiom on the refined language spoken by the aristocracy Karamzin obtained harmonic effects ranging from the adoption of a simple, albeit lyrical phraseology to a carefully balanced syntax" (Tosi 205). In the story of "Poor Liza" that concludes this volume, Karamzin's sense of "harmony and elegance," as Alessandra Tosi puts it (205), is evident at every turn: in his expressive diction, which has been purged of unwieldy high-style Slavonic vocabulary; his short, well-crafted, and often verse-like sentences; and the efficient and well-structured exposition of his little jewel of a story. From the standpoint of contributing to the development of the Russian literary language, the three works that follow will tell the tale not only of Karamzin's genius but also of how much progress had been made in this quest during the roughly twenty years separating *The Comely Cook* from "Poor Liza."

As regards the first challenge noted above, the creation of a secularized literature on a Western model, the impact of the works in this collection roughly corresponds to the date of their initial publication, with the slim text of "Poor Liza" casting a disproportionately large shadow across the landscape of Russian letters. The first of the three to roll off the presses, Chulkov's *The Comely Cook* enjoyed only one printing in the eighteenth century and would have to wait almost 230 years before it was reissued in post-Soviet Russia. Given these facts, Chulkov's narrative would at first glance appear to have a rather limited literary legacy, but in reality it holds a seminal place in the annals of Russian literary history. Scholars disagree as to which work merits the title of the first Russian novel, yet if this honor does not belong to *The Comely Cook*, then Chulkov's tale stands very close to the beginning of the tradition. More significant than the exact epithet accorded this text, however, are the two quite important foundation stones it provided for the edifice of Russian literature. First, Chulkov proved that a traditional fund of native artistic resources was not incompatible with the quest for literary modernization. In addition to the Western models—including the genre of the novel itself—that a host of Russian writers was busily attempting to imitate in their quest to construct a new, modern-style secular literature, Chulkov added a healthy dose of Russian folklore, *lubok*, and the mentality of the carnival. Second, and even more important, Chulkov used these various forms of native expression to infuse the beginning of the novel tradition in Russia with a sense of skepticism regarding the very process of appropriating foreign values. To paraphrase Nikolaev's comment about the literature of the Petrine period (51), Chulkov taught Russians how to laugh, only now the target was the Western-inspired novel and the culture that gave birth to it. By employing risqué proverbs, material taken from *lubok* broadsides and chapbooks, and an anti-heroine and plot inspired by the irreverent spirit of the carnival to mock virtually every aspect of the literature of his day—from chaste, purehearted heroines to the power of reason—Chulkov sounded a clear note of independence for the Russian novel from its very inception.

Standing on the opposite end of the spectrum from Chulkov, who, despite his status as a pioneer of Russian prose fiction, never attained great popular success, Matvei Komarov was Russia's first best-selling writer. In an age when prose fiction had come to dominate the literary scene, Komarov gave readers just what they were looking for. Mingling a modicum of Enlightenment moralizing with the story of a roguish anti-hero, devices taken from the worlds of folklore and *lubok*, and a mocking sense of humor cultivated in the Russian carnival, Komarov's first entry in the novel genre was a smashing success, as attested by the seven printings *Vanka Kain* enjoyed in the eighteenth century alone. Underscoring that such an eclectic blend of high- and lowbrow literature was indeed a winning combination, Komarov's next novel, *The English Milord George*, went through six printings itself in the eighteenth century. Moreover, Shklovsky calculates that at least thirty editions of Komarov's works were published through the first two decades of the twentieth century (*Komarov* 16), and yet another printing of *Milord George* was set to roll off the presses in 1918 (Schaarschmidt 434) when the Soviets confiscated it and then banned all of Komarov's works. Apparently scenes such as the one in which a Moorish queen bares her "magnificent," "pleasing," and "tender" breasts in an attempt to seduce the English lord (65) were not what the authorities had in mind to enlighten the reading habits of the new Soviet man and woman. The prudishness of totalitarian censors notwithstanding, Komarov's novels, and especially *Vanka Kain*, no doubt had a far-reaching and long-lasting impact on what the lower strata of Russian society thought the genre should be. Such was the conclusion of no less a figure than Count Leo Tolstoy, who wrote in the early 1860s that "just as in the past, the people aren't reading what we want them to read but rather what they like: Dumas, the Cheti-Minei, Paradise Lost, Korobeinikov's Journey, Frantsyl Ventsian, Eruslan, [and] the English Milord" (*Polnoe sobranie* 363).[46]

Although Komarov appealed mostly to the literate peasants, tradesmen, merchants, and soldiers who constituted the bulk of the readership of the subculture, his work also did not fail to make an impact on the upper reaches of society. As Tolstoy himself would put it later in the same text quoted above, many respectable citizens were also intimately familiar with works like *Vanka Kain*. Chastising those who looked down on such stories, he writes: "If those who are saddened by the fact that the people read Franstyl Ventsian asked themselves in good conscience how they attained their love for good reading, they would surely have to admit that they are obliged to the very same books they now consider evil for the greater part of their development" (*Polnoe sobranie* 363–64). Prominent Russians who knew of Komarov's fiction included the influential critic Vissarion Belinsky (1811–48), who in 1839 "used the word 'immortality' in reference to the popularity of *The English Milord George*" (Schaarschmidt 436), and Alexander Pushkin (1799–1837)—the poet, dramatist, and prose writer Russians refer to as "Our Everything"—who had a copy of *Vanka Kain* in his personal library (Schaarschmidt 432). Nor did Tolstoy simply pay lip service to the impact Komarov had made in Russian culture. In the last decade of the nineteenth century, in an attempt to reach the common folk at their level, he cofounded the successful publishing house The Intermediary, whose goal was to issue cheap editions in the style of *lubok* literature, and even tried his hand at writing an adapted version of *Milord George* (Schaarschmidt 428). Thus, over seventy-five years after Komarov's death and more than a century after he published his last work, the former serf managed to extend his influence throughout Russian society, even encouraging a response from Count Tolstoy, one of its most privileged members and by far Russia's most well-known literary figure.

Unlike Komarov, whose accomplishments were mostly overlooked or only grudgingly acknowledged by polite society, Karamzin had achieved the pinnacle of his profession by the time he voluntarily left the field of belles-lettres in 1803 to concentrate on writing his history of the Russian state. Even more impressively, his fame would remain at high tide for years—"during the first two decades of the nineteenth century scarcely a literate person in Russia was unacquainted with Karamzin's works" (Kochetkova, *Karamzin* 134)—and his influence would extend even beyond that as new generations of writers and critics engaged with his numerous and varied accomplishments.[47] Many of Karamzin's pioneering efforts in the realm of Russian prose fiction have been mentioned earlier in this essay—among others, he was Russia's first professional author, became the leading representative of Russian Sentimentalism, popularized many new genres, and led the way in molding a new, more modern type of reader—yet this impressive list is far from exhaustive. By the first decade of the nineteenth century, Karamzin had not only made "prose genres palatable for educated readers, thus setting in motion a process of legitimization that was to produce long-term results" (Tosi 196),[48] but owing to "the success of stories such as *Iuliia* and *Bednaia Liza* . . . [his tales] were treated as ready-made narrative models and slavishly imitated" (Tosi 76). From plot construction and the depiction of the inner lives of literary characters to the metatextual rapport established between authors and readers and even specific themes (friendship, the country idyll, and the threat posed to it by the temptations of the city), Karamzin provided his immediate successors with all the building blocks they needed to carry on the work he had started—or, in some cases, even to challenge it (Kochetkova, *Karamzin* 114–17; Toporov 85, 177; Tosi 198–204). Moreover, in a national literature known for its great psychological novelists, Karamzin merits the title of "the true founder of Russian psychological prose" (Orwin 15), and with his belief in the intrinsic goodness of the soul, he also stands at the beginning of a Russian tradition of essentially moral, and often transcendental fiction that finds its fullest expression in the works of Turgenev, Dostoevsky, and Tolstoy (Orwin 28). Despite working mostly in the smaller genres, Karamzin managed to extend his influence over some of the most celebrated novels in all of world literature.

Given that "Poor Liza" is Karamzin's most famous work, it is only fitting that it should have a long and productive history of influencing the course of Russian literature in everything from the finer details of style to the larger units of character, theme, and plot. Concerning the former aspect of the author's craft, Toporov notes that the specifics of the way punctuation is used in the original, 1792, version of "Poor Liza" "more often than not sharply distinguish Karamzin from other writers of the eighteenth century and, strictly speaking, [they] only acquired an important and frequently new semantic significance at his hand" (51). For example, his proclivity for italics was "picked up in the next generation by Zhukovsky and several other writers" (52), and his frequent insertion of ellipses "became an important element ('device') in the poetics of Sentimentalism and then, later, Romanticism" (64).[49] At the level of character and plot, the basic dichotomy of "the morally strong woman who, against all odds, wields moral power over a seemingly stronger man . . . was already a *topos* in Russian fiction [of the first decade of the nineteenth century], as testified by authors as diverse as Mariia Izvekova (*Milena*) and Nikolai Gnedich (*Don Korrado*), who, following the example set by Karamzin's famous story *Bednaia Liza*, opposed their principled heroines to fickle, or outright evil, male counterparts" (Tosi 125). And such tales do not include the many stories and novels that were "directly inspired by *Bednaia Liza*, such as A. Izmailov's *Bednaia Masha* [*Poor Masha*] (1801), the anonymous *Neschastnaia Liza* [*Unfortunate Liza*] (1810), Prince Dolgorukii's *Neschastnaia Liza* (1811) and N. Brusilov's *Istoriia bednoi Mar'i* [*The History of Poor Mary*] (1805)" (Tosi 208n68).

As Russian literature moved into its Golden Age in the middle of the nineteenth century, Karamzin's chef d'oeuvre continued to extend its influence.

> Both Pushkin and Dostoevsky read "Poor Liza" as part of their Russian prose heritage, and . . . they weave mention of it into their works as a tribute to its effects on them. The female protagonist of Pushkin's "Queen of Spades" (1834) is called Liza; so is the heroine of Turgenev's "Diary of a Superfluous Man," who is abandoned by her prince; and so are heroines betrayed by men they love in Dostoevsky's *Notes from Underground* and *The Demons*. (Orwin 15)

Furthermore, Liza's interior monologue registering her disbelief that Erast has abandoned her foreshadows a similar passage by the title character of Tolstoy's *Anna Karenina* (Toporov 201–2), and Erast himself is the literary ancestor of the protagonist of *Notes from Underground*, for like Erast, the Underground Man "first loves [his] Liza, then betrays her, then regrets his betrayal" (Orwin 25). In addition to this impressive list of literary characters who are indebted to Karamzin for at least part of their motivation, "Poor Liza" initiated two of the most important themes in Russian prose fiction of the nineteenth century: the "little man" and the peasant question. Regarding the former theme, Evgeny in Pushkin's *The Bronze Horseman*, Akaky Akakievich in Gogol's "The Overcoat," and Goliadkin in Dostoevsky's *The Double* all can trace their lineage to Karamzin's depiction of the meek and eventually overwhelmed Liza (Kochetkova, *Karamzin* 135). As for the latter, Turgenev's often positive and always balanced portrayal of the peasantry in *A Sportsman's Sketches*, Father Zosima's faith in the basic goodness and spirituality of the Russian peasant in *The Brothers Karamazov*, and the sound worldly wisdom espoused by Platon Karataev in *War and Peace* also have their genesis in the sympathetic representation of Liza and her mother. Like so many aspects of Karamzin's literary activity, his myth of the Russian countryside and its modest inhabitants continued to inspire future generations long after he had passed from the scene.

ПРИГОЖАЯ
ПОВАРИХА,

или
похожденіе

развратной женщины.

Часть I.

Въ Санктпетербургѣ 1770 года.

Title page of the original edition (1770) of *The Comely Cook*

M. D. CHULKOV

The Comely Cook,

or The Adventures of a Debauched Woman

To His High Excellency,

State Chamberlain

And Holder of Various Orders,

My Most Gracious Sir!*

---

    *   His name will not appear here for the reason that I do not wish to err. Books are dedicated to a person according to their content and the disposition of the person to whom the book is offered. I have personally seen many such books that have been presented to people of noble birth, but instead of magnifying their virtues, they served as a satire of them. It is as though the author in wishing to praise his Maecenas,[1] yet knowing neither good sense nor restraint in his praise, instead abused him most absurdly. Fearing such an outcome and, moreover, not knowing the value of the book I have written, I am therefore not dedicating it to any one person. The title of Your High Excellency adorns a man, and therefore I too have used it for the adornment of my book, not desiring, however, to adorn it with some High Excellency's name but only with the letters from which this word is composed and printed. I therefore proffer the following dedication to any most noble and loftily virtuous general, court chamberlain, or courtier whose superlative qualities, condescension, and mercy I desire to praise indefatigably from the bottom of my heart.

Your High Excellency!
Gracious Sir!

Everything in the world is perishable; consequently, this book, which I am dedicating to you, is perishable as well. Everything on earth is inconstant, and so this book is here now, will remain for a time, and then will eventually decay, disappear, and vanish from memory. A person is born into this world to behold glory, honor, and wealth; to experience joy and comfort; and to pass through misfortune, melancholy, and sorrow. In like manner, this book has also come into the world that it may endure controversy, criticism, indignation, and abuse as well as accrue its trifling share of praise. All this will come to pass, and then it will eventually be transformed into dust, just as the person who praised or defamed it.

With the form and title of this book, it is my desire to entrust myself to the protection of Your High Excellency, which is a desire common among all those people who do not possess a portrait of the tsar at home. Worthy people are promoted; consequently, your intellect, virtues, and condescension have elevated you to such high rank. You are inclined to exhibit favor to those in need, and it would suit me quite well to acquire it. Society will have the opportunity of knowing precisely who you are when it has the pleasure of enjoying your good deeds.[2]

Your High Excellency,
Gracious Sir,
I am your most humble servant,
The writer of this slim volume.

Preface[3]

The beasts of field and forest have no faculty for learning,
Nor do fish and reptiles know how to read;
Flies do not congregate to debate about verse,
Nor do the spirits transported on air.
They never speak, be it in prose or verse,
And so it follows, they've never even glanced in a book.
    For this obvious reason,
    My dear reader
    Shall most certainly be
    Someone who has toiled his whole life through
    Over learning and other weighty matters,
And who paves his way beyond the clouds with his mind.
And in his thoughts he never sets
A limit to his will and reason.
    I leave behind all other creatures
And address my words to you, O Man!
        You are a reader,
        A doer,
        A writer of words,
And to sum it up, you comprehend a lot.
You certainly can't read this book upside down,
But instead will look it over from the start
And see in it all of my art.
Find in this book all my mistakes,
Just please, my friend, don't judge them harshly;
Errors are normal for us, weaknesses acceptable,
And all mortals are accustomed to making mistakes.
Though we have traipsed through the fields of learning
    from the beginning of this age,

We've yet to find a man so wise
He has not made at least one error in his life,
Even though he be the type who knows how to dance.
But I've not been schooled in either music or dance,
And am, therefore, quite capable of committing a blunder.

THE COMELY COOK

I WAGER THAT MANY OF OUR SISTERS would call me immod-
est; however, as this vice is for the great part inherent in women, then
not desiring to contradict nature and extol myself as modest, I embrace
it wholeheartedly. Society will see my actions and will certainly dis-
cuss them, and when it has discussed and weighed them all, let it call
me whatsoever it pleases.

It is known to all that we were victorious at Poltava, the battle
where my unfortunate husband was killed.[4] He was not a nobleman
and owned no estate; therefore, I was left without any means of subsistence: I carried the title of sergeant's wife yet was poor. I was at
the time nineteen years of age, and therefore my poverty seemed all
the more unbearable to me, for I did not know the ways of the world
and could not find a situation for myself, and so I became free for the
reason that people like us are never given anything.[5]

At this time in my life I inherited the proverb *Sew large sleeves for
yourself, widow, so you'll have somewhere to put all the scandalous
words*. The entire world fell on top of me, and people hated me so
much in my new life I didn't even know where to lay my head.[6]

Everyone talked about me, accused me, and defamed me with
things I could not at all understand. I was about to break into tears
when an honest old woman who was known to the entire city of Kiev,
for that is where I found myself at the time, took me under her protection and so pitied my misfortune that the very next morning she found
a stately young man for my diversion. At first, I was obstinate, but in
two days' time I gladly set about following her advice and completely
forgot about my grief, which I had felt for almost two weeks straight
following the demise of my husband. This man was more young than
handsome, but I am tolerably comely, and *the bee always flies to a
pretty flower*. He was the man servant of a certain nobleman and spent
money without end, seeing as how it was his master's and not his own.

Thus money served as proof of his love for me and his eternal pledge.[7] Soon thereafter, almost the entire Merchants' Arcade[8] came to know that I was a great fancier of buying all sorts of things, necessities as well as trifles, and the belongings in our house increased almost by the minute and our estate swelled.

I knew well the proverb that *wealth gives birth to honor*, so I hired myself a female servant and set about playing the mistress. Whether or not I knew how to be in charge of people, even I do not know, for at that time I had no need to enter into such trifles; rather, it will suffice to say that I had no wish to do anything myself and so drove my servant as a fool rides his ass. My dear valet wished to command others no less than I, so he hired a boy to serve him during our conversations, and since he was with me ceaselessly, our reign was therefore never interrupted even for a minute. We shouted at our servants just as though we owned them and beat and cursed them as much as we pleased, according to the proverb *You get nothing but misfortune when a fool has his way.* You could say that we handled the situation *by beating them with the stick and paying for it with the ruble.*

The more finery a woman has, the more she feels like parading herself about town, which is why so many of our sisters are corrupted and come to a bad end. I was content with everything and went out to promenade every day when the weather was clear: many people recognized me, and many men wished to strike up an acquaintance with me.

On one occasion, close to midnight, we could hear a man banging on our gate, and he was not so much requesting to be let in as breaking in by force. We would not have let him in but didn't have the strength to resist, and since my dear valet was not with us, I sent my servant to open up. My old woman prepared to meet him, and I, for my part, hid myself and wondered was this not Paris who had come for his Helen,[9] my reasoning being that I was a desirable woman in this city, or at least that's how I thought of myself.

The gates were opened, and the pair of them strode into the room: one of them appeared to be a servant and the other his master, even though the latter was dressed somewhat worse than the first one. Without saying a word, the gentleman sat down at the table, and after sitting there a short while, revealed a snuffbox covered with diamonds. As soon as my old woman laid eyes on it, her timidity transformed itself into joy, and she ceased considering these men enemies of our kind. The young and handsome man inquired of her if this was where Martona lived, and since this was my name, she answered: "I do not know but shall ask the master of the house." Running up to my room, she said I should appear before them, for the gold snuffbox assured her things would turn out well, and then she uttered the proverb *"I'm not blind, I've got eyes in my head."* In such situations I was no one's fool, and to my good fortune, since I had not yet undressed, I appeared before my new Adonis[10] with a triumphant face and noble bearing, and, to tell you the truth, although he did not confuse me with Venus,[11] I was still received as a middling goddess according to the proverb *They greet you according to your dress but see you off according to your sense.* From the very first moment he seemed so tender to me that to please him, I would have gladly abandoned my valet, and no sooner had he made me a gift of the snuffbox, than I was struck by how vile it was to have dealings with a lackey. From this gift with its gold and diamonds, I concluded that this man was not of common birth, in which I was not mistaken. He was a gentleman, and not one of the lowest rank either. This first meeting of ours was an auction, and we talked about nothing else until we concluded our contract: he bargained for my charms, and I ceded them to him for a proper sum, and then we pledged ourselves to each other with a contract in which love was the middleman and my landlady was the witness, but as this type of contract is never reported to the police, it remained inviolable for us even without any formal order. My gentleman resolved to visit me often, I promised to receive him at any time, and so with that we parted.

After his departure, I admired the snuffbox more than Venus had rejoiced over the golden apple.[12] I fondled it as much as I wished; showed it at least a hundred times to the old woman and the servants; and whenever I uttered even just one word, I always gestured and explained myself using the snuffbox. And when my extreme joy permitted me to ease my mind, which had been enraged by the gift, and my body, which had been fatigued by my excessive affectation, I put the snuffbox on the nightstand next to my bed and fell asleep; however, even in my dreams, it appeared vividly before me according to the proverb *Novelty is always handsome.*[13] To tell you the truth, the snuffbox was somewhat worse for wear, but to me it seemed new, insomuch as I had never in my life possessed such things and had never even hoped to.

At nine o'clock in the evening, my former gallant paid me a visit. I must confess my conscience bothered me a bit for getting rid of him so soon, but since I no longer wanted to keep company with him, I feigned being indisposed; however, I had forgotten to take my favorite gift off the bedside table, and no sooner had he seen it than he picked it up and, having surveyed it, asked me where I had gotten such a thing. I told him I had bought it. "Just a minute, madam," he cried, "for I see things in a different light. This is my master's snuffbox, and as he told me himself, he lost it at cards only yesterday. There is nowhere you could have bought it so soon, therefore it must have been given to you by one of those wastrels who are always following you around, so here is how it will be. Until now I thought I alone was familiar with you, but now I see the entire town is visiting you by turns. I'll show everyone right now how elegant you are; I'm going to get the horses, and after I bring them round, I'll strip you of everything, right down to your last thread. Make a fortune off your other friend, but return every last scrap to me!" Having said this, he took his leave and left me in a terrible fright. We didn't know what to do: there was no place to run and no one to defend us, for people of the sort that I was then do not have friends, the reason being our immoderate pride. So we awaited our certain misfortune and the end of our rule. At this point I wasn't counting very much on my new lover and thought that when he got a glimpse of me as a poor wench, he would certainly forsake me. Any gazing into a crystal ball made things look bad for us, and I would have rather consented to die right then and there than part with my possessions, so much had I come to esteem and love them.

About a half an hour later, to my even greater misfortune, my new lover came to call on me. What was I supposed to do? I was in utter disarray, ruin was at the doorstep, and, to make matters worse, my new man would be the witness of my misfortune and abuse. Seeing me in tears, he drew near and began questioning me. I uttered not one word in response and threw myself on the bed. At that very moment my valet entered the house, and coming into the room, he cried, "I'll get even with you!" When he saw my man standing by my bed, however, he ripped the hat from his head and became so frightened he was unable to add even one word more. My new lover asked him why he was carrying on so and why he had come to this place. His cowardice prevented him from explaining the situation truthfully, so he lied two or three times without compunction, and when my master cried out that he should be gone, the matter came to an end.

In an instant it was as though a huge mountain had fallen from my shoulders, and it seemed the horrible cloud of misfortunes surrounding me had scurried by so quickly it never even had the opportunity to obscure the sun. It was not difficult for me to figure out that I had exchanged a servant for his master, and I knew full well that the anger of a valet posed no danger now that his very master was taking my side. I needed to put on a whole new change of clothes, that is, to transform my emotions from fear into unspeakable joy, but as I had frequently read the chapbook entitled *Women's Wiles*[14] and had applied myself zealously to learn its lessons, such a transformation did not seem very wise to me. Little by little I began to moan in such a way it was as though I had been practicing how to swoon on command my entire life, and I told Sveton, for such was my lover's name, that some manner of fit had overcome me. Right then and there I recognized the kindness and good will he harbored toward me. He immediately summoned the surgeon, and although he came, I really needed him not at all, for with just one word my Sveton had the power to cure me of the most perilous fever. From this time on he appointed two of his servants for my needs and on that very same day sent me a silver service or, in simpler terms, dishes. The very first time I sat down to eat with my old woman, who, to tell you the truth, didn't know how to sit at the table or how to go about using a spoon and who was, besides, even a little less sensible than I was, I pronounced to myself the following proverb:

It used to be that Makar dug ditches, but now he's in the governor's office.[15] Happiness gives no one an accounting of its actions, and it is free to bestow the title of governor on an ass and to promote an owl onto the general's staff.

My Adonis was a man of the world and really knew how to handle himself in matters of the heart. In the morning he sent me gifts by way of his valet, who was still unknown to him as my former amour. The latter brought me an entire wardrobe of clothes and bowed to me as though I were his lady rather than his lover, and when I asked him to be seated, he answered me most courteously that such an honor would be above him. It seemed most strange to me that one night had made me the mistress and sovereign of the man who had formerly been my commander. I received the gifts with the important and gracious air befitting a nobleman's paramour, and taking five rubles out of my pocket, I offered them to the valet, who accepted them and, sighing with the deepest sincerity, entreated me to hear something he had to say in private. When we had gone into the other room, he fell to his knees before me and said the following: "Madam! I am no longer the man who intended to fleece you of everything; I surrender it all to you. Take possession of it according to the proverb *Money is mere metal, and clothes do not last, but we value our skin most of all.* I beg you for the sole favor of not telling my master I was familiar with you, and to show you my gratitude for this, I shall take your side and help you to ruin him completely." I must confess that no matter how unscrupulous and greedy I might be, the valet's zeal for his master seemed improper to me. However, virtue was unfamiliar to me even from a distance, and so in no time my former lover and I agreed to ruin his master; however, we did not manage to transfer our intention into action according to the proverb *Life isn't only carnival time, Lent always comes around as well.* In good time you will be able to see exactly what hindered us, if My Dear Reader has not become bored reading of my adventures.

For some weeks' time I delighted in the virtues of Venus and would not have traded my lot for any treasure in the world; however, as everyone knows that happiness is not long-lived and that there is nothing in the world less constant, my fate slipped and took off in a completely different direction. Sveton received a letter from his father, who wrote him to come home as soon as possible, for he felt very weak and despaired for his life. This letter made my lover so pensive he didn't know what to do with me: his father's illness pained him, but parting from me was unspeakably worse. For a time our displays of love gave way to planning, which began and ended with me, for I was the reason for Sveton's uneasiness and I alone comforted him in his grief, and he would have willingly forfeited his father if only he would not have to be parted from me.

A good horse never wants a rider, and an honest man never wants a friend. Seeing Sveton's great sorrow, his neighbor proposed the following remedy: Sveton should travel with me to his estate, which was situated only four miles from Sveton's lands. The neighbor would send a letter ahead to his brother requesting him to take me in and care for me, and he would say that I was a close kinswoman of his wife and that Sveton ought to be allowed to visit me there whensoever he pleased without interference. It was accomplished just as it was proposed, and for such a wonderful scheme my lover gave his neighbor a ring worth five hundred rubles.[16] On the very same day we got our things together and went on our way. My ward did not wish to follow me, so I left her behind and rewarded her as generously as was necessary for the lover of a nobleman to do. I left her without tears, however, for I didn't know the first thing about gratitude, nor had anyone ever instructed me in its ways, and therefore it seemed perfectly natural to me to go through life without it.

In the middle of our excursion, Sveton announced to me that he was married, and just recently so, but he assured me he did not love his wife for the quite common reason that parents frequently marry their children not to the person the children desire but rather come to an agreement among themselves and compel the children to honor it, which is why there is seldom concord between husband and wife. Sveton assured me this is exactly what had come to pass with him; however, this news was a bitter pill for me, and because of it, in two days' time I had wasted away to such an extent it was as though I had been in bed with a fever for a month. I did not lament that I would be deprived of my lover but did fear something much more frightening than a cessation of our love-making. I would have been able, or so I thought, to endure three separations from my lover in one day rather than just one such welcome with which noble-born wives honor our sisterhood for the theft of their husbands. My heart had a direct presentiment of such a storm, and I would have gladly agreed to go back rather than follow Sveton, but, to my misfortune, he loved me greatly and did not want to hear a word about my leaving, and he tried to convince me that his wife would obey him and accept his word as law.

Such a song would have been agreeable to me in the city, but now, the nearer I approached the estate, the more the fear in me heightened by the hour according to the proverb *A cat knows whose meat it has eaten.*[17] Finally, they brought me to the designated place, where I was received with great joy, for the brother of the neighbor who had written the letter thought in reality that I was a relation of his sister-in-law. Thus I thanked Sveton for his society on the road and remained there content with everything.

The next morning, when dawn had not yet broken, my lover came calling on me for a visit, and he made me greatly happy, saying his father had completely recovered and that we would soon be setting our course for the city once more. "My wife wishes to go with me," he told me, "but this can be undone as easily as two times two is four, and she will end up remaining here." Thus, once more preparing ourselves for the road, we yielded to our passions just as we used to, and, to tell you the truth, Sveton found himself in my company more than when he was at home, which in the end became the reason for my misfortune.

Sveton's wife did not delay in suspecting her spouse.[18] Coming to know of my presence from the servants, even though they were strictly forbidden to talk about it, she sent for the master of the house where I was residing. Without beating about the bush, she immediately made out my status and came to an agreement with him to worm out the truth, for he had already begun to suspect me according to the proverb *You can't hide an awl in a sack*, or *you can tell a falcon by its flight.*

A short time later, at the very moment when Sveton and I were alone and, owing to human frailty, engaged in love-making, an armoire, which to my misfortune stood in the same room with us, flew open, and a woman came out of it and cried: "Greetings, my friends!" My lover jumped off me, and I leapt up. Sveton took his leave from the room, and I endured dozens of blows across my cheeks from his wife's hand—and this was just the beginning, although I won't say a word about the end out of courtesy to myself. Let it suffice to say that in no time I was out on the open road without a companion or a cent to my name. This was a bitter time for me, and I felt the unhappiness that surrounded me on all sides intensely, but what was there to do? *The bear was wrong that ate the cow, so too the cow that strayed into the forest.*[19]

The fields and forests were unfamiliar to me. Unlike my lovers, who were enticed by my charms, they offered me nothing; consequently, I found myself in mortal want. By evening I happened upon a village, where I was forced to barter my silk dress for peasant's clothes, as my conscience reproached me for traveling in such attire, and, at the same time, I had not yet gotten used to going around in it. And so, outfitted with patience and my peasant frock,[20] I set off on my way. While on the road nothing significant happened to me, save that I was one comely unfortunate among many, but not everyone is inclined to read such accounts. The rich man fears impoverishment, and such talk has long since become boring to the poor. Thus will I set aside any commentary about my journey and talk about those things that will divert the Reader.

According to the signs of the calendar, I arrived in Moscow on a Wednesday, the day we signify by the ancient pagan god Mercury, the god of roguery, so it is as though I was appointed a cook to a government secretary with his aid.[21] Some scoffers would opine that I had gone from the frying pan into the fire; however, one can often be mistaken. The secretary was a pious man: he never arose in the morning or retired at night without first praying to God; before lunch and dinner he read the customary prayers aloud and always washed his hands; he never missed a Sunday and always attended the liturgy; and on the twelve Church holidays,[22] he rode about to convey his respects or accepted them from his petitioners. Each morning he stood for two hours in prayer, while at that very time his wife was in the antechamber honing her skills at accepting bribes, of which there was no shortage. When they sat down to tea, their young son presented them a list of all the people who had come to see the secretary that morning, which also included what they had brought and what it was worth, and in this way the secretary was able to resolve the matters before him in his department depending on the amount of the offering. This is when I came to realize that all the secretary's clerks took bribes just like their master. When he arrived at the office, his wife[23] would begin reviewing the gifts, take many for herself, and divide the others among the clerks. One week I received about eight headscarves, and that's in addition to the biscuits and apples with which we contented ourselves every day.

At first the secretary's wife loved me for the reason that *one fisherman can spot another from far away in the stream*.[24] She was an obliging woman, who frequently deceived her husband rather than endeavoring to remain faithful to him, which, to tell the truth, he did not strictly demand, for he looked after his profit more than his honor, and thought that even without it his home would be rich and full, like a cup that runneth over. In addition to this praiseworthy gift, the secretary's spouse confined herself to various faults, which she never held in short supply; consequently, she was only sober when she got out of bed in the morning. I did not have this particular vice and therefore was not able to keep her company in it; however, I was her confidante in everything. I was about to take my happy situation for granted when an illiterate minor clerk who lived in the secretary's house in order to make clean copies of his work called my attention to it. It was quite astonishing to me that not knowing how to read and write, the clerk yet knew how to fall in love with me, for I had formerly thought that love never made an appearance in the hearts of scriveners. He wasn't quite on the mark in his duty as a clerk but showed himself to be even less so in his role as a lover. He recognized love but just didn't know which end to grab and how to hold on to it. In the beginning he winked at me and nodded his head, and I comprehended his intention and began laughing at him. Wishing first to inform myself about his mind, I posed three questions for him to decide: Who is the cleverest person in the city, who the most learned, and who the most virtuous?

The next morning he expressed himself to me this way: "I haven't found anyone cleverer than our secretary, who settles all matters without hesitation and always reports about them in an orderly way; there is no one more learned than a certain attorney, who can recite almost every government decree by heart and frequently forces judges into silence; but I can't really say who is the most virtuous of all, and I think there aren't many among the tribe of scriveners who could, for we hear about virtue but rarely." Upon hearing this, I smiled wryly, and then he continued: "So, do you think Poets with their commas and periods are really more intelligent than all other people? If they came down to our department, they would soon forget about putting in their periods because they would be laboring over them for such a good while they would go hungry. The other day, I don't know how, an ode by someone named Lomonosov was dropped off at work, and not a soul in the entire department could make sense of it, and what's more, the secretary himself said it was pure delirium and not worth the most insignificant official document."[25]

Such is the way my lover understood learned people, and, I suppose, he would not have given even the best among them a place among the copyists. He quickly made out that his mind was not to my taste and that he was not to my liking because of it, so he set about pleasing me with gifts, which is why he began to apply himself so diligently to the recopying of his work. And in fact he did give me rather a lot considering his condition because he always took triple the price for each copy he made. As is well known, that is how it works with his type: once a scribe comes under a secretary's protection, he gets triple for everything. At that time I was grieving for Sveton, and when comparing my clerk to him, I wept bitterly, but this occurred because I was stupid. Nowadays our sisters do not carry on so but instead try to rid themselves of one noble lover in order to seek out another as soon as possible and make another bundle. That is precisely why you would not be able to track down in the entire land even one of our sisters, that is to say, such a comely cook as I, who is faithful and would not want to have three or four lovers at the same time.

Through the care and pains of my civil servant, the dress I wore was a little cleaner, and therefore the admirers who came to visit the secretary's wife began to glance at me a bit more tenderly than at the mistress of the house. This pleased her not at all, so she dismissed me from her service.

When I had quit that house, I did not grieve so much, for there was no one there to part with, and therefore I wasn't being deprived of anything. The next day a panderer called upon me, and from the look on his face I could tell he had found me a tolerably good position that would also turn a nice profit for him, since he was paid according to the type of place he discovered. He told me I should smarten myself up somewhat, since where I was going to live, it was not my services that were required but rather my looks. I confess I knew how to dress, the only question being in what, but after I had outfitted myself nicely enough, we set out on our way. When we arrived at our destination, the procurer ordered me to stand by the gate while he informed the master of my arrival and inquired of him if I should come in. In no time he came running back out of the house and ordered me to follow him. When I entered the chamber, I saw a man of already advanced years who had a long, curly mustache and an aquiline nose. He was a retired colonel, who had served in a regiment of hussars.[26] At that moment he was sitting in an armchair counting silver coins; when he caught sight of me, he managed to straighten up a bit, said "Hello, my dear," and requested that I sit down. Then he commanded his servant to heat some water for tea and set about conversing with me.

"I, madam, am a widower, and soon it will be eight days since my wife has died. I'm already getting on in years and have already reached my seventh decade, which means that looking after the household is a great burden for me. I absolutely need a young woman like you who can look after things everywhere, that is, in the pantry, the cellar, the kitchen, and my bedroom, because it is the case that I am already beyond the age when I should be dragging myself around to all these places every day. I am not pinning my hopes on the servants even though I have a cook, for she has attained more than forty years and consequently is not as nimble as a young person, who could keep an eye on many things. As far as wages are concerned, I by no means intend to bargain, but I will be grateful in proportion to the services I receive. After all, I won't live to be as old as Methuselah, and when I die, everything will be left behind and I don't know to whom it will go, for I am a foreigner and have no kinsmen here. Should my overseer find a place in my heart, I shall make her the heiress of my entire estate. I hear, madam," he said, "that you are seeking such a position, so if you like, please remain here with me. I will be extremely glad to have you and have no doubt that you know how to keep house exceedingly well." I was not so dull as to talk myself out of such a proposal. The old man's possessions pleased me, and I immediately set about winning the favor of his money. When I consented to his conditions, he paid the panderer five rubles and gave him a little something extra from the household stores for finding him an overseer who was to his liking, which I could tell was the case not just from the colonel's generosity but from the look on his face as well.[27]

I told him I needed to run home to retrieve my meager belongings, but he would not consent to this and said I would not want for anything. "Here, madam, are the keys to all my wife's clothes; they will fit you just right. Use them as you wish, and they will suffice." Thus, in one hour I took control in the house and had the entire estate in my hands, and not much more than two hours after that I had command of the master as well, for he did not hesitate to reveal that he had fallen head over heels in love with me and that if I were to leave him, he told me, he would pass away before reaching his natural end.

My greediness for fine clothes did not permit me to delay long, so I rushed among the trunks, where I found some rather handsome clothes, but the most pleasing catch of all was some pearls, the likes of which I had not only never worn before but had never in my entire life even seen. Rejoicing excessively in my fortunate discovery and neglecting the demands of decency, on that very first day I began restringing them to my liking, in which task, having put on his glasses, my dear colonel the hussar assisted me by selecting huge pearls, handing them to me, and then kissing my hands. When it was time for lunch, I ate with him, then I had dinner with him and stayed with him afterwards.

From my lover's perspective the days flowed by in deep satisfaction, and, to be completely truthful, even I was not discontented: his riches made me happy according to the proverb *Although gold doesn't talk, it does create a lot of good*. To be sure, his age disquieted me somewhat, but I bore this burden patiently like a magnanimous and constant woman. However, I was not permitted to go anywhere out of doors other than to church, and even that was but rarely, only on the twelve holy days. This seemed rather uncharitable to me because for a woman who had reached the age that I had then, it was not so much spiritual nourishment that I required as good times,[28] but I was content with everything, and when you are in a state of high contentedness, domestic bondage is worse than the strongest prison. We were living at the time near the Church of St. Nicholas (the one on chicken legs).[29] Thus, on one of the Church holidays I wished to attend the liturgy and therefore arrayed myself as magnificently as I saw fit, and, under the watchful gaze of my superannuated lover, I arrived at the church and took my place where the ladies of noble birth commonly stand.[30] Since the colonel was escorting me with great courtesy, no one made so bold as to crowd me or discomfit me in any way, insomuch as my dress and my lover's admiration made me a great lady, and in order not to injure others' esteem for me, I looked haughtily at everyone and said not a word to a soul.

On the right, alongside the dais for the choir, stood a fashionably dressed young man who was not known to me but who was quite pleasing to the eye. The entire service through he never removed his eyes from me and, after an appropriate amount of time, between whiles made all manner of signs to me that are known only to us women—and also jealous husbands and lovers. My old colonel observed this, and not waiting for the end of the service, approached me and called upon me most courteously to accompany him home. I considered this most indelicate and so would not consent to his request. My lover, fearing to anger me, was forced to stay to the end of the service; however, he did not leave my side and remained rooted to the spot. I observed, as I think others would not have done so well in my place, how the expression on my lover's face transformed itself by the minute: sometimes he seemed so pale it was as though he were preparing to enter the lists; at others, he went hot and cold all over, first turning redder than a tomato then breaking out in a cold sweat all over his face, so that, in a word, he found himself in such disarray he could have been taken for a madman. At the end of the liturgy, he took my hand so firmly I was forced to call my pain to his attention, and his hand shook so violently I found myself in motion as well. Thus, in such an indescribable state of disorder, we found ourselves at home.

As soon as we entered the chamber, the colonel proclaimed the following: "No, madam, little do I know how to comprehend feminine beauty and charms; you are more beautiful than I had thought, for which you may charge me guilty. In truth, one may say you are the Russian Helen, and as for what they say about Venus, I give no credence to such nonsense. All these mere youths have set their sights on becoming Paris, and their eyes betray their intentions concerning you. May the Fates save me from sharing the lot of the unfortunate Menelaus.[31] However, I will resist these ravishers with all the power remaining in me. I possess intelligence, power, and wealth, but what good are they to me if you, O Beautiful One, do not feel a love for me equal to the one I feel for you?" With this he threw himself on his knees before me and melted into tears. Thus was I compelled to assume the duty of a passionate lover; I raised him from his knees and, as a sign of my assurance, kissed him on the lips and spoke these words: "My Dearest, is it possible I could be untrue to you and betray my ardent love at its very inception? Death alone will separate me from you, and even in the grave, I shall recall your admiration for me.[32] To please you, I shall renounce the society of all men, and not one of them will be able to entice me; rest assured, Dearest One! Your faithful and sincere lover Martona bids this of you with her tears."

Upon hearing such sentiments, my toothless Adonis calmed himself to some degree; however, so heavily did the young man's gazing upon me weigh on him that he retired for the evening without eating, and in just one half hour he broke his rest repeatedly, shouting at times "Forgive me!" and at others "Desist!" at the top of his voice, and at still others "I am done for" because he was dreaming that I had been carried off or had betrayed him.

Some few days later a man arrived at our house and asked the colonel, would he accept him into his service? The old man refused him the first time, but the man intensified his efforts and sang his own praises to the skies. Taking out his passport, he wanted to show it to the colonel, for he said there was not an honest man around who had as many references as he did.[33] His words seemed sufficiently persuasive to me, for whoever takes it into his head to fend for himself in this way needs to apply himself assiduously in order that he may practice his trade to perfection. This is how I came to take the references from him, and while looking through them, discovered a letter addressed to me. I extracted it carefully, put it in my pocket, and returned the references to the servant, and then I told him to come back tomorrow in the morning when we would have resolved whether or not to take him on.

Although I was not a great adherent of betraying my lovers, the inconstancy inherent in us did not permit me to delay any longer, so I took myself to another room, tore open the letter, and found in it the ensuing declaration:

Dear Lady!

It is not in our power to love someone. All that is beautiful in the world attracts our mind and senses. You are most fair and therefore captivated my heart from the moment I caught sight of you in the church, where it seemed to me that your beautiful eyes spoke as the servant of your heart. And so, assured by this sign, I have made so bold as to express myself to you in the certain hope that although you have not yet come to love me, perhaps you have discovered no reason to hate me.

An Admirer of Your Beauty,
Akhal

I could not say whether there exists even one person in the world who could be commended for having remained firmly on the path of virtue at every moment, and while satisfying its severe demands, refused himself superior, more natural pleasures. I have always held the opinion that everything on earth is inconstant: when the sun is in eclipse, the sky is completely obscured by clouds; the seasons change four times in one year; the sea ebbs and rises; the fields and mountains first turn green, then are covered in white; birds shed their feathers; and Philosophers recast their systems—so how, then, can a woman, who is born for change, love one man to the end of her life? I even laugh at those men who unceasingly commend the faithfulness of their spouses, for it seems to me it would be better to remain silent about such things that reside fully within a wifely domain. I did not belong to the sect of Stoics nor in any way adhered to their system,[34] and therefore did not want to refuse the one who required my indulgence. In the morning, when the servant called, of whose agile mind I was assured from the look in his eyes, I answered him thus: "I consent to whatever is required of me, but the master of the house, the colonel, does not wish to accept you into his service; it seems to me, however, that you have no need of such a position, for even without it you can find the road to your well-being."[35] "This is true," cried my lover. "There are many people in Moscow, and you can catch on with someone else if not with me." The servant was satisfied with our answer and, after expressing his gratitude, took his leave of us.

Our life is based on cares, thus I began to fuss about the situation, and the handsomer Akhal seemed to me, the more I desired to betray my gray-haired Cupid. When new love had begun to reside in my heart, any thought of showing gratitude to him never entered my thoughts, for rare is the woman who is subject to this virtue. I was one of that number of beautiful women who think of themselves as not being obligated to anyone in the world and who dispense their benefactions generously.

The first thing I did was rush off to our cook and confide the secrets of my heart to her. It seemed odd that without any reassurance from me she promised to serve me with her entire being, which made me understand that anyone will consent to serve a rich person, whether his intentions be good or ill. From this time on diverse schemes came to mind for my meeting with Akhal, and you could say that one invention was better than the next. I offered some good ideas, but my confidante was better still. We fixed upon the idea of transforming Akhal into a woman for a time and by such means introducing him to me so that we would always be able to meet without suspicion, and we found no other solution to the problem, for after that time they kept me under such tight watch, I was rarely even permitted to go up to the window.

A sheep craves salt, a goat freedom, and a flighty woman new love. We did not wish to delay our scheme but even for an instant, whereupon the next day my counselor flew to seek out my new lover, and although she didn't know where his house lay, she found it quickly according to the proverb *Your tongue will take you to Kiev.*[36] Akhal received her with great joy and directly rewarded her in the way that lovers do. She relayed to him our intention, to which he concurred without hesitation, and he released her to me with a letter, in which he assured me that to please me, he would go all the way to the bottom of the ocean.

It is true that to please me, he immediately carried out my command. He told the landlord of the house in which he was living that he had received permission to take a leave in the country and would be departing tomorrow but that he would leave his servant behind with some portion of his possessions, which he entrusted to the landlord's safekeeping. When morning dawned, he gathered what he needed and made his way to the Coachmen's Suburb.[37] Then he sent his servant into town or proceeded there himself—I know not which—and purchased more than enough woman's clothing for both himself and the servant. Thus they slipped into their clothes and prepared for their roles in a comedy of the latest fashion. Akhal sent his servant to seek out rooms for them and ordered him to say that they had arrived from another city to visit his sister here. They found a place, rented it, and moved.

Our cook hurried to them and arranged things. When she returned, she said that Akhal would call himself my sister and would send me his servant with the name and in the guise of a young woman, and she also told me what their names would be and taught me how I should greet the supposed maid. So it was that I began to anticipate the fulfillment of my wish with overwhelming joy.

Evening had already turned to night when my servant told me a certain girl was asking for me. When he heard this, the colonel commanded that she be escorted into the chamber, for he observed all my actions most assiduously. At that moment, however, the cook winked at me warily, from which I conjectured that this girl was in fact Mercury who had been sent to me by my Jupiter,[38] and as soon as he entered, I cried at the top of my voice: "My dear, by what chance do I see you here? Could it be that Mother has come?" "Not at all, madam," he answered me. "Your mother remains at home, but your older sister has come. You have not deigned to write us for some time, so she has come here to see you." Then, making his way up to me, he kissed my hand and performed all the proper formalities. I asked him was everyone at home in good health and about many other things, and he answered me so well it was as though he had spent at least the last decade studying how to deceive people. I inquired where they were staying and intended to live, to which he responded that it was quite a distance from us. Since it had already grown late, I delayed the rendezvous with my dear sister until the morrow and entreated my benefactor to order the servant to fly to her to bid her welcome from me and also to invite her to dine with me the next day. "Even though this is discourteous, for I should go to see her myself," I instructed the servant, "one ought not to stand on ceremony with a close relation, and, besides, since she has not yet been able to collect herself, I might inconvenience her with my arrival." Thus the prelude was rather well played, and our servants went to see my dear sister.

I must confess I have never rejoiced as much as I did when I was able to deceive my vigilant overseer so successfully, but the boy was so artful in representing himself as a girl that had I not known, I most certainly would have been deluded myself. At that time my old man came to his senses and began asking me about my family, which is a question that had previously never entered his head, for excepting love, he really had nothing on his mind. I gave him such a wonderful account of my familiars that neither he nor I could in reality come to apprehend what my ancestry was; however, I did not give him the opportunity to prolong such a conversation, which would not have brought me much profit, but rather ventured to commend the exceptional qualities of my visiting sister and above all noted that she was handsome and far more charming than I. "Do not fall in love, my dear," I proceeded to tell him, holding him by the chin, "for I am afraid you will become fascinated with her and will abandon me." "Better that the whole wide world abandon me," he responded in a firm and confident voice, "for I am an adherent of loving until death and consider myself not at all like our present-day Don Juans who exchange lovers daily and seek occasions to betray them yet more frequently. No matter what a beauty a woman might be, she could never entice me, my dear, so long as you love me from the bottom of your heart most true. I shall confess I have rarely courted a woman such as you who is so faithful that you would not even consider betraying me, and, after all, such behavior is truly depraved." After such a pledge from him, I assured him that I was more constant than anyone in the world, which promise he believed, and he esteemed me to such a degree that he was prepared to jump headfirst into the river if only that would have pleased me.

At night, in the morning, and during the day I thought of nothing so much as my designated rendezvous, for the sake of which I spared no pains to heighten my charms. At last the time arrived, and my sister came to call, and although our meeting was not of blood relatives, it was exceedingly loving, and once we had thrown ourselves into each other's embrace, it was only by force that we were pulled apart. Pleasantry followed pleasantry, and kiss followed kiss: my sister pressed me tightly to herself and kissed me quite frequently on the bosom, and I reciprocated with an equally fervent gratitude so that, in a word, even the most meticulous mathematician would not have been able to calculate all our kisses without being in error. We were not just exemplary sisters but, I wager, the type this world has never before encountered. We ate nothing at dinner but contented ourselves solely with gazing at one another, and with each passing minute I found new charms in my sister, as she did, perhaps, in me as well, and we supposed we could live our entire lives without nourishment if only we remained inseparable from one another. My ancient lover confessed that he thought us some manner of marvel, "for," he said, "in my entire life I have never seen such ardent love between sisters. To put it plainly, you could be considered lovers, and were one of you dressed in men's clothing, no one would believe you were blood sisters. I commend your virtue and sincere hearts; here are true relations worthy of great respect."

"We have not seen each other for five years now," my sister said to him, "and we have been parted almost from the time we were infants; therefore, kind sir, it should not astound you that we never tire of looking at one another. We are few, just mother and we two, and we have been orphans since father's passing." "Your virtue is even more praiseworthy because you have not abandoned each other in your poverty and continue to love each other to a degree that is beyond my ability to express. It appears, however, that you do not resemble each other in the least, but enough of that, for it is true that children of the same father are not always created in the same image. I as well had a brother who nevertheless shared no likeness with me."

This is how dinner ended, whereat my old man drank more than was common. It never even entered his head to keep an eye out for anything, and woman's clothes suited Akhal so well there was no occasion for him to hold any suspicion. However, my dear sister delighted me so, I did not want to release her to spend the night at home and therefore begged her to remain with me. Akhal did not consent to this with the intention of forcing the old man to request it, and when I showed myself to be discontented that she had not agreed to my invitation, the colonel took up the question and convinced her she must certainly stay. And what's more, out of respect for our guest he surrendered his bed to us and, wishing us a good night, retired to other rooms.

My conscience bothered me not in the least, for I thought there were people in society who were more audacious than I by far, who in one moment caused more injury than I do in three days' time. It's worth giving yourself up to vice, for it will always seem sweeter and more pleasing than virtue.

Thus my sister and I passed the night together in complete pleasure and in the morning parted at dawn so that our cunning might in no way be observed. I proceeded to my old lover, and excusing my sister, told him she was obliged to leave so early to attend to several necessities. On that very day we dined at her house, and when we returned home, my lover praised her for all he was worth and could not find words enough to express his approbation. And so we were together every day without fail, and everything unfolded for us as well as we could desire. My old man was content to be deceived so artfully, and I was grateful that he conducted himself without showing the slightest awareness of my deception. For his part, Akhal considered himself fortunate to have received from me without any pains that which one often can't obtain with two years of unceasing industry, and, moreover, that he was dealing with the type of man who was so easy to fool and who never thought to take notice of it.

I knew that in our age constancy in love was the type of guest who, upon arriving, cries out "Greetings!" but at the same time has "Farewell!" waiting on the tip of his tongue. A lover remains faithful only when he fails to see any favor from the person he loves. Then he sighs, moans, and, kneeling before her, sheds feigned tears and vows the type of constancy which reigns only in the theater. But when he receives everything from her, then, owing to the feebleness of human memory, he forgets all his oaths in a minute and drives them from his mind. I endured this more than once in my life, but right now my narrative is about my love for Akhal, and it will catch up with the others in due course. Some time later he made known to me his feeling that my life was calamitous and might soon come to the brink of a great misfortune, and, moreover, that it was in fact depraved. I knew all this myself, but as I could not find nor even see a way to change it, I had to remain in such a condition against my will. "I, madam," he said to me, "have dedicated my life to you up to the grave and flatter myself with the hope that I shall never be deprived of your favor. You have offered me your heart, and with this I am content, but in order to show you that I am grateful, I intend to join myself to you in marriage, if only you will have it. I am a nobleman, and although not wealthy, do not consider myself poor. I have no father and no mother as well, and therefore live according to my own free will. There is no one who could prevent me from joining myself to you in marriage. Thus, if it be agreeable to you, give me your word, and we shall prepare ourselves for it. You must leave this city without fail in order to escape the impediments before you. My estate will be a refuge for you, and the obligation of your spouse will serve as your defense and protection. Only then will no one have the right to demand you from me. In this way, your life will assuredly become happy and prosperous." There was no need to ask me twice, for I knew how to distinguish ill from good and what was useful to me from what was harmful. I accepted Akhal's proposal most willingly, and, it seemed to me, he was as a result exceedingly happy. Although I saw things more clearly than others assumed I could, I was not able to make out his dissembling, and on this occasion I truly realized that however keen and resourceful a woman might be, she is always subject to the deceptions of a man, especially at that time when she is most passionate concerning him.

Our compact followed without delay. We immediately kissed the icon and betrothed ourselves to one another, and from that day forward I began to call my sister my husband, and she called me her wife. The next day Akhal proposed that I should receive a goodly sum from the lieutenant colonel[39] for my stay with him, but since he would not consent to this, my husband counseled me to steal everything from him I could lay my hands on so that before entering into marriage, I would be able to clear my conscience with the things I carried off. As my intended spouse was always found near me in the guise of my sister or I always attended him, it was not difficult for us to carry off my ancient lover's belongings, and we were inclined to transfer pearls and money from him, for these things are more obedient than others, and it is possible to pack them away in a trunk or suitcase without raising any suspicion. Finally, when we felt we had carried off enough and that we could live on it in contented prosperity if not for our entire life then at least for two-thirds of it, we began to plan to leave, and with the aid of money, everything is accomplished quickly. Horses were made ready, and my husband set off on the road, saying he would await me at a certain post station.

During the night, when my aged lover found himself in the full pleasure of sleep, I arose stealthily from my bed and successfully quitted the house. After hurrying to the place where horses awaited me, I entered a carriage and flew after my spouse; however, to my misfortune and without any warning, I inherited the fate of the unhappy Phyllis. My Demophon had deceived me and gone away, whereto I did not know.[40] In this instance, I reasoned, he had greater need of my lover's possessions than he did of me, and had been captivated not by my charms but by gold coins and pearls.

I inquired at the post station about Akhal but was told they had not seen anyone passing by who resembled my description. Thus, after having a good cry, I was compelled to turn back, only I didn't know where to go and therefore took lodgings at an inn in the Coachmen's Suburb. The real Phyllis did not bewail the treachery of Demophon but rather only regretted it. I, on the other hand, was so overcome by malice I would have consented to tear Akhal in half had he been in my power and had I the strength to do so, but however much I strained to do this, it was impossible to relieve my fury. My own life was dearer to me than the life of a scoundrel, and therefore I began to reflect upon my condition. Doubt, fear, and despair tore at me ceaselessly, and I didn't know what I ought to venture at that moment. The lieutenant colonel's immoderate love for me assured me he certainly would forgive my error, but the shame of acknowledging myself to be unfaithful, stupid, and deceived completely prevented me from presenting myself before him, and I would have more readily consented at that time to suffer any manner of poverty than to confess I had been betrayed.

The Reader might ponder, I suppose, whether love for my fellow man could have resided within me at that time. I will hasten to clarify this doubt for him by saying that even debauched women are not completely deprived of common sense, and had their inconstancy and frivolous luxury not conquered them, they would assuredly be more virtuous than the money lender and the miser. That I might soothe my old man, I scorned both vexation and injury and ventured to go to him to acknowledge my fault, while relying as well on my artfulness which, in the event of his severity, I knew I could use to deceive him easily.

Thus I called on him full of fear and the very least hope for my well-being. No sooner had I entered the yard than I was met by his steward, who rewarded me with such a sound slap on the face that I saw stars. Such a show of respect did not bode well for my return, and I resigned myself to all the severities of a destiny whose wrath I had provoked because it was already impossible for me to leave. I hastened to find my lieutenant colonel, for I hoped I would discover greater leniency in him than in his servants. I found him in his room, where he was lying in bed surrounded by doctors. The moment he saw me he cried out so forcefully that he frightened everyone in attendance upon him. Then he jumped up from the bed and, embracing me, began to sob inconsolably, and when he had come partially to his senses, he exclaimed the following: "Is this not a dream which delights me so with this agreeable vision? Is this not a seductive hope that deceives my mind? Beautiful Martona! Is it you whom I have in my embrace? Are these your lips I am now kissing, your charms I see, you who are before me? Speak! Answer, Beautiful One! or have I already lost you forever?" I do not recall with what alacrity my sadness was transformed into joy, but after I had embraced him in all sincerity, I shed the tears that had been laid in store for me in the courtyard by the blow of the steward, who, while preparing to strike me, had ordered me not to step aside. My lover accepted my tears, which were flowing from me in a stream, as a sign of my remorse and the sincere acknowledgment of my misdemeanor against him; however, I told him I had left him only because I desired to test his fidelity to me: Having been deprived of me, would he be shattered or not? To this the lieutenant colonel replied that not only was he shattered but he had even been preparing for his end. Thus I inherited his former love and his former esteem for me as the favorite among all his servants; as for what I had carried off and given to my deceiver, he never mentioned these things, for he considered me dearer than life itself.

From this time on my lover began preparing for his demise, for upon my leaving, he had run around everywhere and sought me in all places, but as he ran around too carelessly and in great despair, that is, without his wits and without his glasses as well,[41] he quite carelessly flew off the porch from the very top step of the stairs and fractured his sacrum, from which action his weak constitution began to deteriorate from hour to hour. I had been so offended by the steward that I attempted to avenge myself on him at every turn, and no sooner had I

told my lover that he had behaved uncivilly with me than the lieutenant colonel struggled to come to his senses at this news and, not brook-
ing any justification from the steward, punished him most severely and
ordered that he be turned out of the house without being paid for his
service, which made me greatly happy.

No good deed ever goes unrewarded; sooner or later, accounts will
be settled. Just as soon as my dear lieutenant colonel passed over from
this world, they put me under guard and locked me in a sturdy dungeon. Upon my lover's death they tracked down his sister, whom during his life he would not even admit into his house and whose name he
did not wish to hear. The steward had wormed his way into her good
graces and given her an account of all the things I had arranged in the
house of her brother, which is why she intended to demand an accounting from me in court, the thought of which seemed more dreadful than
even death itself. I was thrown into a stone cellar and not even given
anything on which I could repose at night. I was given nourishment
two times a day, but it consisted solely of bread and water, and so I was
compelled to maintain a Lenten fast, which is something that formerly
had never entered my mind. Such an abstemious life banished all ideas
of love from my head, and I no longer thought of adorning my body
or enticing lovers to me. I found myself in this situation for about two
weeks or more, and each day I shed as many tears as there were in my
eyes and was quite unspeakably shattered.

One time at night, while I was lying on the stone floor, the door
of my dungeon swung open, and Akhal entered accompanied by another officer. Upon seeing me in such a melancholy condition, he was
overcome with remorse and asked the officer who had come with him
to extract me from this place and look after me well, while he, in the
meantime, released me completely from captivity. I thanked him, and
after kissing me, he told me he felt obliged to deliver me from my captivity, and thus pitying me, they both took their leave. A quarter of an
hour had not elapsed when they took me from this hell and placed me
in a handsome room, where a bed, a table, and a chair had been made
ready for me. I am not able to express how I rejoiced at that time and
thanked Akhal in his absence from the bottom of my heart, and then

I lay down on the bed, and not having had much rest in a great while, slept all the way through for about half a day. The officer on guard duty, as I afterwards discovered, came to my room four times, and seeing me fast asleep, did not wish to disturb me; he recounted all this to me with such great respect that I concluded he had fallen in love with me, in which opinion I was not deceived. He was on guard there for an entire week and remained with me constantly, and when another officer arrived to relieve him, he prevailed upon him and remained one week more. Finally, Akhal and he, through their united efforts, delivered me from captivity, and having taken me from my keep, they handed me over to a far-from-impoverished old lady, who on that very first day outfitted me with all the sorts of things I required. My face and my actions proved to her that I did not sell my charms very cheaply and that I never let them out of my hands at bargain prices, which is why she tried yet more zealously to attire and soothe me.

Misfortune is more quickly forgotten than prosperity, especially among people in my line of work. In three days' time I had entirely improved: my face had regained its former beauty, my body had re-acquired its former whiteness and softness, and there were no signs at all that I had sat in prison and been most cruelly altered for the worse, but rather it appeared to everyone that I was only now beginning to distribute my charms to the male sex in accordance with my benevolence.

I don't know why, but for four days my liberators were not with me; finally they arrived together, and laying eyes on me in my former or even better condition, they melted, and one more than the other sought to gain an advantage in my heart. Akhal was closer to me and therefore acted more freely with me, but Svidal (such was the other one called) was exceedingly courteous and tender and feared to provoke me with the slightest act, which led him to seek a place in my heart through tenderness. It was not in my power to forbid Akhal to treat me freely, as he had in our former acquaintance, but such actions made Svidal think I loved Akhal more than him. Thus it was my duty to assure Svidal at a time convenient for such a communication that I had conferred the advantage to him in everything over his rival.

It is only with difficulty that two persons divide inherited property, but it is impossible for them to share a lover without a quarrel. Akhal always had the advantage over the other, and although it was against my will, I was obliged to obey him. No matter how much I tried to assure Svidal that I loved him more than Akhal, to a certain extent he did not believe me and began to become jealous, and jealousy, as is known to all, makes for a queer business and never concludes well. All too soon I came to apprehend that it is overly burdensome for our sisters to become involved with military folk, especially at such times when they are enflamed with jealousy and do not think fit to share their booty with each other. One evening all three of us were sitting at table in the form of a triangle, viz., we were playing ombre.[42] According to the rules of the game, no one is permitted to look at another's cards, but Akhal did not heed this rule and quite often broke the shape of the triangle and moved close to me. At first Svidal told him courteously not to look into my hand; then he pronounced with anger in his voice that Akhal was being uncivil by thrusting himself upon a lady against her will; and finally they quarreled. Akhal told him he had complete mastery over me and that he ought not to enter into matters that did not concern him, but Svidal answered that it would be better to inquire of me which of them had the greater power. Such is the question they put to me. I said nothing in reply to it, however, and tried to persuade them to cease their quarreling, but my words did not help, and they proceeded to squabble to such a degree that they nearly came to blows. Svidal took his leave and relinquished me to Akhal, who rejoiced that he had gained a victory over his enemy and commanded me quite strictly not to have anything to do with Svidal, whom I should refuse to admit into my presence. This command was quite intolerable to me; however, to satisfy Akhal, I falsely promised to carry out his will. This is how I discerned that Akhal was desperately in love with me, and that it was not vexation which had acted upon him on this occasion but rather his true love.

A half an hour later one of Svidal's servants called and placed the following letter into Akhal's hands:

Dear Sir!

I have been insulted by you, and you know how the defamation of honor must be paid for, so do me the pleasure of bringing yourself tomorrow at nine o'clock in the evening to the Marian Grove,[43] where I shall await you. If you are not there, then mark my words: I will deal with you as though you were a common scoundrel.

Your servant, Svidal.

When he finished reading the letter, Akhal blanched and apparently became frightened, for he was quite unskilled in accepting a challenge to a duel, this being the first time it had happened to him in his entire life. However, gathering his last drops of strength, he told the servant he would satisfy his master as he desired, and after sitting with me for a very brief time, he parted from me without any show of affection and left in a state of great agitation and fear. I must confess that their appointed duel threw both me as well as my overseer into an extreme commotion: we didn't know what to do, where to turn, or where to hide, for I already knew how pleasant it is to sit in prison under heavy guard. We wept the whole night through and didn't sleep at all; I feared an ill outcome and from the bottom of my heart pitied Svidal, which is why I realized that I had come to love him. Two inexpressible passions tore at my heart and gave me not a minute's peace, and when the hour arrived wherein their battle had already begun, I swooned, threw myself onto the bed, and lay there in unconsciousness for two hours or more. All our servants gathered about me and wept, and they felt sorry for me even as they feared for their own ruin. In a word, our house was full of wailing and sobbing, and I was in a state of unconsciousness. Although I didn't make a very flattering presentation, however, in this instance I had no doubt that these virtuous people saw me as someone who was pitiable and worthy of their aid.

As the clock struck twelve, Akhal came running into my room, and taking hold of my hand, he raised me from the bed. He was barely able to control his breathing, fell to his knees in fear before me, and spoke thus: "Madam! Although I have treated you badly, I have loved you greatly. My shortcomings were the reason I deceived you, but having abandoned you, I soon realized it was not possible for me to remain at peace without you. I therefore returned to Moscow, and discovering that you had fallen into misfortune, summoned all my power to aid you, in which I at last succeeded. Finally, I resolved to carry out the promise I had given you and intended to marry you, but unmerciful fate is depriving me of this pleasure, and I must immediately leave Moscow and then all of Russia. I am an ill-fated man who is now subject to a cruel torture. Forgive me, Beautiful One, forever. I have shot Svidal." With these last words I swooned and fell on the bed; after kissing my hand, Akhal tore himself from me drowning in tears and greatly aggrieved, ascribing my fainting to my separation from him.

At that instant I clearly realized precisely what true amorous passion is. Upon hearing of Svidal's destruction, my blood ran cold, my throat dried up, my lips became parched, and I was able to breathe only with difficulty. I thought that since I had now been deprived of Svidal, I had been deprived of the whole world, and at that moment the forfeit of my life was of no consequence to me, for I was quite prepared to follow him into the netherworld. Any disaster I could imagine could not compare with my unhappiness. The wellsprings of my eyes were thrown open, and tears rolled down my face without measure. Svidal appeared before me so vividly; all of his charms, tenderness, and civility were before my eyes incessantly; I was tormented without mercy; and an unappeasable sorrow devoured my tormented heart. At that moment no prospect of ruin could frighten me, and I was prepared to endure anything and to meet death without hesitation just to repay Svidal for the loss of his life, for which I, the unhappiest of all women in the world, was the cause.

My overseer visited me many times and advised me to flee the city, but I didn't think as much about my ruin as I regretted Svidal's demise. I passed that day and the ensuing night in the most tormented state of anxiety and despaired for my life no end. In the morning, I lay in bed in great disorder and pictured to myself my departed Svidal. Suddenly, he appeared before me, and rushing to me, kissed my hands. I began to cry out with all my might and fainted. All the servants rushed into my room and assured me Svidal was standing before me, not dead but alive, and that this was no vision but actual fact. Within me I could feel how difficult it was to pass from great despair to excessive joy, which is why I afterwards fell ill for a great while. Jumping up from the bed, I threw myself into his embrace, but even then I still could not believe he was standing alive before me; however, at such moments assurance comes quickly. Svidal began to speak and to convince me of his love with the type of tender passion the dead are never able to muster. Thus I knew for certain that he was alive and loved me as much as I him, or perhaps somewhat less, but we didn't bargain over this and loved each other without any haggling. At this point I will not depict our delight because it would be superfluous to recount in detail all the words and actions and movements that are produced in a frenzy of passion, many of which have already been confirmed by various experiments, and also because after the passage of time, the passion of the enraptured one vanishes and she completely forgets everything her lover said at that moment, exactly as it happens with a patient after a fever or a madman after recovering his senses.

From the birth of the world we have had but one obligation, and it compels us toward goodness, which is why it is not beloved by every-one and why we have arbitrarily created various other duties which bind us to all sorts of things. Of all these responsibilities, I chose but one: viz., I asked my lover by what means he had been liberated from death, to which he responded with the following words: "True love is always attended by jealousy, and they, conjoining,[44] made me shrewd and wise. First I sought an opportunity to quarrel with Akhal, and when I had succeeded in this, in order that I might have my revenge, I conceived the idea of getting even with him over swords; however, a quite superior plan then came to mind, and I feared only that he would refuse the duel. Yesterday, at the appointed hour, I was already in the grove when he arrived, alighted from his carriage at a distance of five hundred paces, and came over to me. Baring my sword, I ordered him to make himself ready, which he set about doing in great fear, so I, in-dulging him and wishing to deceive him all the better, inquired would he not wish to settle this affair by taking up pistols. He consented to this more willingly, for he shoots exceedingly well. So from my pocket I pulled two pistols that had been prepared without bullets, which in his fear he had not the power to notice. I offered one to him while retaining the other for myself, and walking away in opposite directions for some distance, we gave each other the signal for battle and both shot at the same time. I fell and feigned that I had been shot. My servants rushed up to me and began to wail and shout as they had been commanded to do; Akhal thought his shot had hit the mark and hastened to his carriage, and on the evening of the very same day, he left the city." After this account we began to laugh, and when we had stopped laughing, we thanked fate for her condescension to us. Thus I fell completely under the power of Svidal's will, and he rejoiced more than a vainglorious general on the conquest of an enemy stronghold. As for Akhal, however, at that very moment I suppose he was driving his horses to leave the scene of his imaginary ruin.

My lover read somewhere that Cupid had gilded his arrows and with this act of cunning had subjugated the entire race of mortals. That is why in the present age each heart wishes to be pierced with such an arrow, for when it comes to poverty, even beauty is not highly captivating. Thus, for the confirmation of our mutual passion, Svidal assigned me an allowance of two thousand rubles per year, excluding gifts and other caprices; moreover, he promised to present me with a thousand rubles[45] if I bore him a son who looked like him. For this reason, I began praying to God, but then I had forgotten that heaven is not obligated to give its blessing to our transgressions even if we start them off with a prayer. Such riches did not make me happy, for I had seen enough of them already, but I resolved to be a trifle more cautious and took it into my head to stock up for a rainy day. I appointed a small box into which I put my shiny gold coins, so they might support me in the event of a turn of fate.

At that time fate had gifted me with a friend: she was a merchant's wife but a nobleman's daughter, a woman who in reality possessed only a middling estate yet who was most skillful in pretending to be someone of vast wealth who, out of modesty and from being a good contriver in the keeping of her home, did not want to be considered prosperous. A merchant had taken her solely for her beauty rather than her name or dowry. He loved her in the extreme yet lived with her in separate rooms for the preservation of his personal honor and, even more, his life. His wife was resourceful and capable of all sorts of designs, which he feared like the plague. Before the first month of their marriage had come to an end, he already had a great desire to leave her, for she was one of those women who compose novels with verse prefaces in them.[46] That is why there congregated around her a host of witty young men who always managed to visit her for an excellent education[47] when her husband was absent. He who was the most skillful among them found rich rhymes for the merchant's wife, and since she was thus occupied with the science of rhyme-making, she rarely slept with her husband.

The first time I called on the merchant's wife I found her to be quite magnificent: she was sitting in bed, and a multitude of learned men had assembled around her, each with a handwritten paper protruding from his pocket. One by one they read their compositions before the gathering and deferred to the taste and judgment of their mistress. It was not surprising that the courteous gentlemen requested her counsel regarding their work, but it did strike me as strange that she applied herself to everything and praised or defamed each composition as she saw fit. Moreover, it struck me as even stranger that when her husband entered the room, everyone rose, bowed, and ingratiated themselves with him as though the entire assembly consisted of his true and sincere friends. The mistress of the house and I got on quite tenderly and without any stiff formality, for the two of us belonged to the same trade, and at the beginning of our acquaintance we talked over more things in just a few hours than an entire school could learn in a week. I realized what sort of person she was, and she informed herself in detail about me, and so we became fast acquainted and called ourselves sisters right up until the day when there was a reason for us to have a falling out.

The next day I was at a party in her house, where I got to see all I cared to of various interludes. Her house struck me as an abode of love, for everyone in it strolled about or sat together in pairs. The oddest of all was an old man who was trying to persuade a girl of thirteen years to marry him. As much as he tried to blandish her with words, he also added the enticement of apples and oranges, which he quite frequently pulled out of his pockets and proffered to her with great courtesy. Not understanding the rules of the game, however, the girl devoured them so swiftly it was as though she had never in her life even seen such things.

In the corner there sat a certain fine young fellow, who was talking very modestly with an old lady. I was about to commend the young man for the respect he was showing his elders and for spurning the lure of frivolous entertainments in deference to his grandmother, but then the mistress of the house assured me this was a pairing of lover with lover. The young man was trying to convince the crone that he was very much in love with her, and avoiding the subject of chronology, which aged coquettes find so abominable, he told her: "You, madam, are exceedingly pleasing, and there cannot reside in you any caprice or any of those other numerous vices which are so agreeable to the young; mature years have their worth, and you will be the harness of my youth." He harbored the intention of marrying her in the hope that this toothless Grace[48] would not pass another year on this earth and that her sizable dowry would provide a tolerable diversion for a fine young fellow.

A tall, potbellied, husky lad was the freest of anyone there, for the reason that in the event he was needed, he served completely at the mistress's pleasure, and he laughed so loudly he drowned out the bass fiddle. He was playing cards with a certain young maid who was so corpulent she quite resembled a skeleton. This was his fiancée, whom he, from the summit of his sagacity, had selected for his marriage bed.

Over there, a gilded officer hovered about a judge's wife and taught her the facts of life. In another place, a young charmer attached herself to a pensive dandy and offered her services to him. In the middle of the room sat a stunted poet, who shouted verses from a Tragedy he had written; sweat rolled off him in sheets, while his wife wiped a field officer's brow with a white handkerchief.[49] In a word, I had discovered there a school of love—or a house of iniquity. However, the mistress of the house possessed an advantage over everyone: no matter with whom any of the cavaliers began his love-making, he always concluded it with the mistress, for she was a woman worthy of all praise who loved her husband from a vast distance. Svidal came for me, and so, having said my farewells to all, I went home, where a discourse about women took root in me. Many of us are extraordinarily flighty, and that is why certain learned people as well as all of our esteemed Philosophers generally hate us; however, by my calculation, I have discovered their abuse in and of itself signifies nothing, for our esteemed Philosophers have often made fools of themselves over the charms of our sex. Socrates was nearly the chief enemy of our gender, yet he could not manage without marriage, and in retribution for his contempt for us, he had a most willful wife, who devoured his heart as rust does iron.

I had in my service a Ukrainian, a quick and obliging fellow who could do diverse tricks: he could somehow swallow knives and forks, release baby doves from their eggs, pass a needle through his cheek, bolt his lips shut with a lock, etc., which is why we concluded he was a sorcerer. One morning he told me that the female servant of my friend the merchant's wife had confided a certain secret to him: namely, that for half a year already her mistress had been seeking someone who would take the life of her husband, but it had to be accomplished inconspicuously. She was offering to pay one hundred rubles for such a deed and had asked of my servant if he would undertake it. "I did not refuse," he continued, "and wish to serve her." When I heard this, I became frightened and told him I would not consent to it and would certainly broadcast his intention to one and all. In reply, he grinned and said: "You, madam, are still not completely versed in the ways of the world and think that people willingly become their own worst enemy. I know it is difficult to get mixed up in something like this and will certainly not let myself in for any dire consequences: I intend to perform a comedy, for the staging of which I shall receive one hundred rubles, and the innocent merchant will escape alive. I will begin the first act today; allow me to attend to it." I dismissed him, and he left; however, I resolved that I myself ought to be present at the playing out of this comedy and that I should reveal the scheme to Svidal so that no harm should come of it. And that is exactly what I did.

My servant came back and brought with him fifty rubles, which he had taken from the merchant's wife for the preparation of a poison, for he had told them that the poison, whose effects begin only in a week's time, was very dear. Svidal asked him precisely what he intended to do. "I am going to make the poison," he said. "You know I am not the worst medic,[50] and after I have put it together, I'll drink off a glass in front of you, so you will not fear any evil consequences from it." So he brewed some grasses and made the poison in about two hours, and when we asked him how much it had cost him, he told us it was just a little more than six kopecks. Having poured it into a vial, he drank off the remainder in front of us and said that if this concoction were taken in beer, then in five days' time a person would become so angry for half an hour's duration that he would be prepared to slaughter his entire household and whosoever else crossed his path, yet afterwards he would feel no ill effects. We believed him and gave him leave to convey the concoction to my friend, to whom he gave directions on how to act when the poison began to work on her husband. Five days later, just as we were told, the merchant became enraged and threw himself at all his servants; consequently, they bound his hands and feet and laid him on a bed. My friend sent for all her relations to have them come view her misfortune, to which gathering I too was invited. Svidal also wished to see this, so we set off together. By the time we arrived, the poison had already ceased to work, and the merchant found himself in his former right reason; however, all present protested that he was mad and that his mind was quite disturbed. Even though he demonstrated that he was in full possession of his faculties, no one believed him or wanted to untie him. Finally he began to beg them to set him free, yet out of concern for him did they not think fit to do this. Then he began to rail at everyone and said that on that very day the world had undoubtedly lost its mind; as a result, his friends and relatives tried to calm him, but his wife, who was sitting across from him, cried and ordered the servants to hold him more firmly. He gnashed his teeth at her and wanted to tear her in half.

His wife assured everyone that he was hopeless and therefore wanted to examine before everyone present how much he had in promissory notes and other bills. Just as they began to pull the keys for these things from his pocket, however, the merchant began to shout, "Help! Robbery! They're stealing!" and the like, whereupon many present counseled to fumigate him with incense and to make the sign of the cross over him incessantly in order to expel the unclean spirit which was invisibly tormenting him so. At this point the unfortunate merchant did not know what to do, and broke into tears and began to weep most bitterly. Everyone responded to his tears with tears of their own; however, no one wanted to untie him, for his wife and all the servants said he had been about to cut everyone in half and they should no longer believe anything he had to say because he was off his head. The merchant could not expect his deliverance from anyone there, so he began asking for a priest. One was sent for directly, and when he arrived, everyone quitted the room and left the two of them alone.

A half an hour later the priest emerged and told everyone he found the merchant completely in his right mind and fully normal. "You are treating him so severely for no reason," he pronounced. "Untie him; I assure you he is not in the least disturbed." Thus he left the house, laughing, perhaps, at their folly. Everyone present wished to obey the priest's command unquestioningly, but the wife alone opposed it and bade everyone with tears in her eyes not to untie her spouse. They did not heed her, however, and untied him. A person so aggrieved will assuredly forget all decorum and conceive a way to avenge himself on his offender. The merchant rushed at his wife, and seizing her by the hair, threw her on the floor. All the people there assembled rushed at him, and notwithstanding either his resistance or his pleas, they tied him up again and put him in bed, resolving: "Now you will not deceive us again; be good enough to sleep deeply, for you are agitated."

Not seeing any means for his deliverance, the merchant fell silent and began to rage against the misfortune afflicting him; he thought his condition would improve with the passage of spiteful time and that after people had come to their senses, they would acknowledge that he was not mad, so he resolved to submit to his evil fate.

As dinnertime approached, the merchant was still struggling in his hempen fetters, and he was finally forced to confess that he had truly taken leave of his senses and that now, owing to fate, he had once more come into his right mind; thus, after swearing an oath that he would no longer trouble anyone, he was permitted out of his bonds. It was amusing to see how he walked about the chamber lost in thought, and how everyone feared to approach him and instead circled round him. What could he be imagining when everyone wrongly considered him a madman? At last the table was set, and everyone sat down, but on the entire table there was neither knife nor fork, for everyone feared that the merchant would break into a frenzy and stab them. At this very moment more guests arrived, and they were informed while yet in the entryway of the host's misfortune. Upon entering the chamber, they stood at the door and cried to him from there, "Hello, good sir!" and feared to approach him, and when they finally sat down at table, they looked at him with astonishment, just as though he were an utter fool. Vexation was written across the merchant's face, and he desired at this very moment to avenge himself on his malicious spouse, but he feared being bound yet again. He would have liked, if even just little by little, to be apprised of his fate, but just as soon as he inquired, "Why do you think me mad?" everyone was ready to rush at him and tie him up, for they thought a darkening of the mind had once more descended upon him. In truth, he seemed pitiful to me, being the master of the house yet unable to utter a word either to his wife or servants.

With the permission of the hosts, Svidal left the table for an hour, and when he returned, he told the merchant he had a servant who was a great master of telling tales: "If it pleases you, let him tell one in order to dispel your agitated thoughts." The merchant was so pleased with this suggestion that he had to hold back tears when speaking with Svidal. Svidal called out to our Ukrainian and ordered him to recite, and while walking away, instructed him on what to say and how to say it. Our servant was utterly obliged to fulfill his command, and so he began his narrative, which astonished not only me but everyone because we had not at all foreseen it. Svidal did this solely out of pity for the master of the house, however, with whom he deeply condoled.

A Tale

Having attained the age of majority, a certain rich merchant who had lost both his father and mother took it into his head to marry. He did not seek a dowry but rather a beautiful and virtuous woman who had been instructed in all the arts and skills that would make her a wise mother, a diligent mistress of the household, and a woman worthy of love; however, since it is so exceedingly difficult to find such a woman nowadays, he came across the daughter of a secretary who was tolerably handsome and knew those skills by heart which would not allow her to leave a young man wanting. She was not without a dowry and brought with her a quite large estate, which consisted of void, legally contested bank notes, a vast number of claims, and the unflattering hope that she would receive an inheritance after her uncle, who is presently attending to business in Siberia, passed away, should he die without marrying, childless, and not having left a will. . . .[51]

Interrupting this recitation, the host turned to the servant and said, "Please, give me a moment," and then he said to Svidal: "My dear sir, this is my very own story, and, I would say, it would not be in the power of the very best writer to describe it in so lively a manner." "With your permission," Svidal said to him, "the ending will be most agreeable to you and defamatory for your mistress, but vices are always punished publicly. I am doing this out of pity for you and know you are not mad; be the master in your own house and command her to remain seated and listen." At that time my friend was about to get up and go her way, but the host commanded her to remain in her seat. "If you have in truth perpetrated something foul, then let your parents hear of it, for they are with us now. Proceed, if you please," the host told our servant. "I am exceedingly obliged to the mercy of your master, and I see my madness is now coming to light, for which I am extraordinarily glad."

They were married, and within a half month's time the merchant's wife became bored with her husband and began to appease her natural loathing for him with certain weavers of rhyme, who visited her at any hour. Although her spouse[52] considered such visits suspicious, he did not venture to speak to her about this, for noble blood courses through her veins, and thus he feared to dishonor her. In conclusion, she became acquainted with a certain woman who is called Martona and who has in her service the Ukrainian Oral. This servant knew various tricks and therefore was considered a sorcerer. The merchant's spouse instigated a plan to have him poison her husband and promised him one hundred rubles for this deed. Oral agreed to the task and explained it to his mistress, who, fearing evil consequences, inquired of her servant what manner of poison he intended to make. He informed her that he had no intention to enter into such a vile undertaking but only wished to receive the money promised him and to deceive the merchant's wife. Having concocted the poison, he drank off a glass of that very liquid beforehand in the presence of his mistress, which acted as real proof that it was not harmful. The servant had taken fifty rubles from the merchant's wife for the making of the poison, but he made it for just more than six kopecks and then put it in her hands. She administered it to her husband with the intention that he would die, and when a type of fit came over him, he was tied hand and foot and laid on the bed. And the conclusion of my tale has been written by you, our host: you know it as do all your guests; therefore, I will not recount it to the end.

After this recitation, the host leapt up from his seat and kissed our servant on the forehead, thanking him for his deliverance from death. Then he gave him four hundred and fifty rubles more and said: "Instead of one hundred rubles, take five hundred for your virtue. As for my wife, I shall cite the rule given to us by the righteous—'*Shun wickedness and do good*'—and do not at all intend to seek revenge against her for her transgressions. If you be satisfied, madam," he said to her, "I shall buy you a village in your name; please be good enough to go there and live happily. I do not need you and do not intend to live with you any longer, but so as not to defile your honor, I shall not speak a word about my misfortune to anyone."

So concluded this comedy, in which my servant, who was greatly pleased with the host, was the principle player. The merchant did indeed bring himself to buy a village, to which he sent his wife, and he thanked my lover Svidal for the disgrace of his spouse. Thus we parted with them that evening, and although we thought it would not be for long, contrary to our expectations, it was forever.

All our life consists of the passing of time. Some people spend it in various labors and enterprises useful to society, others in idleness and trifles, notwithstanding that luxury and idleness, like the twin teats of all vices, under the guise of sweetness infect our body and soul with a pernicious evil and inflict penury and fatal contagions upon us. Nevertheless, in their leisure, all people like to engage in love-making.

Svidal was continually free of civic responsibilities, and I was not bound by any manner of duty; consequently, we were idle, or superfluous, people and thus let not one hour nor even one minute pass by without practicing the lessons of love.

After the passage of quite some time, I received a letter with the following content.

Madam!

Nature puts man on earth in order that he will eventually die after experiencing the trials of countless vicissitudes; consequently, no one is able to escape his appointed lot. Fortunate is the man who dies happily, and not experiencing any misfortune, leaves this world without regret. But I, the unhappiest of mortals, lost my lover forever the day I deprived my friend Svidal of life, and so for that very reason I am now forfeiting my life. . . . Unbearable torment! Horror takes possession of me as I venture to inform you of my misfortune. I have taken poison, am preparing for death, and expect it very soon, and I make so bold as to ask that you favor me with one last opportunity to see you. My servant will tell you where I am situated and impatiently await you.

Akhal.

Although the oppressors of wisdom and confidants of Venus, my dear sirs the lords of fashion,[53] say that compassion is not in the least

innate to our sisterhood, I, on the other hand, would maintain that they
are as knowledgeable on this count as are those Philosophers who set
out to prove what constitutes a kiss. Having read this letter, I felt an
awful contrition arise within me. Akhal's foul deed against me was utterly obliterated from my memory, and only his good deeds appeared
strikingly before my mind. I wept over his impending end and pitied
him as a sister would pity a dear brother who had rewarded her with a
dowry and from whom she could not hope to receive even one more
drop in inheritance.[54] I immediately sent someone to inform Svidal
about this, and he came to me without delay and ordered me to prepare
myself to go to Akhal so that I might yet find him among the living.
Thus we arranged ourselves in great haste and traveled together along
with Akhal's servant, who served as our guide.

The place in which Akhal found himself was about a dozen miles
distant from Moscow, and when we began to approach it, Svidal alighted
from the carriage and ordered me to go on alone, for he wanted to
present himself to Akhal later. He asked Akhal's servant and me not
to tell Akhal that he was yet among the living, for he himself wished
to apologize before him and solicit his forgiveness for such a vile and
unintentional transgression.

No sooner had we ridden into the courtyard than we heard a terrible
wailing issuing from all the servants, for this was Akhal's house, which
he had purchased with my money. I thought he had already passed on:
my legs buckled, and I was beside myself as I stepped out of the carriage; however, I was informed he was yet alive. When I entered the
room, a most dreadful scene presented itself to me: everything was obscured—the floor as well as the walls and ceiling—with black flannel.
The bed had just the same manner of curtain about it, on which a delicate white pattern had been embroidered; the table was also draped in
black, and a second one stood in front of it, on which a cross was visible
and under which lay a human skull and two bones. An icon-lamp stood
before an icon. Akhal was seated at the table reading a book. He was
wearing a black robe and a black nightcap with white braid, and while
reading, he wept most pitifully. Hearing that I had entered, he glanced
at me with great sorrow, and gushing forth even more tears, spoke thus:

"Madam, you see before you a man who is leaving this world and departing on a road unknown to him. Diverse images torment my heart, and my indomitable conscience, as the first judge of our actions, represents clearly to me that I am vile to everyone on earth having spontaneously become a suicide. I believe the soul which has been struck down by my hand stands at the throne of justice and requests a righteous vengeance upon me; and so, averting the wrath of fate, I have punished myself for the villainy I have perpetrated. Be seated, madam, and I will give you an account of my misfortune.

"When I had entered upon my loathsome deed and slain Svidal, you were, I fancy, informed of this by someone, but I, owing to the derangement of my mind, had not the strength to tell you. Parting from you, I wished to run from my transgression and absent myself from the place which so strikingly recalled my villainy to me and which threatened a just and shameful punishment for it. I distanced myself from the place but had not the power to outstrip the torment of my conscience: it followed me everywhere, tormented me everywhere, and unceasingly drove me to repent. In the end, a terrible fear descended upon me, and when I fell asleep at night, then Svidal, entering my chamber, would awaken me, and standing before me, would weep most bitterly. Terror seized me, and I could find no peace either day or night. Wherever I went, fear followed at my heels, and finally my own shade induced terror in me. Not seeing any means for my deliverance, I ventured to end my wretched life and forfeit this world, which I, perhaps without foundation, abhorred and which had justly come to hate me. I returned here, and as soon as I arrived, arranged everything for my demise. I took poison and now consider myself already deceased, and on the brink of death I see I am once more happy and able to part with the one for whom I lived and suffered. I assured you during my life that I loved you, and now, at its end, I confirm it. Here is the deed for this house, which I have purchased with your money: it is written in your name. And here is my will: I am childless and have bestowed my entire estate on you. With this I give witness that you were dear to me."

After hearing these words, I was not able to restrain my tears and no longer had it in my power to conceal the secret which Svidal had asked of me. Just as I was about to take it into my head to tell Akhal of it, I became aware that his face had become altered, his eyes were frozen, and a dreadful tremor had settled into all his members. He spoke not another word and pressed my hand quite firmly. I thought the final hour of his life had commenced and that the poison he had taken had begun its work, so I screamed in order that his servants might attend us. From the sound of my voice he came partially back into his right mind and began to beg my forgiveness for anything he may have done to make me uneasy. He was already speaking so confusedly it was not possible to make out either the beginning or the end of his speech, and he appeared to me to be entirely despairing of his life. I asked of his servants that they find Svidal to inform him that Akhal was already departing and that he should hasten to bring him his apology. Upon hearing the name Svidal, Akhal was thrown into even greater confusion: terror embraced him, and his barely coherent mind completely abandoned him. In a great frenzy, he spoke thus: "O Dreadful Shade! though I be drawing my last breath, leave me in peace. I know your vengeance is just, just also is your anger, and your murderer is worthy of any punishment he receives from you. I quake and dare not look at you without a great dread. You arise before me in blood, without breath and without voice. For all that I took from you, I am deserving of any torture in hell. I am prepared for every torment that pleases you and the fate I have offended. I am loathsome to myself and therefore have put an end to my hateful days, and I regret that cruel death yet hesitates to rip my soul from me without mercy. I am already prepared, and everything has been appointed for this moment."

All of us who were there tried to give him aid. I cried inconsolably, and his servants howled unspeakably, for he was a kind master to them. I sent for doctors but was told it was forbidden under the threat of Akhal's curse to have one attend him and that they had given him their oath on this; consequently, I used whatever came to mind to treat him. He partially returned to his senses and entreated me not to labor in giving him aid, "for it is no longer necessary for me," he cried. At that very moment Svidal dashed into the room. As soon as the almost insensible Akhal caught sight of him, he tore himself from our grasp and fell into a dreadful frenzy: he beat and tore at himself, shouted as much as his strength would allow, and completely took on the aspect of a madman. Using all our strength, we restrained him and at last covered him with a blanket so that he might partially gather his shattered reason and rid himself of the terror he felt upon seeing Svidal, the person he had slain, for he thought and imagined that his villainy was greater than any earthly transgression.

The End of Part One[55]

The True and Detailed Account

of The Good and Wicked Deeds

of The Russian Rogue, Thief, Robber,

and Former Moscow Police Spy Vanka Kain,

And of His Entire Life and Strange Adventures

Written By

M . K .

ОБСТОЯТЕЛЬНОЕ

и

ВѢРНОЕ

ОПИСАНIЕ

ДОБРЫХЪ И ЗЛЫХЪ ДѢЛЪ

РОССIЙСКАГО МОШЕННИКА

ВОРА,

РАЗБОЙНИКА

и

бывшаго московскаго сыщика

ВАНЬКИ КА[ИНА]

его жизни и стра[нныхъ]
похожденiй.

Сочиненное

М. Х.

Title page of the first printing (1779) of *Vanka Kain*

PREFACE

Dear Readers!

In offering you Kain's history, I consider it my duty to make public the reason that prompted me to write this work.

It is well known to many, I would say, that the reading of books, which enlightens the mind, has become a common occurrence in our country, and that time which was darkened by the shadow of ignorance, in which those who read the writings of Aristotle and various other books were anathematized, has already passed. Nowadays, not fearing the anger of an empty, ancient anathema, our good citizens, and not only the nobility but even people of the middle and lower stations and especially the merchant class, are most willingly practiced in the reading of all manner of books. Being not infrequently in contact with such people, I have heard that some of the young people among them who have read the life of the French thief Cartouche, which has been translated from German,[1] were astonished by his roguish deeds, adding that in Russia there have been neither villains similar to him nor other adventures worthy of curious note.

That this opinion is unjust is known well enough by those reasonable persons who are familiar with the affairs of their country, and furthermore, as proof, the following can be said:

Whereas according to geographic calculation the vastness of Russia surpasses all other European states joined together, it cannot be the case that in such an expansive empire there has not been the very same type of adventures which occur in other countries that are the smallest fraction compared to her, for nature brings all people into the world equally, Russians as well as the French, Germans, and others, and therefore a number of virtuous and depraved people are to be found in any nation.

In our native land there have also been remarkable occurrences in nature and great deeds and many changes worthy of notice in society: there were and still are wise town governors, great heroes, and fearless commanders; many people have experienced the types of adventures worthy of occupying a place in histories; and there were and yet are infamous rogues, thieves, and robbers. What we have too few of, however, are industrious writers, for had we at present as many writers of history as there are poets and writers of comedies, and if certain people kept a diary of their life, then without fail, in due course no small quantity of books worthy of our curiosity would appear in society, and with even greater pleasure our descendants would read in them about the deeds of their ancestors rather than the acts of foreign peoples.

For this reason, as long ago as 1773 I had the intention of undertaking an account of the deeds of the notorious rogue Kain, about which I had heard directly from him. In 1755 I was attending to business in the Department of Criminal Investigations,[2] where he was being held while a commission was convened concerning his criminal activity and where he recounted all his adventures to the nobleman Fyodor Fomich Levshin, who at that time was in that very department.[*] No matter how sharp human memory may be, however, after eighteen years it is quite impossible to recollect everything clearly, and therefore I resolved to leave off this undertaking, but in 1774 I by chance came across a brief record of the deeds of this rogue. Unfortunately, it was written in the type of style the lower classes commonly employ to tell fairy tales or whatever manner of adventures, and, in addition, great mistakes had been made by the copyists because some things were so confused with others that it was barely possible to make them out.[3] From the content of this record, however, it was necessary to think that the original was written either by Kain himself or by some other person from his words. Moreover, on several occasions I had

---

[*]   By the grace of the secretary, Kain was not held in the Department of Criminal Investigations like other prisoners, who were never allowed out of prison, but with only fetters on his legs, he was given the freedom to walk throughout the building and frequently went into the front chambers of the department and openly conversed with the clerks and also with the nobles who were sometimes there. To understand why the secretary was so well inclined toward Kain, look on page 158. {All footnotes in this text are Komarov's, except for material in brackets. *Trans.*}

the opportunity to talk with such persons who knew Kain rather well, and some of them had been acquainted with him and had much to say about his many activities, and so I, not wanting to become like the lazy servant of the Gospel who hid his master's money in the ground,[4] considered the aforesaid record together with my recollection and wrote this account.[*5] Although our Kain does not bear a resemblance to Cartouche, his history, however, is worthy of some note, which I offer to your good will while remaining, with proper devotion to each reader, your most humble servant.

Matvei Komarov,
Resident of the City of Moscow

---

* If it had been possible to view all the evidence concerning Kain's deeds produced by the Moscow police, the Secret Office, and the Department of Criminal Investigations, then this history would be still more sizable and substantial; however, even now there is incomparably more truth in it than in an empty prognostication by Zadeka. {See endnote 5.}

THE HISTORY OF
THE ROGUE VANKA KAIN

Good is sometimes born of evil,
And evil quite often arises from good.

IVAN OSIPOV, OTHERWISE KNOWN AS KAIN, was born during
the reign of the wise sovereign, the Emperor Peter the Great, in the
year 1714 to parents of low estate, who dwelt in Moscow, the capital
city of the Russian Empire.[6]

According to a fate that is unknown to us, Nature endowed this
scoundrel with a keen mind, mental agility, boldness, and a quick understanding, and it conferred upon him the type of fortune that favored
him greatly in all deeds, both good and bad, and more than once delivered him from the most unfortunate situations, from which even
he himself at times did not expect to be saved. Notwithstanding these
natural gifts, however, the one thing he did lack during his youth was
a good upbringing, through which he would have learned to use his
natural understanding of things not for evil deeds but rather for good
ones. Wise people liken human reason to a spring, whose flowing
water, should it go through sand and stone, will emerge as the purest,
crystal-clear source, but if its course goes through slime, swamps, and
unclean places, then its water will be cloudy and not good for anything.
So no matter how wise a person may be by nature, when he does not
have a good upbringing in his youth and begins to grow up in the society of depraved people, then he himself will be depraved, for it commonly happens that not only young children but also people of complete
maturity, each according to his own inclination, imitate both good and
wicked actions from each other, and for the most part good manners
and morals are derived from contact with well-behaved people. As it
is well known that we in Russia have a great many lowborn people, so

their children grow up without any manner of good upbringing, and
like reeds waving in the wind,[7] bend farther to the side where the wind
blows stronger. So it was that while growing up, Kain always circulated among such people who passed their lives in idleness, drunkenness, willfulness, and all sorts of pranks,[8] from whom, beginning in his
infancy, he imitated all their villainous acts and wanton deeds and made
such a strong habit of them*[9] that having come of age and being well
off, he was in no way able to break himself of them. That is why, having
become first a petty criminal and then a great thief and robber, he committed such acts that eventually plunged him into irrevocable ruin and
that led to the following history about him:

At first Kain found himself in the service of the Moscow merchant
Peter Dmitrievich Filatiev.**[10] Owing to his innate dexterity and keenness of mind, Kain carried out the duties entrusted to him tolerably
well, although, as was his habit (which he himself explained afterwards), he not infrequently committed minor thefts both in the house
of his master and also from nearby neighbors: that is, he laid his hands
on pewter dishes, plates, copper tableware, and other not so valuable
things which were simply lying about. In addition, he was not lazy, as
he arose in the morning much earlier than anyone else to take small
game to Hunters' Row,[11] viz., geese, ducks, and various sorts of chick-
ens, which he had stolen at times from the neighbors and at others
from Filatiev and his servants. He also frequently got drunk, did not
spend the night at home, and instigated arguments and fights, about
which folly complaints repeatedly made their way back to his master,
for which Filatiev was sometimes compelled to punish him with excessive severity.*** Such a life seemed not very agreeable to Kain, and
he therefore devised many ways of saving himself from the yoke of
slavery and making himself free, knowing that freedom is the best
thing in the world and that under the yoke of slavery not even all vir-

---

*   Learned people sometimes call habit our second nature. {See endnote 9.}

**   In former times rich and important merchants were called *gosti*. {See endnote 10.}

***   As evidence for curious readers that in his day Kain was famous for his activi-
ties, I have placed two songs in which his name is mentioned together with other of his
songs at the end of this history. {Despite this statement, the songs mentioned above were
not appended to the first printing of Komarov's account of Kain's life and are therefore
omitted from this translation.}

tuous people are happy. As he was Filatiev's serf, however, he was not able to discover any means of attaining freedom for himself other than fleeing his master, and so in order not to leave the house of his benefactor empty-handed, he resolved at an opportune moment to visit the trunk full of money in Filatiev's bedroom, at which he had often directed his gaze so pleasantly.

Before setting about this enterprise, Kain became acquainted with a certain retired sailor nicknamed Kamchatka who was living at the sail factory,[12] and he struck up a great friendship with him because Kamchatka was from the same station in life as Kain, and we usually like to have friends who are the same type of person as we are. One time when they were together in a tavern, among other conversations Kain revealed his aforementioned intention to Kamchatka, who, praising Kain's evil design, advised him to carry out this undertaking without wasting time. Then each of them drank down a healthy measure of vodka to affirm their friendship, and they swore oaths to each other that if one of them fell into some misfortune, the other would seek all possible means for the liberation of his friend.

Having come to an agreement, they each made their way home. Kain had promised to carry out his plan without fail that very night, which is why he ordered Kamchatka to come to Filatiev's house and wait by the gate.

At nightfall, after Filatiev and his entire household had gone to bed, Kain, as was his custom, undressed and also lay down in his place; however, he did not have sleep on his mind but instead impatiently awaited the hour when everyone would be in a deep sleep. After several minutes, he noticed that his master and the entire household had fallen sound asleep. Rising, he dressed quietly, and, with the utmost caution, entered his master's bedroom, opened the trunk with the aid of tools he had made ready beforehand, extracted from it no trifling amount of money, and, putting on some of his master's clothes, left the house with all haste. When he had passed through the gate, he nailed a previously prepared piece of paper to it, on which were written the following words:

"Drink water like a goose, eat bread like a swine,
but let the devil work for you, not I."[13]

Then Kain joined up with Kamchatka, who was waiting for him
outside the gate, and they went their way. Kain was unspeakably happy
that he had succeeded in carrying out his plan without any obstacles,
and with his pockets full of money, considered himself a happy man.
Amid this joy, however, it came to them that it would be dangerous to
walk past the sentries' boxes to the place they had designated, fearing that because Kain was dressed in his master's clothes and both
of them were out after curfew,[14] they would be considered suspicious
people (which in reality they were) and be put under arrest. They did
not find themselves in such doubt for long, however, for Kain, given
the keenness of his mind, immediately invented a useful means for
overcoming this hazard. He knew that a priest resided not far from the
house of his master and agreed with Kamchatka to drop into the house
of this clergyman. When they arrived at the house, Kain climbed over
the fence, unlocked the gate, and admitted Kamchatka, but as soon
as they entered the yard, the church guard who was stationed at the
priest's house caught sight of them and inquired who they were and
why had they climbed the fence into someone else's yard at night-
time. "We are your parishioners," Kamchatka answered the guard,
"and have come to the priest for our spiritual needs. We knocked at
the gate for a good while, but you were sleeping so soundly you didn't
hear a thing, and we have extreme need of the priest; if it's your job to
unlock the gate for parishioners, you have no time for sleeping." The
guard, realizing what type of people they were, was about to cry out,
but Kamchatka hit him with a club and knocked him off his feet, and
standing over him, threatened to take his life should he try to resist
or cry out. In the meanwhile, Kain entered the priest's chamber, and,
after finding where he kept his clothes, put on a long, wide cassock
and outfitted Kamchatka in a short caftan.[15] Thus arrayed in the priest's
clothes, they left the house, and as they passed along the streets, the
sentries standing by their pikes hailed them, asking who they were
and where they were going, to which questions Kain reported that he

was a priest and Kamchatka a deacon and that they were on their way to give confession to a dying man. With this cunning invention they passed all the sentry booths without any suspicion and arrived at the Stone Bridge,[16] under which there was commonly gathered an assemblage of robbers and thieves, and they found there several of the same type of "respectable" folk as they were themselves, who immediately upon their arrival asked Kain for some money to purchase vodka. Pulling twenty kopecks out of his pocket, he offered the money to them, and one of them rushed with it to the tavern and brought back a full bottle. The scoundrels who were under the bridge drank up first and then presented the bottle to Kain and Kamchatka, and when Kain had drunk some off, one of them hit him on the shoulder and said: "It's clear, brother, that you are cut from the same cloth as us" (this meant he was the same manner of person). "Live here with us awhile, for we have enough of everything: our scales are weighed down by what we have not, and there are barns full of hunger and cold; while living by this bridge, we rent out our rooms, giving silent alms to those who pass along at night, and, truth to tell, we have nothing but dust and soot and sometimes not a thing to eat."[17] At the conclusion of this cunning introduction, the scoundrels set about their business, and Kamchatka went with them, but Kain stayed under the bridge with his loot to rest and slept through until it was light. When the morning star began to show itself on the horizon, he embarked for Kitai-gorod*[18] to look for lodgings for himself, and while approaching Pansky Row,[19] he ran into one of Filatiev's men, who, without saying a word, laid hold of him with the aid of others, bound his hands behind him, and led him to the house of his master.

Kain, knowing his guilt and the severity of his master, gave himself up to despair, and not foreseeing any means for his deliverance, at every instant expected the harshest punishment. Seeing that he had the ravisher of his beloved trunk in his power, Filatiev rejoiced unspeakably and had a well-deserved punishment prepared for Kain: he ordered that an iron chain be put on Kain and that it be affixed to a

---

*   Kitai is that part of the city of Moscow where the Merchants' Arcade, Customs House, and Ambassadors' Court are located as well as all the merchant shops and rows. {See endnote 18.}

post in the yard, near which a bear of no small size had been tethered; moreover, he imposed a fast on Kain, firmly enjoining all his servants from giving him either a crust of bread or a drop of water.

In such a desperate state, Kain passed two days tormented by hunger and thirst and could imagine no other fate for himself than that his master had taken it into his head to starve him to death. However, sometimes beyond all our hopes, human happiness unexpectedly delivers us from the very abyss of misfortune, as indeed then happened with Kain.

One of Filatiev's female servants was appointed to feed Kain's comrade—the bear chained with him to the post—and Kain begged her most pitifully to bring him a piece of bread. The magnanimous servant, taking pity on his situation, secretly brought him some bread and water, with which he appeased his hunger and thirst. One day the servant walked up to him and said: "You don't know, Ivanushka, that our very master has now gotten himself into no small amount of mischief because a soldier of the Border Militia has been killed in our house and thrown down the well."[20] When he heard this, Kain cheered up somewhat, thinking he would be able to save himself from his misfortune by reporting this incident to the government. Although it is true that happiness and unhappiness and good and evil do not manifest themselves according to our desires and that human intentions are not always fulfilled, Kain, to his delight, found great success with his scheme.

Several days later, thinking that Kain's high spirits were sufficiently pacified by the fast that had been placed upon him, Filatiev ordered Kain to be brought before him. After having Kain stripped naked, Filatiev wanted to whip him, but first he asked what had forced him to flee. At that point Kain answered with courageous audacity: "I did it to frighten you a bit, and after stealing from you, ran away so that you would not sleep longer than me. And now you will be so good as to not to beat me, for I intend to declare a crime against the sovereign."[*21] Upon hearing this, Filatiev was seized by fear and didn't know what to do with Kain,

---

* At that time this charge was considered to be of such importance that if an actual thief or robber who was caught in a distant city were to say these words, no one would dare to punish him in any way, but instead they were obligated to send him to Moscow to the Secret Office, where there arose no small number of delays in cases, during which thieves found a means to escape. {See endnote 21.}

but a guest who happened to be at his house, Colonel Ivan Ivanovich Pashkov, advised him not to hold Kain at his house any longer, not to threaten him further, and to send him, as he was obliged to do, to the authorities. Following this advice, Filatiev ordered that Kain be once more chained to the very same post and closely guarded, and then himself passed almost the entire night without sleep. As soon as daylight arrived, he presented Kain along with his report to the Moscow police, where they immediately set about asking him if he were declaring a crime against the sovereign. With unflinching audacity Kain answered that he truly was declaring it, that he was not going to deny it, and that what it consisted of he would testify in the proper place for such things; therefore, without any delay and under heavy armed guard, they led him to the Secret Office in the village of Preobrazhenskoe.[22] As soon as they delivered him there, the secretary asked Kain by what point he could prove his accusation of a crime against the sovereign. "I know neither points nor pounds, nor weight nor overweight,"[23] Kain answered the secretary, "but I will explain my case to the head of this office and not to you." The secretary, chafed by such a coarse answer, beat him mercilessly about the face and head with a ruler; however, he was unable to learn anything further from him and therefore ordered that great iron fetters be put on Kain's hands and feet, and after putting him in a cell, he reported about this to Count Semion Andreevich Saltykov, who was the governor general of Moscow at that time.[24]

The next day in the morning His Excellency arrived at the Secret Office and ordered that Kain be taken from prison and brought for examination into a torture cell, and when Saltykov entered the cell, he asked Kain why he had not gone to the secretary for interrogation and what important information he knew. Kain fell at the count's feet and answered: "Kind Sir! I have only to report to Your Excellency that my master is a murderer: the other day he killed a soldier of the Border Militia in his house, and after wrapping him up in a bast-mat bag, ordered him thrown down a dry well where all sorts of garbage is thrown and where the corpse is right now. I did not declare this to the secretary because he is a friend to my master; I frequently saw him visiting my master's house and for this reason was afraid he would withhold my declaration out of friendship for my master."

The count, upon hearing Kain's evidence, ordered that he not be punished and further commanded that after nightfall a proper military escort be sent to Filatiev's house for the collection of the corpse. Thus they went at nightfall to his house, and placing a guard around the entire premises, began knocking on the gate. Filatiev's servant, the one who had captured Kain, came out beyond the gate and asked what they wanted, and Kain, upon catching sight of him, ordered that he be put under guard and cried: "You caught me in the morning hard by Pansky Row, and I am taking you at night in your own house, so you and I are even now." Then, after entering the yard, they went on Kain's instruction directly to the well, and having pulled out the dead body, they seized Filatiev himself and transported him to the Secret Office. After arriving the next morning, the count asked Kain once again whether his master was present at the murder. Kain testified that the soldier was in fact murdered and thrown into the well on Filatiev's order.

After a fair investigation, Filatiev turned out to be partially guilty of the death, for which he was dealt with according to the law, and for his testimony, Kain was released and also given a document emancipating him from serfdom by the Secret Office.

Having attained his long-sought freedom, Kain was indescribably happy as he set off from Preobrazhenskoe to Moscow, and when he reached the Foreign Suburb,[25] he found his friend Kamchatka in a tavern, where he was carousing in honor of Kain's joyous emancipation with four ruffians from the gang of scoundrels that congregated under the Stone Bridge. Between conversations Kamchatka told Kain that they intended to go to the Yauza River that very night to rob the home of the court physician,* who lived near Lefortovo Palace.[26] Kain asked that they take him with them, and so, having waited for night, they entered the doctor's garden and sat down in a pavilion. When the watchman who was in the garden discovered them, he asked who they were and why they had come there. "We are peasants," they answered, "and extreme necessity has forced us to stop off in this place. Please come in, and we will give you an account of our situation." As soon as the

---

*   The name of the doctor in one record is given as Yelvakh, in another as Yalvikh, but I think both of these names are incorrect, for in our country people of the lower classes commonly both write as well as say foreign names incorrectly.

watchman entered the pavilion, they seized him, bound his hands and feet, and, threatening to kill him should he cry out, asked what was the best way to get into his master's bedroom; the watchman, realizing he was in the hands of merciless people, was forced to point out the window through which it was possible to climb directly into the bedroom. Leaving the watchman tied up in the pavilion, they went up to the window and pulled out one pane of glass from the frame. Pushing the bolt aside and opening the casement, Kain climbed into the window first, and, sitting down on the sill, took off his boots in order that he might move barefoot through the rooms and also in order to run faster in case this became necessary. After he had taken off his boots, Kain entered the chamber, and seeing that the doctor and his wife were tossing about in a deep sleep, he covered them with the blanket that had been pushed down to their feet. Then he went into the other rooms, and when he entered the nursery, one little girl who was lying there asked him why he had come. "Quiet!" Kain told her. "We are merchants who have come to your house to find some things we have lost." Then, putting a knife to her chest, he said: "Should you put up even the slightest resistance, I will take your life this very moment." In the meantime, Kain's associates came up to him, and tying the girl up, put her on her parents' bed between the doctor and his wife.* Going through all the rooms, they collected all the best things, including a small dressing table with silver objects, all of which they gathered up, and then they crawled back out the same window and made their way to the Yauza River, where there was a raft for crossing. They got on the raft and set off for the other side, but just as they were approaching the shore, they heard pursuers behind them. In order to cover their escape, when they reached the riverbank, they cut the cable on which the raft ran so the people pursuing them would not be able to cross the river. Then they ran to the Danilov Monastery,[27] where they took refuge with the groundskeeper who was living there and gave him the silver items they had stolen from the doctor for safekeeping and sale.

This successful foray emboldened Kain to undertake other thefts.

---

*   Some people say that Kain killed the doctor and his wife, but nothing is said about this in any of the records I have.

Therefore, after the passage of several days, he recruited four accomplices who were called 1. Zharov, 2. Kruzhinin, 3. Mitlin, and 4. Kamyshin, and he went with them once more to the Foreign Suburb to rob the palace master tailor.* Waiting for evening, Zharov quietly went into the house and hid under a bed, while Kain and the rest of his companions entered the garden and awaited an opportune moment to break in. At nightfall, when the aforementioned tailor and his household had fallen asleep, Zharov crawled out from underneath the bed, unlocked the necessary doors, and, going out into the yard, gave his accomplices waiting in the garden a signal, whereupon they entered the tailor's rooms, stole some money and various things worth about three thousand rubles,[28] and with that set off on their way. When they had taken themselves a short distance from the tailor's house, they saw a man running after them whom they suffered to come up to them and then seized, and taking him to the Yauza River, they tied him up and said that if he tried to resist or cry out, they would throw him in the river. Being in their power, the servant swore by every oath he knew that he not only wouldn't scream but wouldn't say even one word about them if only they would spare his life. Kain ordered the bound man to be placed in a boat standing along the bank, and after pushing it off from the shore, they went to New Savior Monastery,[29] where they took refuge.

Some time after this Kain went for some necessity to Red Square, where he came upon the very servant girl of his former master Filatiev who had provided nourishment for him when he was chained to the post. Upon seeing her, he thanked her for her kindness at that time and promised to show her his gratitude in due course. Among other things, the servant told him that two of her master's storerooms, in which there was no small amount of money and sundry goods, were under her supervision, and she wondered would he not wish to try his luck in visiting them; Kain, smiling wryly, answered that he would think this over with his friends and then parted from her. Four days later Kain purchased a live chicken, and going to the yard of a certain

---

* The name of this tailor, or his nickname, was given as Gets in one account and Reks in another.

Tatishchev, he threw it into the garden and commenced knocking on the gates, whereupon the caretaker, having come out to him, asked what he wanted. Kain asked that he be allowed to come into the garden so that he might capture his chicken, which had flown in there, and the caretaker, not knowing Kain's design, permitted him to enter. Having entered the yard under the guise of catching the chicken, Kain secretly observed the locks and grates on the windows of Filatiev's storerooms, diligently noting the best way to break in, because the windows of these storerooms looked out on Tatishchev's garden. Then, after surveying everything, he went his way. When he returned to his comrades, who awaited him by the wall of Kitai-gorod near the Ilinsky Gates,[30] he assured them it would be much easier and safer to carry out this venture against Filatiev's storerooms than it had been to rob the doctor and the tailor, and he counseled them to make this assault on Filatiev's stronghold without putting it off for long. Having agreed among themselves, the next evening they went to Tatishchev's garden and broke the iron lock off the window with the tools they had brought with them, and then placing a log into the window grate, they broke it open, climbed through the window, and then broke open the trunks they found in the storeroom. They took as much of the money, silver plate, and other things in the trunks as they could carry off, including a little velvet-covered box containing gold and diamond objects that Kain had come across, which he hid from his accomplices. After cleaning out Filatiev's storeroom, they returned to their lodgings greatly satisfied; however, a search for them was soon organized, or perhaps so they fancied, because it often happens that everything frightens a suspicious-looking fugitive and even the smallest accidental noise creates a great fear in him. In their fear they ran along the wall of Kitai-gorod with all possible speed, but burdened by their loot, they became so fatigued and grew so weak they could not carry their booty any farther and therefore stopped opposite the house of Count Chernyshev, where at the time there was a large expanse of mud, in which they buried everything. With empty hands they traveled beyond the Moscow River, and arriving at the house of General Shubin, began knocking at the gates in the back of the yard, as a result of which knocking the sentry on duty came out to them and asked what they wanted. Kain answered that by the side of their yard lay some sort of drunk person or perhaps even a corpse, and when the sentry had come through the gate to see the person who according to Kain's tale was lying there, they seized him and then pulled the sheepskin coat he was wearing over his head and tied it so tightly he was unable either to stand up or utter even the faintest cry. Leaving the sentry on the street in this condition, they harnessed some horses from the stable to a carriage standing in the yard and took it to Miliutin's factory,[31] whence they picked up a factory woman they knew. After helping her into the carriage, they drove to Chistyi prud,[32] where they stopped alongside a merchant's house, and Kain together with one of his accomplices climbed into the merchant's attic. Discovering some few dresses and scarves hanging there, they took them and arrayed the aforesaid factory woman in them, and seating her once again in the carriage as though she were a noblewoman, they continued their journey to the house of Count Chernyshev, where the things they had stolen from Filatiev were buried. When they reached that spot, they stopped, and taking a wheel off the carriage, they ordered the so-called noblewoman to get out, and under the guise of putting the wheel back on, they pulled their booty out of the mud and put it in the carriage. In order that passersby would not suspect them, on Kain's instruction the so-called noblewoman cursed, beat some of his men across the face, and screamed at them, asking why they had set out in a faulty carriage without having inspected it at home. When they had pulled everything out of the mud without leaving anything behind, they put the wheel back on, helped their factory noblewoman back into her seat, and set off for their destination. Upon reaching the Mint,[33] they noticed it was already beginning to get light, and fearing that their horses and carriage would be recognized, they stopped there, took their ill-gotten gains out of the carriage, and left it along with the horses at that spot. Taking the would-be noblewoman by the arm, they led her to their lodgings, and after rewarding her for the careful way she had played her role, they let her return to the factory from which they had taken her.

After the passage of no small amount of time, Kain was once again in the city, where he saw Filatiev's aforementioned female servant. She gave him an account of how her master had greatly suspected her in the theft of his goods from the storeroom, for which she had been given over to the police and, while being interrogated under cruel punishment, was asked whether she had conspired with anyone in the robbery. She endured these beatings and insisted she knew nothing, whereupon she was returned to her master. Since Filatiev thought these beatings were unjust, he soon thereafter set her free, and she then married the cavalryman Nelidov, who was in a mounted regiment of the Life Guards.[34] Wishing to show his gratitude to her, Kain pressed her to come to a public house, and after finding a seat for her there, rushed to his lodgings and brought back the velvet casket he had stolen from Filatiev, which he gave to her with all its diamond and gold objects as a sign of his gratefulness. Staying in the pub for quite some time, they both became rather tipsy, and therefore the woman asked Kain to accompany her to her lodgings, where, when they arrived, the woman's husband asked her what sort of man she had brought home. "He and I served the same master," his wife told him, and Kain answered with the following words: "I'm neither a thief nor a robber but just look that way; however, please be good enough not to doubt me, for I have a document declaring my freedom given to me by the Secret Office."[35] Pulling the paper out of his pocket, Kain showed it to him and then asked Nelidov if he would conceal him in his lodgings until morning and give him leave to spend the night. At his wife's request the cavalryman agreed to this. Kain, even though he was exceedingly drunk, was not able to sleep through the customary thieving hour of one o'clock in the morning, and so, arising quietly, he betook himself from his room and crawled over a fence into the garden of a harness-maker who lived alongside Nelidov's quarters. Entering the harness-maker's room, he stole 340 rubles from a portmanteau in his chamber and returned directly once more to Nelidov's lodgings. When he heard Kain enter, Nelidov reproached him for having left so early without telling him. "Quiet! My Dear Cavalryman," Kain answered him, "keep this to yourself," and pulling the money he had stolen from the harness-maker out of his pocket, he handed it to Nelidov's wife, reciting to her as well this Russian proverb: "Take the priest's onion, it's already peeled. Just think of me always, and pray for me when I die."[36] At daybreak he took his document of emancipation back from the cavalryman as well as a small amount of money from Nelidov's wife, and after bidding them farewell and thanking them for his stay, returned to his lodging. Not long after this Kain found out that upon being notified of the thefts of the doctor, the tailor, and the merchant Filatiev, the Moscow police had sent strict orders regarding the discovery of the thieves throughout all quarters of the city, and among all the houses signed statements concerning the stolen goods had been taken. For this reason, even though he took all precautions, Kain still feared that should any of his companions fall into the hands of the police for whatever reason, then he too would not be able to avoid the same fate, so he gathered round himself a band of six men, whose number included Kamchatka, and declared his intention to them, which consisted of retiring from Moscow for some time in order to avoid the searches being undertaken by the police. His comrades were immediately won over to his proposition, and without putting things off, they gathered together the very next day and set off on foot along the Vladimir Road for the Makariev Monastery, which stood on the left bank of the Volga 300 miles from Moscow and 40 miles from Nizhny Novgorod. Kain considered this area convenient for his thieving handiwork because every year after St. Peter's Day it is the site of a great fair which attracts many merchants who come with all sorts of goods not only from nearby Russian cities but also from Siberia and the borders of Persia, Turkey, and Poland in order to trade the entire month.[37] While on their journey to the monastery, not far from the city of Viazniki,[38] Kain's gang came across a drunken peasant who was riding on a cart filled with straw; after stopping him, they asked where the town governor lived, but instead of giving them an answer, in his drunken state the peasant set about cursing them. Such a response vexed Kain, and he ordered that the man be dragged off the cart and lashed to the shaft bow with the reins, and after striking a fire from the flint he always carried with him set the straw in the wagon ablaze and then hitting the horse with a cudgel, Kain sent him coursing down the road. The horse became so startled that it dashed off the side of the road and galloped and thrashed through the field until the cart with the burning straw fell off the front axle, and with just the peasant who was tied to the shaft bow and the front wheels of the cart in tow, the horse flew all the way to the village where Kain and his accomplices needed to spend the night. Fearing that they might be recognized there, however, they were obliged to pass by to another village even though it was late. This inhuman joke provided great amusement for Kain and his cohorts: while watching the horse galloping across the field with its burning cart in the approaching darkness, they laughed without measure, and the poor peasant, who was wrongly punished by these villains, remained barely alive.

We shall leave this unfortunate peasant, be he dead or alive, to the mercy of fate, for it is not possible to get information about him, and we shall return to Kain's affairs and see what sort of adventures befell him at the famous Makariev Fair.

Several days later they reached the Makariev Monastery, and on the day after their arrival, having surveyed the entire area and the merchants' shops and storehouses situated there, they noticed a storehouse in which Armenian merchants had combined their goods. Stopping alongside this storehouse, they diligently observed where the merchants kept their money and then took it into their heads to steal it, for which they employed the following ruse: Arising quite early the next morning, they approached the storehouse, and seeing in it two Armenian merchants, they awaited their departure. In a quarter of an hour one of the Armenians set off for the market to purchase some meat. Kain sent one of his gang to follow him and ordered him to summon the police on the merchant, which in fact was carried out. After the Armenian was taken to the guardhouse, Kain's man, who had mingled in among the people who had come running at the sound of his shout, went his way, and Kain along with his other associates approached the Armenian who had remained in the storehouse and told him his friend had been taken into custody. The Armenian locked up his wares and went to the guardhouse for information about his friend. Using this opportunity, Kain knocked the lock off the storehouse, entered it, and stole two leather pouches and three bags of money, and carrying them some distance away from the storehouse, he buried them in the sand. In order that no one besides his gang would be able to find the money and also to make it easier for them to get it out at the right time, Kain hurried down to the wharf, bought some few sheets of tree bark,[39] and made a shelter resembling a shop on that very spot. After buying quantities of lace, some leather pouches of the type in which peasants carry money, and sundry cheap ribands, he hung them up in the shelter under the guise of wanting to trade them. Waiting for night, he pulled the money from the sand, took it to his gang, and left his trading stand with all its goods where it stood.

This not insignificant treasure, with which Kain might have lived for some time without resorting to his villainous trade, did not in the least restrain him from his criminal ways, for several days later, when he was at the Merchants' Arcade, he noticed some merchants counting their money along Bell Row. When they had finished counting it, they put it in their shop, covered it with a mat, and, leaving the shop on some necessity, began talking with other merchants; Kain immediately leaped into the shop, grabbed the bag from under the mat, and broke into a run, but instead of money, a bag of silver icon frames had found its way into his hands. This adventure did not work out as happily for him as the theft of the Armenians' money, however, because a woman selling honey cakes near the shop, having caught sight of this, cried out to the merchants, who rushed after Kain and caught him. After leading him to their office, they immediately took the document of emancipation given to him by the Secret Office, and then putting an iron chain around his neck attached to a vast block of wood and stripping him naked, they began to whip him with an iron wire. Kain, unable to endure this cruel beating, cried out a crime against the sovereign; the merchants, not delaying in the least, led him away to the Department of Criminal Investigations and Colonel Redkin,[*40] who ordered that he be put in prison. The next day, after discovering this turn of events, Kain's closest friend Kamchatka bought a great number of *kalaches*,[41] and under the pretence of

*   At that time this colonel had been given a large command and appointed the chief investigator for the eradication of thieves and robbers, and full power had been given to him not only to interrogate robbers with the use of force but also, as the law allowed, to punish and hang them. {See endnote 40.}

handing them out as charity, he went to the prison in which Kain was being held. While giving the prisoners one *kalach* each, Kamchatka gave Kain two, in which he had baked sundry keys and silver money, and handing them to Kain, he said in thieves' cant that there were keys in the *kalach* for opening the lock.* After taking the *kalaches* and furtively pulling the keys and money from them, Kain asked a dragoon to buy him some vodka, and when the dragoon had brought it to him, he first treated the dragoon standing watch and then himself quaffed a good glass for courage. Having drunk it off, he took himself to the latrine, where he opened the lock that held the chain round his neck, lifted up a board, and ran; the sentry, after waiting a considerable time for Kain's emergence from the latrine, lost patience and looked in. But what did he see there? Only the block of wood that had been around Kain's neck, and his prisoner was completely gone. Frantic, the dragoon directly roused the entire command. They rushed out to recapture Kain and were right on his heels, but owing to the crush of people involved in a fistfight on the street, they could not catch up to him. In the meantime, Kain had run out into a field, where he came upon a herd of Tartar horses, and not far from them he saw sleeping in a tent a Tartar prince who had a small chest full of money under his head.[42] Approaching stealthily, he tied the Tartar's leg to a horse standing next to the tent, and striking it with a stake, set it free, and the horse dashed off into the field at full speed, whisking the Tartar away. Kain took the headrest full of money, returned to his gang, and, after telling them of his adventures, advised that they clear off for Moscow directly, for their crimes had reached such proportions that it had been ordered by the Department of Criminal Investigations to search for them everywhere. Not wasting any time, they went to the wharf, and crossing the Volga, arrived in the village of Lyskovo,[43] where they changed clothes so that they might not be so easily recognized; however, this trick was

---

* Many people, I suppose, will consider these words an empty, vulgar fabrication, but whoever has dealt with horse dealers knows well enough that during the buying and selling of horses they employ among themselves the sorts of words that others cannot at all understand. For example, they call a ruble a *birs*, a *poltina* (50-kopeck coin) is a *dior*, a *polpoltina* (25-kopeck piece) is a *sekana* or *sekis*, a *grivna* (ten-kopeck coin) is a *zhirmakha*, and so on. In similar fashion, thieves have many made-up words which, besides them, no one can understand.

not able to conceal them from soldiers of the Department of Criminal Investigations, for six dragoons who were in that very village began searching among all the yards for any suspicious people. Seeing the danger, Kamchatka and the other members of Kain's gang ran off in various directions, while Kain himself ran through the coaching inns to the Makariev dock once more, and recrossing to the other side of the Volga, ran into a public bathhouse, thinking to conceal himself there from the dragoons who were searching for him. No sooner had he entered the bathhouse, undressed, and stepped out into the yard, however, than he saw a multitude of soldiers encircling the entire bathhouse. There was nothing else for him to think than that they were searching for no one other than him. He sprang back into the bathhouse, and after rolling up his clothes and throwing them under the bench, he came out in just his breeches and walked right past the soldiers. Going directly to the officer of the guards at the guardhouse, he reported that while he was in the bathhouse, all his clothes, some money, and the passport he had been given by the Moscow Magistrate had been stolen. The officer had no choice but to send him back to the aforementioned Department of Criminal Investigations, which he did after first dressing him in a soldier's cloak.

Anyone can imagine what fear Kain felt at that moment, realizing that if they recognized him as the same criminal who on the eve of that day had fled from this very office, then not only could he not hope for his freedom but also for any mercy from the severe Colonel Redkin. However, do you think, Dear Reader, that the end draws nigh to Kain's criminal adventures? No! If you are not bored reading this modest volume to the last page, then you will see that the following adventures are vastly superior to the previous ones, for such changes occur in our fortunes that no human wisdom is able to foresee. Frequently, something good will be ripped from our hands at the very instant we are preparing to enjoy it, and it not rarely happens that when a person experiences some manner of misfortune and becomes deprived of all hope, he suddenly receives what he desires. Although they say fear drives all remedies and reasoning from our thoughts, which prevents a person from knowing which measures to take for his deliverance, this is not so with everyone. Although Kain had become extremely frightened, he had not completely lost his ability to reason, and he found a means whereby he not only saved himself from punishment but also received a passport from the colonel.

When they had brought Kain from the guardhouse to the department, the colonel asked him who he was. Kain, adopting a bold and courageous front, answered: "I am a Moscow merchant, Your Excellency, and have come here with my goods. While I was in the public bathhouse, all my clothes, some money, and the passport given to me by the Moscow Magistrate were stolen, and that is why I went voluntarily to the guardhouse to make this declaration, from where the officer sent me to Your Excellency." The colonel ordered the clerk to interrogate Kain in writing, and when the clerk began his questioning, Kain whispered in his ear: "Three pounds plus of flour from me is professed; in other words, a caftan with a long sleeveless vest."[44] The industrious pen-pusher, upon hearing Kain's pledge, exhausted all the treacherous power of his stunted mind to justify Kain's acquittal in his report, but unfortunately for Kain, at the very moment the clerk was questioning him, the very soldier from whose guard he had escaped walked in the room. At the soldier's entrance, Kain's alarm increased greatly, and he became so fearful thinking the soldier would recognize him that a change came over his face. It never entered the soldier's mind, however, that the same prisoner who had run away from his guard just the day before could cross his path once more; therefore, he did not examine him closely, and for his part, Kain dissembled as best he could so as not to be recognized.

Upon interrogating Kain, the duplicitous clerk reported to the colonel, who, after carefully examining Kain's interrogation, was not convinced; therefore, he ordered the clerk to go with Kain to the fair and to inquire among the merchants from Moscow whether they knew him and whether or not he was in truth one of their brethren. When he heard this, Kain became unspeakably happy, knowing that, without a doubt, the treacherous department clerk would do anything for money. Happily, with the help of his companions, money was something he did not lack, for excluding what had been stolen from the Armenians, the money taken from the Tartar's headrest alone was all that was needed, and then some, for the purchase of the clerk's conscience.

With this intention Kain led the clerk to a merchant he knew in a public house, at which place his gang immediately appeared as well, bringing him a change of clothes and a sufficient sum of money. Their spirits brightened immensely, and both the aforesaid merchant as well as Kain's comrades, who also called themselves merchants, assured the clerk that Kain really was a Moscow merchant. Moreover, they gave him ten rubles, for which sum the clerk would not only have willingly consented to sell his conscience but also his soul lock, stock, and barrel. When they returned to the department, the clerk reported to the colonel both orally and in writing, assuring him on his honor as a clerk* that Kain was in reality a merchant from Moscow, that many merchants knew him, and that they vouched for him as an honest man.

Firmly convinced by this report, the colonel ordered Kain to be freed. Upon hearing this, however, Kain fell at the colonel's feet and importuned him with feigned tears to do him the paternal charity of ordering that he be given a new passport from his office to replace the one stolen in the bathhouse, for he intended to travel with his goods to various cities. Owing to the diligent efforts of the perfidious clerk, such a passport was issued for two years, with the department's seal and the signature of the colonel himself.

Although subordinates might not be people of far-reaching intellect, it quite frequently happens that they completely deceive their superiors. This arises from the fact that dishonest people generally have more control over their hearts than sincere people do. The honest soul cannot conceal what his heart feels, everything is depicted on his face, and his attempts to dissemble are in vain, for true virtue cannot be concealed. Depraved people, on the other hand, know how to dissemble so skillfully that the viler and more dishonest their intent, the more artfulness they have to conceal it because their cunning heart, without feeling any horror for the abomination of their crime, does not display any outward uneasiness, and their intellect, which has become inured

---

* In the opinion of honest people, among a half dozen of even the very best clerks, there is less than an ounce of clear conscience combined.

to their fraudulent ways, employs all its artfulness to conceal this deed from those who could perceive it. Judges who do not enter deeply into the cases entrusted to them but instead place vast confidence in all matters directly in their subordinates are particularly susceptible to this error, for very few clerks are conscientious people.

However, Dear Reader, we shall leave these civil servants to rattle their bones, we shall leave them in peace and let them, as is their wont, practice their insidious, slanderous deceits, for this pertains to us not in the least; only may God grant that we never have anything to do with them. We would be better served to turn our attention once more to Kain, who, saving himself from misfortune and obtaining a passport by means of the aforementioned fabrication, gathered his gang, and after purchasing horses and tents, embarked for the city of Nizhny Novgorod. When he arrived, Kain encamped on the mountain Sokolka, as it is called, and leaving his associates there, himself set off to the stalls of the market to practice his accustomed trade. He had not succeeded in reaching them when he came upon five soldiers from the Department of Criminal Investigations, who, laying hold of him by the collar, accused him of being a fugitive even though Kain showed them the passport which had been given to him by their chief commander. They did not accept his explanation, however, and instead began leading him off to their post. While walking with the soldiers along the street, Kain noticed a tub full of water standing alongside one yard, and tearing himself away from the soldiers, he leaped onto the tub, jumped over the fence and into the yard, then dashed from the yard into the garden, and thus was able to escape. After hurrying to his comrades, Kain immediately departed with them for Moscow, which they safely reached several days later. After selling off their horses at Horse Square Square, they set off for Nizhnie sadovniki,[45] and at first not knowing where to find lodgings for themselves, they discovered in one place an old, empty hut, where they decided to spend the night. Waiting for evening, they entered the hut, and making a pane of paper for the window, they passed the night without any difficulties. When they awakened the next morning, they spied a peasant who was selling boiled meat walking by the hut. While gazing out the window, Kamchatka called him over, and having bargained for a large piece of beef, he offered it to his mates, telling the peasant he would bring the money out to him directly; however, after Kamchatka closed the window, they all left the hut. The peasant waited for his money, standing at the window quite some time, but when they did not bring it out, he looked in the window and, not seeing anyone, went into the hut, where he found neither people nor even any manner of animal. According to a superstition common among people of the lower classes, the meat seller concluded that his beef had been taken not by people but rather by devils, and therefore he rushed from the hut in great fear. And this is the story he repeated to many people as the truth. Kain and his gang then found refuge for themselves with Aleksei Nagibin, a cloth factory worker who lived near the Paupers' Home,[46] and after staying with him for some time, one evening they agreed among themselves to set off to the Greek Monastery[47] in search of spoils. When they arrived at the cell of the Greek Zephyr,[*] they were informed that he was at the all-night service and that only his workman remained in his cell, where he had locked himself in. Having approached the doors, Kain began to knock quietly. Hearing this, the workman asked, "Who's there?" "Your master has ordered you to bring wax candles," Kain answered the workman, who, believing him, grabbed the candles and started off for the church, but no sooner had he opened the doors than they leaped into the cell, tied him up, and threatened to slash his throat should he begin to resist or cry out. Then, gathering up some clothing, money, and two small pistols, they returned to the home of the cloth factory workers.

The following day a servant living in the cloth worker's house stole

---

[*]   As with the doctor and the tailor, I am also not able to confirm whether or not this name or nickname is correct. It most certainly is not true, however, as one unknown writer of a short tale about Kain has claimed, that this Greek is a monk, for just as Kain himself did not call him a monk, this person is also referred to simply as the Greek in all the accounts I have compiled, which have come to me from various sources. Besides, the pistols taken by Kain give witness that the Greek was no monk, for there is neither the slightest need nor any proper reason why a monk should possess a firearm, and, in addition, there would have been no great profit for Kain to take a monk's clothing.

Evidently, this author does not know that Greek merchants rent and live in many of the cells in the Greek Monastery, and therefore the Greek robbed by Kain was in reality a merchant and not a monk. I think any properly reasoning person would agree with this conclusion.

the pistols and went to Red Square to sell them. Unfortunately for her, the owner of the pistols came across her path and began to bargain with her for them, and when they had agreed on a price, he summoned her to the Greek Monastery for the exchange of money. As the monastery was near to Red Square, the woman consented. The Greek, having led her to his cell and then tied her hands behind her, presented the woman along with the pistols to the police. There, under interrogation, she testified that she had taken the pistols from the house of her master and that they had been brought into the house by some persons living with him. A police detachment was immediately sent to the worker's house, where, after seizing Kain and his accomplice Zharov and confiscating all the belongings stolen from the Greek, they took them to the jail. At the initial interrogation Kain and Zharov issued a denial, for which they were placed in a cell. An order was given to interrogate them a second time under the cat-o'-nine-tails and to arrange a confrontation with the witness; consequently, several days later Kain and Zharov were brought abovestairs from the jail for punishment and interrogation. First they put Kain under the lash and led Zharov onto a porch so that he would not be able to hear what his accomplice testified, intending through this procedure to break them in the interrogation and discover the truth. While on the porch, Zharov spied freedom and ran, but Kain bore up under the cat and stood fast in his contention that he knew nothing, and thus after this cruel punishment he was led away again to his cell, where he was kept no short time.

About three weeks after this, Kamchatka sent an old woman to Kain who, while pretending to dispense alms, told him he should find a means of running just as Zharov had. At the very moment when Kain was conversing with the old woman, however, he was taken anew for interrogation to the chief of the city police, who admonished him to confess to the theft of the Greek, but Kain was steadfast in his contention that he knew nothing and that he was being unjustly slandered, so they led him away once more to his cell.

During the time Kain was being held in prison, his gang did not fail to seek out various means for the deliverance of their leader, and finally Kamchatka happily succeeded in putting his secret scheme into action.

He found an opportunity to bribe the cavalry sergeant on duty at the prison so that he would allow the woman who had accused Kain to be taken under guard to the bathhouse. (What can you not do through money?) The cavalry sergeant consented to this and sent one soldier as a guard. After arriving at the bathhouse, the woman immediately undressed, and after wetting her head with water, immediately put on a change of clothes that had been brought there for this very purpose. Covering her head with a veil, she came out of the bathhouse and walked past the soldier who was guarding her at the bathhouse gate and who was in no way able to recognize her.

Upon the departure of this woman, there was no longer anyone to make the case against Kain, and he maintained toward his acquittal that the witness had fled knowing the injustice of what she had wrongfully undertaken against him and because she feared a deserved punishment for it; consequently, soon thereafter, the belongings that had been stolen from the Greek were returned to him by the police, and Kain was entrusted into the custody of the aforementioned cavalryman Nelidov.

Upon gaining his freedom from the police, Kain resolved to quit Moscow, fearing that he would be returned for his actions to that very same fortress from which he had barely escaped because he was, out of habit, utterly unable to leave off his criminal trade. He found Kamchatka and yet four other fugitives who were nicknamed 1. Stolop, 2. Kuvai, 3. Legat, and 4. Zhulza,[48] and persuaded them to retire for some time from Moscow. After agreeing to Kain's proposal, they all set off for Horse Square, purchased horses, and embarked for the city of Kashin,[49] and when they arrived there, they called themselves merchants from Moscow and began living in the house of the elder in the Coachmen's Suburb.[50] They lived in that city above half a year without committing any crimes, whence they set off for the Frolishchev Hermitage.[51] Along the way they came across a band of Gypsies, and noticing that their Cossack lieutenant lagged somewhat behind, they seized him along with his horse and cart, led him off into the forest, and, after tying him up and leaving him in the forest, took all his belongings with them. Later they arrived at Silk Cove,[52] which is downriver from the Makariev Monastery, where they spied merchant ships sailing along the Volga, from one of which a man disembarked and set off on dry land. Kain and his gang followed him, seeking a convenient opportunity to rob him along the way, but he dropped in at a distiller's factory and did not come out, and so not wishing to wait there long for him, they set off toward the Makariev Monastery for the purchase of provisions. As they approached it, they spied six persons sleeping in the monastery meadow, from whom they stole the purses and clothing lying near them, and then they dropped into a tavern called the Sand, in which there were at that time up to seventy brigands, among which number was the ataman Mikhail Zaria (birds of a feather flock together).[53] Kain gave him an account of his situation and that of his companions, and wondered would he accept them into his command. The ataman was not content at that moment to attach them to his band, but perceiving in Kamchatka skills well suited for the criminal trade, he appointed him an *esaul*.[54] After purchasing some guns, powder, and other implements useful to a gang of outlaws at the Makariev Fair, they then set out to pillage a distillery. Before reaching it, they stopped a very short distance away, built a fire, and began to boil kasha, and then the ataman sent his incendiary* to the distillery so that he might inform him of the best way to attack it. Because the owner of the factory recognized the incendiary as a suspicious person, or, perhaps, because he had tidings concerning the activities of these brigands, when he caught sight of the incendiary, he ordered that he be captured and tied to a post. After waiting about two hours for the return of his agent, the ataman also sent his lieutenant Kamchatka to the factory and ordered him to give a sign should he meet any resistance. After arriving at the factory and seeing the bound incendiary, Kamchatka asked the distillery workers why, without any reason, they had treated his comrade this way. In response, the owner of the factory ordered that Kamchatka be caught and tied to the very same post. At that very moment, however, Kamchatka began whistling and crying out as loudly as he could, and hearing this sign, the ataman ordered all his men to take up arms and rush to the factory. First they entered the malt barn, in which they locked no small number of people they had seized there; then they

---

*   Criminals call the person who carries the tinder, steel, and flint an incendiary.

set off directly for the owner's house, and although the owner of the factory shot at them with his guns, to the good fortune of the brigands, or, perhaps, because he shot without letting them approach the proper distance, he neither killed nor even wounded anyone. Seeing them rushing toward him most boldly, the owner was overcome with fear (and perhaps he may have also thought, as some maintain contrary to common sense, that the brigands had cast a spell over his weapons), whereupon he ceased firing at them and locked himself in his chambers. Taking up a log, the brigands smashed the doors into smithereens with it, and they had only just entered the chambers when a guest who was then with the owner drew his sword and struck the brigands' incendiary across the neck with it, and he fell dead onto the floor. Immediately rushing at him, the bandits seized this hero, and taking away his sword, locked him in an empty storeroom, telling him "we'll deal with you later." Then they turned their attention to the owner, to whom the ataman said, after spying a star designating an order of merit on his caftan: "We won't touch you, but since you've fallen into my hands, it's time to settle accounts with me." Placing the owner once more under guard, he ordered his men to gather up money, silver and copper plate, and other objects, and in addition they took several horses and dray carts. When everything had been collected, the ataman ordered the aforementioned hero to be brought before him and asked him who he was. "I am Bakar, the Georgian Tsarevich,"[55] he answered the ataman. Upon hearing this, the ataman commanded of all his brigands that no one should venture to do the Tsarevich even the slightest injury, and so, leaving him there with the owner, they traveled to the Kerzhensk Forest.[56] After selecting a convenient spot, they remained there an entire month, eating, drinking, and making merry, because they had collected a goodly portion of both vodka and victuals from the factory they had robbed. From there they went to the village of Rabotki,[57] where they stopped and lived three weeks. During their time there, the steward came to the village and asked them who they were: "We are Don Cossacks," the ataman answered him; however, recognizing them as suspicious people, the steward forced them to ride from the village. While the ataman was talking with the steward, however, Kain approached a Kalmyk who was with the steward and asked him who the master of this village was. "General Vasily Yakovlevich Shubin," the Kalmyk replied.[58] Grinning, Kain proceeded with his discourse: "Is it not so your general always goes around in a fur coat, and that is why he is nicknamed Shubin? Well, tell him we'll send some tailors for the sewing of his summer clothes." Then, having ridden from the village, they continued their journey along the Moscow road, and when they arrived at the Lisinsky ferry, they began crossing the river Oka on a raft. As they were crossing the river, an officer who also happened to be on the raft asked them who they were and where they were going, but they made him no answer at the time; however, just as soon as they had reached the other side and stepped out onto the shore, the ataman stopped the officer and cried: "You asked about us on the water, but we will speak with you here on dry land. You ought to mind your own business and just be on your way, and as for those traveling along the high road, what business is it of yours; you, after all, aren't the police detective Redkin." Having pronounced this, he ordered his gang to take the officer's sash, the medal from his neck, and his hat[59] and then gave him some money for these things. Leaving him at the ferry, they proceeded on their journey towards Moscow, where, upon arriving, they separated into two parties: one remained in the Pereslavskaia Coachmen's Suburb and the other in the suburb of Rogozhskaia.[60] While living there more than a half year, they questioned everyone passing through about General Shubin. One time a landowner's servant stopped in Rogozhskaia, and, while conversing with him, the brigands asked him whose man he was. "General Shubin's," the servant answered them; "When is your general in the village of Rabotki," the brigands continued their questions. "In the summer," he replied, and with this went his way. Waiting for spring, they agreed among themselves to go to the village of Rabotki to rob the aforementioned General Shubin; consequently, the ataman sent Kain, Kamchatka, and yet one other bandit ahead of him along the Vladimir road for reconnaissance and the renting of lodgings in anticipation of the arrival of the entire robber gang. Their destination was the village of Izbylitsy, where they frequently found refuge at the dwelling of a certain peasant. Thus, in accordance with the ataman's order, the three advance quartermasters betook themselves quite early in the morning along the designated path, and when they had gotten out of Moscow and had begun to approach the menagerie,[61] they saw before them three persons, one of whom was a woman whose head was covered down to her neck in a white sheet. Coming abreast of them, Kamchatka inquired who they might be and where they were taking the woman. "We're taking the woman to give birth," they replied to him. Out of curiosity, Kamchatka stopped the woman in order to look at her face and then began removing the covering from her head, which action led to a quarrel breaking out among them. One of the men who were escorting the woman snatched out a knife and wanted to run Kamchatka through with it, but anticipating him, Kamchatka struck him so forcefully on the head with his mace that he knocked him off his feet; upon witnessing this, the other accomplice abandoned the woman and went off into the forest. In the meanwhile, Kain managed to come up to Kamchatka, and having seized the unknown man, he tied his hands behind him and asked the woman who she was. "I am the maidservant of the landowner Likharev," she replied to them, "and these two men lured me from my master's house, but where they were taking me I myself do not know." From this declaration Kain recognized that they were taking her into the forest with the intention of murdering her, and pitying her condition, they took both her and the man they had captured to the suburb of Lefortovo[62] and handed them over to the guards at the cheval-de-frise. What happened with them after this is not known, so let us therefore leave them in Lefortovo and direct ourselves to the continuation of Kain's journey.

Several days later they arrived in the village of Izbylitsy and took lodgings for themselves at the house of the peasant they knew. There Kain prepared four large boats for the ataman's arrival, and not long after that the ataman entered the village with his entire robber gang. Leaving their horses with the aforesaid peasant, they boarded the boats and sailed for the village of Rabotki, in which place a fair was being held where a vast multitude of people from various hamlets and villages had gathered. At that time, however, General Shubin himself was not in the village, but rather he had set out into the fields after game.

When they made shore, they went directly to the general's house, and locating the bailiff and the estate manager, they locked them in a hut. Next they entered the general's chambers in order to look for money and goods, all of which they swept up, and then taking the bailiff, the estate manager, and the previously mentioned Kalmyk with them, they boarded their boats once more and sailed off down the river Volga.

After Zaria's gang departed the village, the peasants gathered themselves up into a vast host and ran after them along the bank of the river. When the ataman caught sight of this, he told the bailiff and the estate manager they should forbid the peasants from pursuing them, for if they didn't, they would be thrown into the water; the bailiff and the estate manager, trying to save their lives from an innocent death, cried out to the peasants that they should stop pursuing them. The peasants obeyed their overseers and stopped, and the brigands, upon sailing some distance away, made shore. Taking the bailiff, the estate manager, and the Kalmyk out of the boat and tying them up hand and foot, they left them on the shore and themselves once more set their course down the Volga. And although in this manner they delivered themselves from the peasants of General Shubin, as I mentioned above there was a fair that day in the village of Rabotki. From this fair a crowd of people ran throughout various settlements, shouting everywhere "Robbers! Robbers!" and in many villages they sounded the tocsin, whereupon a vast multitude of people assembled from many places and ran after Zaria and his gang along both sides of the river Volga. Moreover, also pursuing them were several persons and soldiers of the Department of Criminal Investigations who chanced to be not far removed from that village and who took the opportunity to shoot at them with their weapons. No matter how courageous these villains might have been, seeing a vast number of people pursuing them on foot and horseback, they began to be gripped by fear, and therefore, applying all their efforts, they sailed to a safe, wooded area. When they made shore, they disembarked from their boats, took as much money and as many of the best goods as they could carry, and left what they could not take in the boats. Furtively continuing their journey through forested areas, in several days they arrived in the city of Murom,[63] where they stayed just two days. Some men were sent ahead to the peasant in the aforementioned village of Izbylitsy with whom they had left their horses, and they inquired of him whether he had heard of the alarm being raised after them in the village of Rabotki. The peasant replied that guards had been posted in many places along the Vladimir road, including even in the tavern of that very village of Izbylitsy, where there was a member of the city council with an escort of five soldiers. Upon receiving this news, Zaria's gang continued their journey directly from the city of Murom to the village of Izbylitsy, and knowing that such a small detachment could do them no injury, they went directly to the tavern, bought some vodka and beer, and, finding some seats, set about drinking and singing songs as much as they pleased. For their part, when they saw these far superior numbers, every one of which was armed, the soldiers did not even venture to utter a word to them. Then Zaria and his gang took their horses and set out for the city of Gorokhovets,[64] and when they had ridden off some distance, the ataman said to his men that after they had selected a good place, they should rest up; consequently, when they arrived in the village of Yazykovo on the bank of the river Sura,[65] they stopped and lived there about three months without giving anyone even the slightest offense. Some time later an Armenian merchant vessel arrived at the village, and when the ataman saw it, he assembled his command and counseled them to rob it, whereupon they waited for night and then went to the shore where the boat was anchored. When he detected their presence, the Armenian recognized them as a genuine robber band, and after firing at them several times with his gun, he hid himself among his wares. Having come on board the boat, Zaria's men found the chief bargeman[66] and forced him to indicate the place where his master had gone to hide. Dragging the unfortunate Armenian into the open, they demanded money from him, and although he vowed and pleaded that he had no money on his boat but only goods, he was not able to deliver himself from these unmerciful people with such an accounting. Seeing that the merchant did not want to share with them of his own accord, the ataman ordered that he be completely tied up with a rope, and taking him by the arms and legs, they cast him into the river. After waiting awhile, they dragged him once more onto the boat, and stripping him naked, lit a fire and wanted to burn him. Who could withstand such barbaric torment and not speak the truth? Not foreseeing any means of saving himself, the poor Armenian was forced to give them all the money he had, but not satisfying themselves with this, the brigands also seized some of his very best goods. After disembarking from the boat, they harnessed their horses and with all possible speed made off for the village of Boriatina,[67] where they were informed that they were being pursued. Not delaying in the least, they continued their excursion farther, and upon arriving at a Tartar village standing on the bank of the river Piana,[68] they went into the yard of a Tartar abyz[69] and forcefully took several horses from him to add to their own. Then they proceeded on their journey to the Bogoliubov Monastery, which is close to the city of Vladimir,[70] and when they arrived at the monastery, they encamped in the farmyard and lived there an entire week. After dividing all the booty they had taken from General Shubin and the Armenian, the ataman sent Kain and Kamchatka to Moscow to reconnoiter for lodgings.

Kain received his portion, and, in addition, the ataman gave him some money and a pair of horses for the journey, on which Kamchatka and he departed for Moscow.

While on the road, Kain was seized by a feeling of regret, reflecting on the notion that although fortune had so far greatly favored all of his many criminal actions, in the future it was quite possible that it might abandon him and therefore betray him to a fitting fate (for nothing on earth is unshakable and firm, nothing is constant, but rather fickleness and vanity alone constitute life). In addition, it also occurred to him that many famous brigands, viz., Senka Razin, Sennoi, Gavriushka, and others,[71] had brought their lives to a premature end with a shameful death befitting their actions no matter how much success they had enjoyed in their criminal trade. For these reasons, he resolved to leave off his life of crime and to live for the time being on the money he had acquired, and he expressed this intention with an explanation of his reasons to Kamchatka, who consented to do the same.

With such good intentions they arrived in Moscow several days later, and after selling their horses, Kamchatka went to the sail factory and Kain to the dwelling of a coachman in the coachmen's suburb of Rogozhskaia, where he had formerly taken refuge. Living there quite some time, he restrained himself from criminal activities, but having about him an abundance of temptation, he abandoned himself to sundry debaucheries, made the acquaintance of many lewd women, and partook of diverse games of cards and dice, whereupon in a short time his iniquitous estate began to diminish greatly; however, there was no way he could acquire money without resorting to his criminal handiwork because he had not been instructed in any trade other than thievery and was not accustomed to working at unskilled labor. This is why he invented a new plan for the restoration of his condition, through which, in a brief time, he became beyond all expectations the happiest of men.

Kain recollected that during his stay with the robber gang, he had heard from their ataman Mikhailo Zaria that every fall or at the start of winter many criminals come to Moscow for the purchase of powder, guns, and other necessities in their way of life, so he contrived to use this occasion to his benefit. In keeping with his general good fortune, this scheme was an utter success, for while traveling about Moscow, he learned in various ways in which places thieves and robbers took refuge. When he had come to know about many of them, he resolved to appear of his own volition at a government office, where he would confess his former criminal actions and, in addition, declare that he could find and catch many thieves and robbers, hoping with this plan to receive a pardon. With such an intention he set off one morning to the Senate,[72] where he stopped by the entrance and awaited the arrival of the senators. Several hours later, when Prince Kropotkin[73] arrived, Kain bowed to him and held out a previously prepared note, in which he had written only that he had some business before the Senate. The prince, after accepting the note from him, put it in his pocket without reading it and went on his way to the Senate, while Kain, standing by the entrance, expected every minute to be summoned inside. Evidently, however, His Excellency, thinking the note had been given to him from the hand of some unimportant petitioner or other, did not recall it, and Kain was not invited into the Senate. When the session ended and the senators began to disperse to their houses, Kain asked among the servants of Prince Kropotkin where his house was located, and several days later he arrived directly at his residence.[74] Stopping by the entrance, he awaited the prince's emergence or expected that someone there, having noticed him, would report his presence to the prince. He did not linger long before an adjutant came out from His Excellency. Spying Kain in his simple gray caftan, he took him to be a vagrant or a petitioner, and therefore not asking who he was and why he had come, ordered that he be removed from the premises. In former times it often happened with us that many judges rarely admitted poor people, especially peasants, into their presence, even though they were in mortal need, in order that they not aggravate them with their petitions.* Although Kain told the adjutant he had need of the prince, they ignored him, and he was led away from the house most disrespectfully, like an uninvited guest.

This first unsuccessful attempt could not deter Kain from a plan that seemed so attractive to him. After leaving the premises, he dropped into a tavern, and after drinking off a goodly measure of vodka, he returned once more along the very same path to the house of the very same Prince Kropotkin, and being even bolder owing to the effects of the spirits, he went straight into the entrance hall. Upon seeing him, the very same adjutant set about cursing and shouting at him more loudly than before, whereupon Kain ventured, for a second time, to enter the house.

"Your Honor," Kain replied, "your anger with me is unjust, for, you see, I'm not a petitioner and have come here voluntarily rather than out of necessity to report a certain important matter to His Excellency." Upon hearing these words, the adjutant reported them to the prince, who immediately ordered that Kain be summoned to him and inquired who he was and what need he had of him. "Your Excellency, I am that person," Kain answered him, "who three days earlier handed you a note at the Senate, and without mincing words, I venture to report to

---

* This in reality occurred about six years ago to a certain widow, a general's daughter who was married to an impoverished nobleman and had come to a certain judge to ask about a particular case. Not only did the judge not deign to admit her into his chambers but, coming into the antechamber and failing to hear out her petition directly, he made such a coarse refusal that she was compelled to return to her home without any resolution and greatly grieved.

Your Excellency that I am a thief and robber, of that I make a sincere confession, but I know of yet many other thieves and robbers not only in Moscow but also in other cities, and if my former offenses were to be mercifully forgiven and a sizable command given to me, then I could net a large number of them." The prince ordered that Kain be brought a glass of vodka, and putting a soldier's overcoat on him, sent him under guard to the Department of Criminal Investigations. He further ordered that a detachment be sent out the following night with enough men to capture any thieves and robbers that Kain might point out.[75]

At nightfall a considerable detachment was dispatched with Kain, which he directed to catch thieves and robbers in the places mentioned below:

1st.) Near the Moskvoretsky Gates in Zariadie[76] they took the thief Yakov Zuev and twenty of his men in the house of an archpriest.

2nd.) Also in Zariadie, in the house of a gunsmith, they caught the thief Nikolai Piva along with fifteen of his associates.

3rd.) Near the powder warehouse, in the house of a deacon, forty-five thieves and pickpockets.

4th.) Beyond the Moscow River in the Tartar bathhouses, sixteen fugitive soldiers and along with them several guns and some powder, which soldiers, upon being delivered to the Department of Criminal Investigations, confessed that they had resolved to rob Avram Khudiakov, the overseer of the Office of Deeds living in Syromiatniki.[77]

5th.) On the Moscow River across from the mouth of the Yauza River, they seized seven fugitive barge haulers with false passports who were hiding on a wooden riverboat.

Thus, on one night on Kain's orders, over one hundred persons were caught.[78] In addition, as many as twenty of the hosts with whom they had taken refuge were also seized, and all were transported to the Department of Criminal Investigations.

The next day in the morning Kain was produced before the Governing Senate along with a report about the previous night's activities. And in this luminous place, in the presence of the senators, Kain made a frank confession of some of his criminal deeds and promised under oath to eradicate all the thieves and robbers concealing themselves in Moscow.

After justly considering this request and agreeing among themselves, the senators not only pardoned Kain and granted him his freedom but yet appointed him a Moscow police spy, thinking that in this manner they would be shielding the inhabitants of Moscow from crime. For this reason, the Senate issued him a decree and also appointed under his command a military detachment consisting of forty-five soldiers and one sergeant, and he found himself in the same relationship to this unit as though he were a captain, only he did not have that rank. Moreover, the Senate sent decrees to the Military Collegium,[79] the Office of the Chief of Police of the City of Moscow, and the Department of Criminal Investigations declaring that upon Kain's request they were to lend him any assistance he might need in the pursuit of criminals.

Thus it was in such a manner that the former swindler, thief, and robber Vanka Kain became a Moscow police spy.

This is how fate plays with human happiness, by procuring the well-being of a thief and robber who, according to the law, ought to forfeit his life or be exiled to the gravest penal servitude. It is true that fortune is inconstant and holds unjust scales in its hands, for on whichever side a person places his hope, he is not able to find equilibrium anywhere. It recklessly tramples and treads underfoot groaning virtue cloaked in beggar's rags, but it looks agreeably upon dishonorable people who are full of diverse vices, and by rewarding them with vast wealth, elevates them to the highest estates.

Do not be surprised at this, Dear Reader, for it is a common occurrence. Were we to examine all human deeds attentively, then undoubtedly we would see an infinite number of examples where criminals, scoundrels, wicked usurers, unconscionable tax-farmers, unjust judges, brigands, and many dishonorable people luxuriate, prosper, and wallow in voluptuousness, whereas honest, wise, and virtuous people labor, toil, struggle with difficulties, and suffer but rarely are happy. For this very reason, one Russian writer has said:

For me three things on earth are rather strange:
The idler who is rich, honest people who are poor,
And that it is the reckless ones who are considered clever.[80]

And why this is so, I think even the wisest people are barely able to comprehend, for the divine fates are not to be put to the test; therefore, let us leave this discussion to men greatly skilled in Holy Scripture because this does not belong to our design. I know that even without this, many will say I have set about something which is not my business, but what is to be done? When you have already begun something, whether poorly or well, it is better to bring it to an ending rather than to leave it thus, for according to the simple proverb, even God is not able to please every temperament because there are as many minds as there are heads. Each person has his own way of thinking, and that is why each person will reason however he wishes, and I will return to the continuation of Kain's deeds.

When Kain became a spy, he considered himself the happiest of men, and truly, had he turned this fortunate opportunity to his benefit and only practiced the one duty entrusted to him, then perhaps his happiness would have continued to the end of his life. Having become so accustomed to crime, however, his deceitful conscience could not long contain itself within the bounds of virtue, according to the proverb "The pitcher goes often to the well but is broken at last."[81] Since he had developed a habit for crime from infancy, Kain was utterly unable to break himself of it.

After receiving the decree and a military detachment from the Senate, Kain rented a house for himself in Zariadie near the Customs House,[82] where he made a billiard table and introduced sundry games, including dice. For this reason, a great number of people of various callings assembled around him every day, and in no time Kain's name began to become famous not only in Moscow but also in distant cities. Many people who were idly roaming about, most of whom were factory workers, came to recommend themselves to his service in the hope of finding a refuge with him. Kain accepted such persons graciously and maintained up to thirty or more of them in his house at one time. Traversing Moscow in the capacity of spies, they learned through diverse means about all sorts of suspicious people and reported this to Kain, and at the same time they themselves frequently engaged in thievery by removing kerchiefs, watches, snuffboxes, and whatever other things happened to fall into their hands from the pockets of people on the street. They brought these things to Kain, from which he took some part for himself and remitted the remainder to these rogues. Sometimes he returned stolen goods to the very people from whom they had been taken, explaining that he had discovered them through his subordinates, and for this he received a reward and no small amount of gratitude.

It was under such circumstances that Kain committed many good and wicked acts, which I have resolved to convey in the following order.

Kain's Acts Committed During His Time as a Police Spy

1.

One time he was told that counterfeit money was being made in Meshchanskaia Street; immediately gathering his command, he snared these craftsmen, viz., Ekim Kholshchevnikov and fifteen of his accomplices, and keeping some of the counterfeit money they had made as well as all of their instruments for himself, he conveyed them to the Department of Criminal Investigations.

2.

In the court district of Kzhel,[83] at a distance from Moscow of roughly twenty-five miles, outlaws had robbed the village elder; consequently, Kain was summoned to the Court Chancery[84] and was ordered to find these brigands. Several days later, while riding beyond the Yauza Gates, Kain spied a drunk man lying in the street and ordered that he be seized and taken to his house. When they began looking him over, they discovered several stolen passports on him. After the drunken folly had exited the man's mind, Kain inquired where he had gotten the passports, reassuring him that if he told the truth, he would be set free. The man was forced to confess that he was among the gang of outlaws who had robbed the village elder of Kzhel, from whom they had taken the aforesaid passports, and he also revealed that his accomplices had taken up residence near the Monastery of the Intercession.[85] Not wasting any time, Kain took the aforesaid informer in the company of his entire command and set off for the place where the alleged robbers had taken refuge, and after capturing forty-nine persons, among which number were the two gang leaders Kazamaev and Medvedev, they transported them to the Department of Criminal Investigations. They found on them no trifling amount of money and various goods, from which Kain did not forget to take an ample portion for himself before conveying the remainder along with the robbers to the Department of Criminal Investigations. Kain took the aforementioned informer back to his house for the purpose of having him expose yet more thieves who he knew were living in Moscow, and therefore the next day he had two soldiers of his command accompany him to seek out criminal gangs. While wandering about the city of Moscow and without having located even one thief, the informer found a way to escape the soldiers attending him and disappeared without a trace.* During interrogation the aforementioned robbers confessed to many thefts, robberies, and murders, and one of them by the name of Savely Viushkin further admitted to being a part of many criminal gangs and to committing so many murders that he could not clearly recollect the number.

3.

Soon after that he caught twenty-seven more robbers, among whom was the leader Bakhtei, and during interrogation they confessed to the break-in of the Koliusky Monastery** as well as to other sizable robberies and murders.

---

* Some maintain as true that the soldiers guarding the informer took money from him and let him go themselves.

** If there is such a Koliusky Monastery, I have not had the occasion to hear of it; perhaps this might be the Kolotsky Monastery on the Mozhaisk Road.

4.

In the village of Pokrovskoe he caught thirty-five robbers who had robbed the landowner Militin of the city of Kashin.[86]

5.

Kain seized the factory worker Andrei Skorobogaty, who was living near the Vasilievsky Garden,[87] along with seventeen of his accomplices for making counterfeit money. With the aid of the very same Skorobogaty, he also found a thief in the coachmen's suburb of Tverskaia[88] who had the same sort of counterfeit money in his possession. In addition, a silver icon frame was discovered in Skorobogaty's lodgings, and upon being brought to the Department of Criminal Investigations, he admitted to robbing a church in the city of Staritsa.[89]

6.

He caught the thief Aleksei Zhurka along with fourteen of his men, and they confessed to the theft of money and goods from Secretary Chubarov as well as to many other crimes.

7.

He found seventeen criminals who had robbed the Siberian Chancery,[90] and during interrogation they confessed to yet many other crimes, for which five of them were punished with death.

8.

He captured nine thieves who had stolen icon frames and mountings as well as other church plate from a church situated alongside the old stone bridge belonging to the Trinity Monastery.[91]

9.

He caught five thieves who had stolen a considerable amount of money from the storehouse of the Maidens' Convent,[92] but it was a nun of that very convent who had incited the crime and who then fled with the thieves and disappeared without a trace.

10.

In the coachman's suburb of Dragomilovskaia[93] Kain captured a gang of thirty-seven robbers led by Aleksei Lukianov, and after being taken to the Department of Criminal Investigations, they confessed to many thefts, robberies, and murders.

11.

On the other side of the Moscow River, on Ordynskaia Street, he caught a criminal known as the Swan, who along with six of his companions had robbed Major Olovenikov, and under interrogation they admitted to still other crimes.

12.

They found the thief Zamchalka along with three of his associates; they had stolen five thousand rubles worth of money from the *kompaneishchik* Demidov.[94]

13.

He caught a thief with gold braid who, when taken to the Department of Criminal Investigations, confessed that he had fled from the St. Petersburg police and had stolen some money and goods from the shop of the merchant Miliutin. Owing to his information, six other thieves were found who confessed to many thefts and robberies, and to fleeing from the authorities.

14.

He snared eighteen criminals, among whom the major one was the leader known as Piva;* they had robbed the *kompaneishchik* Babushkin.

15.

At various times Kain found and captured forty thieves, who in turn informed on more than one hundred people of the same high character as they were themselves, and all of them were found by Kain.

---

*   In one account this name is given as Pava.

16.

An Account of Kain's Wedding

The passion of love resides not only in noble hearts, but even people of low estate are also quite often infected by it. The only difference is that the highborn (in their opinion) nourish this passion in their hearts with a greater tenderness than the lowborn; however, chaste love sometimes finds greater constancy and tranquility among the very simplest village dwellers than it does in enlightened people who reside in magnificent cities where they live in palaces decorated with gold, dress in gold brocade, and adorn themselves in sparkling precious stones. But if we judge this fairly, from an impartial point of view, then all human manners can be found to no small degree in any type of people, whether they do good or ill, according to the proverb "Every family has its black sheep," for the world has been created not solely for the nobly born but for all people equally, and only certain human judgments have placed distinctions between people. But however that may be, one may say that Kain's wedding was unique. Although I have lived on this earth more than forty years, I have not only not seen but have not even heard of a wedding similar to this one, and I think that you, too, Dear Reader, would not be able to recollect a like instance. Although these nuptials were not magnificent, they are, however, worthy of some comment and unfolded in the following order:

Before Kain had entered the ranks of police spies, when he was yet practicing his trade as a thief, there happened to live alongside his lodgings a certain retired sergeant who had a daughter, and although she was not an extraordinary beauty, she was nevertheless not unattractive. Kain, who at the time was calling himself a merchant, had become acquainted with the sergeant, and having fallen in love with his daughter, he strove in various ways to incline her to his love.[95] That is why, in the guise of his friendship with her father, he presented her with rather considerable gifts, and although she accepted them, she nevertheless conducted herself toward Kain with the utmost seemliness in tender conversations alone. However many and diverse intrigues Kain used to find the road to her heart, he was never able to gain even the slightest success, and so no matter how this counterfeit

Cupid strained his feeble bow with its blunt arrows against the settled heart of the sergeant's daughter, all his pains were for naught. Seeing his want of success in this endeavor, he was forced to leave off his scheme with no small measure of regret. However, the chaste beauty who had captivated his rogue's heart never escaped his thoughts, and therefore a short time later, when he had become a police spy, he took it into his head to use this opportunity to fulfill his desire. Kain entertained the hope that upon seeing him in such a position, this constant maiden would more willingly consent to his proposal, and, in addition, he was then dressed not so commonly as he was before, for he wore German-style clothes, curled his hair a bit, and covered his cunning head with powder. When Kain called on her, he was informed that she intended to get married, but he commanded her not to marry any suitor other than him. But whether she knew his true character, or whether her heart was already occupied by another love, and perhaps having an innate antipathy[*96] to him as well, she rejoined that he should not in the least nourish such a hope and should cease to think about it because she had no intention of marrying him, no matter how vast a fortune he had. This unexpected refusal struck Kain more fiercely than a thunderclap, whereupon he became greatly distressed, for generally what seems most precious of all to any man is the thing that he has been denied or forbidden, and our heart never suffers more than when it fears losing the thing that fascinates it and that it loves excessively. Thus Kain, being consumed by this amorous passion and not seeing any means of fulfilling it, took refuge in his criminal imagination. He went to the Department of Criminal Investigations and pressed himself on the forger Andrei Skorobogaty, a prisoner whom Kain had brought there himself for making counterfeit money. Kain promised to petition for Skorobogaty's freedom if only he would slander the sergeant's daughter, saying that she had an agreement with him in the making of counterfeit money. Tempted by Kain's promise, Skorobogaty ordered the secretary to be informed that he had a certain matter to divulge; upon receiving him, the secretary asked what he intended to reveal. "Sir," Skorobogaty said to the secretary with great servility, "there is

---

*   revulsion. {See endnote 96.}

-18セ

a certain sergeant's daughter who knew about the counterfeit money I made and who profited by it."

Why demand more evidence? I think everyone knows that sometimes a secretary's penetrating mind, even without any proof and from human physiognomy alone, can discern the truth, or at least who has more money for the secretary's conscience. A detachment was sent directly, and the sergeant's daughter was transported to the Department of Criminal Investigations, where she was asked why she did not report Skorobogaty even though she knew he was making counterfeit money. The unfortunate and guiltless girl justly pleaded her innocence and assured them with various oaths that she not only knew nothing but would not even recognize her accuser were she to see him; however, not being convinced by her truthful answer and not having afforded her a confrontation with her accuser, the truth-loving secretaries decided to interrogate her under the lash. They tortured her to the point that she barely remained alive and then ordered her to be carried away unconscious on a bast mat and thrown into prison like a common criminal.

On the next day after this agonizing punishment, Kain sent a woman to the sergeant's daughter and ordered her to say that if the girl agreed to marry him, then in two days' time she would be set free; in reply, the virtuous maiden ordered that Kain be told not to harbor any such thoughts. Irritated by such a coarse answer and seeing that his underhanded intrigues were not having their desired effect, Kain took himself once more to Skorobogaty and told him to accomplish all he could to convince the secretaries and the officials in attendance that the girl had indeed known about the making of counterfeit money. Based on such false evidence, the case reached the point where the girl was to be interrogated under torture. As soon as the ill-fated and unjustly suffering girl was informed of this, streams of the bitterest tears gushed from her eyes, and having fainted, she lay there unconscious for some time. When nature had overcome the frailties of the body and she had regained consciousness, she pondered her unfortunate state and, not finding any means for her deliverance, was compelled to take refuge in the arms of this criminal, so she yielded to his demand and sent word that they should meet. Upon hearing this, the inhuman scoundrel rejoiced unspeakably, and that very minute, just as the starving, rapacious hawk covets the gentle dove, he hastened to her in prison with great delight. When he arrived, she told him, while melting in a flood of bitter tears: "I see fate has determined for me to be the unhappiest of women; if you are able to save me from the unjust torment that threatens me, I will consent, against the will of my heart, to be your lawful wife, but otherwise I would prefer to die rather than relinquish my maidenly honor." When Kain heard this, he became overwhelmed with joy and swore various oaths that he would marry her without fail. He immediately rushed to the secretaries, who were exceedingly gracious to him,[*97] and after talking with him in private, they announced to the officials in attendance, with the help of the interpretation of several decrees, that they ought not to interrogate the sergeant's daughter under torture, for although she knew about the making of counterfeit money, as a woman who was ignorant of the laws, she did not report it more out of simplicity and ignorance than by design. As the officials were guided by the reasoning of the secretaries, they did not long tarry over their recommendation and in two days signed a judgment to whip the girl with the knout and release her from custody, which was accomplished according to Kain's request without any mercy.

Here, My Dear Reader, is the inconstancy of human fate! It frequently amuses itself by maltreating good people and tarnishing the brilliance of the just, and instead of them, it favors idlers and elevates those who have no virtue whatsoever. It is true that the secrets of an incomprehensible fate are hidden from us and that we are unable to fathom why it does not reward all with equal happiness, why

---

*   The secretaries at that time were Dnski and Bgmlv {see endnote 97}, and their benevolence toward Kain arose from the fact (as Kain himself told it) that when he was a police spy and brought thieves and their stolen goods to the Department of Criminal Investigations, at night the aforesaid secretaries together with their clerks would select the best things from the goods in the secretaries' chamber and divide them among themselves, and the remainder they left to those bringing petitions before them. When there was not enough left for those people from whom the goods had been stolen, they collected something from those with whom the thieves had taken refuge. Fearing that Kain would denounce them is precisely why these secretaries showed him every benevolence while he was being held there. {See Komarov's preface, page 112.}

it sometimes offers scoundrels the means to increase their wealth and fulfill their desires but determines that honest people must endure poverty and plunges them into an abyss of misfortunes.

After the commission of the unfortunate girl's punishment, Kain took her into his custody, and adding the proverb that broken bones mend stronger than ever,[98] he gave her over for the treatment of her back to a woman he knew who made communion bread. After some time, when the girl had returned to her former health, Kain sent to the parish priest without any ceremonial preparations to say that he would be getting married, and taking his bride with him, he went to the church accompanied by many soldiers of his command. According to the statutes of the time, when the priest arrived at church, he demanded the wedding record,* but when Kain gave it to him, he recognized it as forged, which in reality it was, for Kain had written it himself at home. For this reason, the priest steadfastly refused to marry Kain and took himself from the church. For Kain, however, there among the host of people who had gathered in the church, it would have been embarrassing to go home without getting married, so he sent the soldiers of his command into the streets and ordered them to bring the first drunken priest they came across to the church. Since we used to have no shortage of such types,** the soldiers had little difficulty in doing this, and no sooner had they gone out onto Varvarskaia Street[99] than an intoxicated priest who had come out of a nearby tavern crossed their path, so they seized him by the arms and led him to the church. "Why do you create such a scene?" Kain said to the priest. "Having gotten drunk, you go along the street shouting and singing songs, which is not at all proper for someone of your position to do. Don't you know I could send you

* According to the statute of the time, the record (in its old-fashioned name), that is, an official letter granting permission to marry, was issued from the Cathedral Office for presentation to the parish priest, and it was expressed therein that those entering into the marriage had no relationship between themselves contrary to the law. A small fee was collected in the Cathedral Office for each wedding record, but nowadays, with the monarch's assent, this has been set aside in order to ease the burden on the people.

** In previous times drunken priests were numerous, but nowadays, owing to the prudent decree of the ecclesiastical powers, this is not evident because the now deceased Archbishop of Moscow Amvrosy[100] decreed that whoever saw a priest or deacon in a tavern and brought him to the consistory would receive a monetary reward.

to the Ecclesiastical Consistory, where they will deal with you using all the severity of the law?" Although the priest's head was full of intoxicating vapors, he still became greatly afraid, and Kain, continuing his speech, said: "If you wish me to free you, then owing to the absence of the local parish priest, marry us." And since to a drunk man the sea is only knee deep, the inebriated priest did not at all object and immediately put on his chasuble and began to marry them. When the time arrived in the church ceremony to lead the bride and groom around the lectern, then the priest, whether it was out of fear or from having succumbed to the power of drink, made at least eight revolutions rather than three. Upon completion of the nuptials Kain, laughing, asked the priest why he had led them round so many times. "You'll live longer," the priest replied to him. Then Kain took the priest to his house, and for the want of invited guests there were seated at the table only the newlywed couple along with the priest and the matchmaker, all of whom were lavishly provided for. At the end of the meal Kain gave the priest a ruble, and after tying his arms behind him, he hung two bottles of vodka around his neck and sewed a sign on the back of his cassock, on which was written: "When he drinks the vodka hanging round his neck, then will he be untied." And with this they led him out of the house. After the passage of some time this priest ran into Kain on the street, and when he caught sight of him, he raised his long cassock and set off running, fearing that Kain would once again make the same sort of spectacle out of him.

The day after this marital union, Kain ordered the soldiers of his command to forcibly convey into the yard any merchants walking past his house, of which as many as forty were gathered; he then ordered that they be placed in the middle of the yard, and sprinkling some peas on a plate, ordered his newlywed spouse to serve them in place of vegetables.[101] Each of the merchants took several peas out of courtesy and replaced them with a ruble or fifty-kopeck piece for Kain's young wife, and in this manner the entire marriage ceremony came to an end.

16.

Soon thereafter, during Cheese Week, which the common people call *maslenitsa*, Kain ordered that a snow mountain be built behind the

Customs House for the diversion of his dear wife,[102] and decorating it with fir trees, junipers, and statues, he covered it in certain places with beautiful cloths.* For the duration of the week a vast number of people gathered on this mountain for sledding, and various entertainments took place, while at the same time the scoundrels of Kain's command extracted from pockets whatever came to hand. On the last day of that week, Kain gathered up to thirty people of diverse stations in life and ordered them to perform on the mountain a comedy called King Solomon.[103] Among other scenes, it was ordered that a factory worker should steal money from the pocket of the person who had been named king, and when the factory worker was caught in this theft and taken to the imaginary king, he ordered him to be punished according to the military article. Thus, at Kain's order as many as two hundred people of various callings were gathered and arranged in two rows, since guilty soldiers were commonly driven through such a formation. Each person was given a broom, and then stripping the guilty factory worker naked, they put a peasant's cap on his head, a white kerchief round his neck, large peasant mittens on his hands, and tethered a small bear cub to his back, and in this manner they drove him through the gauntlet six times with the drummer of Kain's command beating the drum. Acting as a major, a worker from the cloth factory known as the Wolf rode on his horse along the gauntlet and compelled those forming it to beat the man without mercy. Thus, instead of a joke, the factory worker was beaten until he bled, for which Kain gave him a ruble and a new fur coat, which made him greatly content.[104]

17.

One time a peasant of the Petrovsky Monastery who traded in Mantle Row[105] came to Kain and said that the steward of that monastery had taken his son for conscription into the army and was holding him in his house under guard. He inquired if it would be possible for Kain to rescue his son from this, for which he promised to give him some money. On that very day Kain took several men of his command and

---

*　The place on which the mountain was built is still called Kain's Mountain to this day.

went to the house of the aforesaid steward, where he told him to free the peasant's son who had been taken for conscription into the army. When the steward failed to agree to this, Kain, becoming angry, ordered his soldiers to seize him and to take him out into the yard. Forcing the steward to his knees, they grabbed a barrel full of tar that was standing in the yard and emptied it on his head, which made him take on the appearance of a Moor.* While gazing at him and laughing, Kain said: "I've previously shorn those who haven't dealt honestly with me; your archimandrite is a fool: it's long past time you became a monk."[106] Then, having taken the peasant's son, he conveyed him to his father, from whom he received the promised amount of money along with extreme gratitude.

18.

Soon after this he caught a fugitive soldier with stolen printed passports, and after being escorted to the Department of Criminal Investigations, the soldier confessed that he had acquired the passports from a certain landowner. When Kain found the landowner, he presented him to the Department of Criminal Investigations as well, where, upon questioning, he confessed to the distribution of passports to as many as three hundred people of various callings and also admitted that they had been given to him by a Senate guard, who had stolen them from the Senate Printing House.

19.

On the day of the feast of St. Nicholas the Miracle Worker,[107] when the merchant Gorsky was at matins, thieves entered his house and threw one of the two servant girls who were at home into the cellar and took the life of the other, very young one, and after ransacking the house, they went their way. Knowledge of this reached the Secret Imperial Office, whereupon Kain was summoned there, and His Excellency Baron Ivan Ivanovich Cherkasov[108] commanded him to

---

*　In all the accounts I have, it is written that Kain covered the steward with tar, but the anonymous author previously mentioned by me on page 136 wrote that it was pitch. This is not only unlikely but completely contrary to common sense because pitch is the type of substance which even on the hottest summer days does not become liquid without the aid of fire, and such heating requires no short time, which Kain had no reason to spend at that moment.

strive to find the accused criminals. Some time after that Kain ran into a drunken sailor on Stretenskaia Street, in whose pocket he found a steel, a tinder, and a torch.[109] Considering him a suspicious person, Kain took him to his house and asked him at times gently and at others with the aid of torture who he was. Seeing that it was not possible to put Kain off, the sailor was forced to confess that he was a fugitive and also one of that number of thieves who had ransacked the house of the merchant Gorsky. In addition, he admitted that they had been urged on by a workman living with the merchant, and from the testimony of this sailor twenty of his accomplices were found.

20.

He caught a fugitive recruit who testified during interrogation that he had been wrongfully conscripted into the army by Miliukov, a landowner from Bezhetsk.[110] Upon finding this Miliukov, Kain presented him to the Military Collegium,[111] where, after an interrogation was carried out, he confessed to unjustly conscripting a vast number of recruits.

21.

One day the factory workers living in Kain's house pointed out to him a fugitive worker from a cloth factory who was walking along the street in gentleman's livery; Kain ordered that he be caught and, after he had been led into his house, inquired of him who he was and in whose service he was established. Since he would not tell the truth, Kain ordered birch rods to be brought and wanted to whip him, threatening as well that should he fail to confess, he would be sent to the Department of Criminal Investigations. The sham servant was forced to confess that he truly was a fugitive worker from the cloth factory who was presently lodging at the quarters of Telesnin, a grenadier in a Life Guards company,[112] with whom, he said, also lived Lieutenant E*** and a soldier of the Semenovsky Regiment[113] named Samson Rudnev, as well as up to fifteen other people of various callings, all of whom rode at night throughout Moscow, indulging in robbery. Not wasting any time, Kain gathered his command and went to the quarters of the accused Life Guard, where he found Lieutenant E, the soldier Rudnev, and several more of their accomplices, whom he seized along with all their belongings and conveyed to the Department of Criminal Investigations. At that time, however, Telesnin himself was not at home, but his companions revealed that he had gone on his way to Yaroslavl.[114] Several days later Kain found him and took him to the Department of Criminal Investigations, where, under the questioning that was undertaken, he confessed that one night, together with the aforementioned Lieutenant E, the soldier Rudnev, and other people living with him, he robbed the merchant Nasyrev as well as Vasily Kupreianov, a merchant living near the Donskoi Monastery,[115] from whom they took no small amount of money and sundry belongings. In addition, they also took from Kupreianov a number of various drinks, for he traded in wine. At another time, they had also broken into the home of the merchant Babushkin. When they came to rob these houses, they proclaimed that they had been sent by the Secret Office on a secret mission to seize these things.

22.

Two persons fled St. Petersburg from the *kompaneishchik*[116] Zamiatnin after having stolen from him a considerable amount of money. Upon arriving in Moscow, one of them found himself in the Office of Contraband Alcohol[117] for some sort of incident, and the other, his comrade, went to Kain and asked if it would be possible for him to find some means of freeing his friend, for which he promised to give him three hundred rubles. Kain immediately agreed to this, and, waiting for evening, took several soldiers of his command and rode to the Office of Contraband Alcohol, where he found the clerk on duty sleeping. Kain ordered the clerk to be stripped, and he flogged him with the lash for being derelict in his duty. Then he conveyed the fugitive from Zamiatnin who was being held there along with the soldier who was guarding him to a smithy on Tsaritsyn Meadow,[118] and removing the fetters from the fugitive, he had them placed on the soldier. He released the soldier to return to that same office and returned Zamiatnin's previously mentioned man to his friend, from whom he immediately received the promised three hundred rubles along with much gratitude.

23.

One time when Kain was on Red Square, he dropped into a public house which he not infrequently favored with his presence, where he saw Sovetov, a clerk of the St. Petersburg Regiment, sitting at a table with a nun of the Passion Convent, [119] who at that time was yet rather young and handsome. Between them stood a bottle of wine. Sovetov was acquainted with Kain because they had previously lived near each other, and he therefore poured a glass of wine and brought it to Kain with the admonition that he not censure them. It was impossible for Kain not to guess what business Sovetov had with the dear young nun, and therefore, having raised the glass of wine Sovetov had brought him, he wished them much success and said: "It's clear, sister, that you take after your mother and that something good will come of you; just live and conduct the affairs you've begun a little more cautiously."[120] After drinking the wine, Kain left them in the public house and returned to his quarters.

Several days later Sovetov coaxed the nun to leave her convent and spirited her away to the village of Cherkizovo, which is about five miles distant from Moscow, where they were married and began living as a lawful husband and wife ought to by enjoying each other in sincere love. However, fate, which has become accustomed to playing with human happiness and transforming our intentions according to its arbitrary rule, became envious of their happiness and destroyed their loving union by an unexpected event.

Soon after their marital union, while in the village of Preobrazhen-skoe,[121] the comely nun ran into the assistants of the Mother Superior of the Passion Convent. Although she was wearing secular dress, they recognized her, and after catching her, they led her away to the Ecclesiastical Consistory, where she was forced to confess that the clerk Sovetov had taken her from the convent and that she had also married him. By the power of church law, the Consistory robed her once again in her black tunic and sent her to the Ascension Convent,[122] where her penance was to be supervised, and it was also ordered that Sovetov be found so that he could be made to answer to the Consistory for his transgression of the laws.

Sovetov was not so stricken by the Consistory's laws as he was by the sad condition of his dear wife and his grievous separation from her; consequently, when he reflected upon his misfortune, he didn't know what to do. Finally, he went to Kain and, recounting his story to him, asked if he would be able to find any means for freeing his unfortunate nun from· the convent, for which he promised to present him with one hundred rubles. "Fine," Kain answered, "I'll try to carry out your request."

The next day Kain put on an officer's caftan,[123] and assembling several soldiers of his command as well as one sergeant of the guard named Nagovitsyn, who happened to be at his house for a game of cards, he set off toward the Ascension Convent. As this transpired on a Sunday, several carriages belonging to gentlefolk were standing alongside the convent, because of which, given the closeness of the street, it was not possible to pass through too freely. Kain instructed Sergeant Nagovitsyn to order the carriages to move away from the convent by informing them that Count Peter Ivanovich Shuvalov[124] would soon arrive for the liturgy, whereupon the carriages dispersed a short distance. Having placed guards in several places, Kain himself went straight to the Mother Superior in her cell and announced that he had been sent by the Secret Office regarding a certain case, that is, to retrieve the nun from the Passion Convent who was being held under her supervision. The Mother Superior, realizing the severity of Kain's demand and not venturing to contradict him in the least, ordered that Serafima (so the unfortunate nun was called) be brought to her that very minute and turned her over from her care to Kain's. Taking the nun by the arm, Kain led her out of the convent, placed her next to himself in his sledge, and said: "The kite has flown beyond the sea. . . ."[125] He then whipped the horses and conveyed her safely to Sovetov.

Those experienced in the ways of the heart know well enough how grievous an involuntary separation of true lovers is; on the contrary, how tender for them is the joy of an unexpected meeting. I therefore consider it superfluous to express here the joy with which the husband and wife united by Kain were overcome. Let it suffice to say that Sovetov immediately gave Kain the promised one hundred rubles along with his hearty thanks, and Kain, while accepting them and laughing, said: "If they gave me one hundred rubles for every nun, then I would drag all of them out of the Ascension Convent."

24.

During Lent several wagons of fresh fish were brought to the Merchants' Arcade, and in one of them the customs guards spied a concealed barrel of vodka, which was seized by their decree, and it was ordered that the vodka along with the carter who had transported it was to be taken to the Office of Contraband Alcohol. The owner of the fish, knowing that according to the power of the laws he would be subject to punishment, went to Kain and asked if he could try in whatever way possible to deliver him from this misfortune, promising him a large gift for his help. Kain ordered him to find out at what time the vodka would be transported to the Office of Contraband Alcohol and to tell him; in the meanwhile, he himself came to an agreement with a soldier who was not of his command, and giving him four of the boldest workers from the cloth factory, who were known as the Wolf, the Ram, the Monk, and the Hat,[126] he ordered them to seize the vodka on the road. Striking out for the Moscow River, they waited there and stopped the wagon; seizing the carter by the scruff of his neck, the soldier cried: "You enlisted me in the army and have yourself now fallen into my hands, so it's time for me to settle accounts with you." Turning to the carter's horse, the factory workers began calling it theirs and acting as though it had been stolen from them, whereupon they tied up the customs guards accompanying the vodka and put them in the sledge. Unharnessing the horse, they mounted the fisherman's workman on it and led it off with them, but they left the sledge with the barrel of vodka and the tied-up soldiers at the Moscow River. When they arrived once more at Kain's house, they reported the safe completion of the commission that had been given to them, for which Kain received a large reward from the fisherman.

25.

A worker for the merchant Klepikov told Aleksei Shinkarko,[127] one of the soldiers in Kain's command, that in a boat anchored on the Moscow River near the Moskvoretsky Gates,[128] there was a considerable amount of money; Shinkarko reported this to Kain, who, some few days later, waited for nightfall and then took the four boldest and bravest soldiers of his command, went to that boat, and asked the guard stationed there, was there not wheat for sale on their boat? Seeing that there was no one else on the boat but the guard, Kain ordered that he be tied up, and upon entering the storeroom, they found a trunk, from which they broke off the lock. After extracting one thousand seven hundred rubles from it, they returned safely to their quarters.

26.

A merchant from Lace Row sent a number of undeclared goods that he wished to conceal from the customs tax from Moscow to the city of Kaluga,[129] which goods were examined at the customs post and confiscated; therefore, he went to Kain and begged him to do whatever was in his power to liberate the aforesaid goods, for which he promised a considerable reward. Without delaying, that very same day Kain took several men of his command, rode out to the customs post, and tied up the guards stationed there, and he took the aforementioned confiscated goods with him and returned them to the merchant, from whom he received his promised reward.

27.

The same merchant from Lace Row came to Kain and said that in a house near the Foreign Suburb,[130] thread for embroidery and weaving as well as decorative beads were being made from illegal gold and silver, in which endeavor state money was also being used.[131] Waiting for night, Kain took several soldiers of his command as well as some workers from the cloth factory who were living with him and went to the house, which he found quite firmly locked and with no way to enter the chambers. He commanded one of the factory workers known as the Wolf to climb into the garret through a dormer and then open the doors, but no sooner had the Wolf climbed into the window than the foreigner living in the house seized him by the hair and set about beating him, and in that fight he bit off the Wolf's ear. In the meanwhile, Kain's other subordinates found a log and broke down the doors, and upon entering the rooms, they took possession of all the gold and silver they could find as well as all of the tools. Then they were about to leave, but a gentleman living alongside the house, upon hearing noise emanating from the house of his neighbor, concluded that it was the work of robbers, and coming out onto his balcony, he cried out to his servants to assemble and run to the aid of his neighbor. Arising from a deep sleep, however, the servants were not able to assemble with alacrity. Kain ordered his subordinates to dash up to the balcony, and seizing the gentleman, they put him in a sledge and transported him to Gorokhovo Field.[132] Having removed one of his shoes, they left him there, and because it was well below freezing, the gentleman was obliged to tuck his bare foot underneath himself like a goose and squat there on the road until passersby found him and conveyed him home. Kain gave the tools he had taken to the merchant who had told him about this scheme and took three hundred rubles from him for his efforts.

28.

Kain found some craftsmen living near the Convent of St. John[133] who were making counterfeit money, and he brought them as well as all their tools and the money they had made to the Department of Criminal Investigations.

29.

On the day of the feast of Pentecost, or as we call it, on the Day of the Holy Trinity, near the Moskvoretsky Gates on the Zhivoi Bridge,[134] there gathered a multitude of women and maidens who, according to an ancient and yet superstitious and idolatrous custom, walked about with birch branches while they sang songs, danced, and threw the wreaths from their heads into the Moscow River. A considerable number of people of all stations had assembled for the viewing of this shameful spectacle, among which number there

happened to be the merchant Grigory Kolosov,* from whose pocket
thieves had extracted twenty thousand rubles in overdue promissory
notes. This loss made Kolosov quite distressed, so he went to Kain
and, humbly bowing, begged him to try to find the promissory notes,
pledging to him an agreeable reward for his help. I would suppose
anyone could understand that for Kain it was much easier to find
the merchant's promissory notes than to carry off the beautiful Serafima from the Ascension Convent because almost all pickpockets
were known to him, and some of them, as was mentioned earlier,
had even taken refuge in his house. To be sure, the promissory notes
in reality had been stolen by soldiers of his command who, while
looking after the affairs of their leader, had themselves turned into
thieves. That is why Kain found the promissory notes in three days'
time, and after going at night to Kolosov's house, he climbed into
the garret, put them behind a picture nailed to the wall, and returned
to his house. The next day Kolosov ran into Kain on the street and
inquired whether or not there was any news about his promissory
notes. "You worry about your loss in vain," Kain replied to him,
"your promissory notes are in your house." Kolosov couldn't believe this, thinking that Kain was jesting with him, but when Kain
assured him with many oaths that the promissory notes truly were
in his house, Kolosov became unspeakably happy and invited him
to his house, and when Kain arrived, Kolosov received him with all
condescension and treated him to the best drinks. After sitting there
a short while, Kain summoned Kolosov's young son and whispered
in his ear that he should dash up to the garret and retrieve some
letters that had been sealed in a packet and placed behind a picture
on the wall. The boy ran up to the garret directly, brought back the
sealed packet, and placed it before Kain on the table. "Here are your
lost promissory notes," Kain told the merchant. "Look them over
to see if they are there in their entirety. Didn't I tell you they were
in your house?" The merchant almost went out of his mind with

---

*   In one of the accounts I have, the name is written as Kolobov, but I will call
him Kolosov because owing to their great wealth, the name of the merchants Kolosov has
been known to many from distant times, and nowadays they own a sizable silk factory. On
the other hand, I have never even had an occasion to hear of the Kolobovs.

joy, and even though he was still not able to comprehend how the promissory notes had come to be in his house, he thanked Kain and asked how much money he needed for their discovery. "Although I have never been a priest," Kain answered, "I know their customs; they are content with whatever is given to them."[135] The wife of the merchant brought a sack of silver coins containing two hundred rubles, and placing it before Kain, she requested that he take from it as much as he pleased. Kain inquired of her how many servants there were in the house. "Sixteen," she answered. Extracting sixteen rubles from the bag, he ordered that they be disbursed to the servants as a sign of his magnanimity, and after putting the remaining one hundred and eighty-four rubles in his pocket, he expressed his gratitude to his host and returned home.

30.

Having called on Kain, the merchant Babkin said that four thousand seven hundred rubles had been stolen from his storeroom, and he asked that Kain apply his efforts to the discovery of the thieves, for which he promised to give him fifty rubles. Such a proposition was not very appealing to Kain because the merchant promised such a trifling amount for the recovery of such a vast sum; however, employing all possible means, he discovered that the money had been stolen by the carpenter who had made the doors for Babkin's storeroom, and after finding the aforesaid thief along with the money, he conveyed them to the Department of Criminal Investigations, whence Babkin received his money, less fifty rubles.

31.

While riding home rather late after visiting someone near the Maidens' Convent,[136] Kain spied a man running through Maidens' Field with uncommon haste, and after overtaking and capturing him, Kain detected blood on his hands. Considering him a suspicious person, Kain took the man to his house, where he put him under guard with the intention of interrogating him well in the morning, but on that very night the man broke out a window, escaped his guard, and disappeared without a trace.

32.

In 1745, while Kain was riding through Moscow, he spied a drunken woman lying in the street and ordered that she be seized and led away to his house, which woman, being exceedingly drunk, said that she knew of some important business. Kain thought the wench was lying solely because she had been overcome by drink; however, given his position, he was quite curious about such things, and for the discovery of the truth he ordered that the woman be placed in his house to sleep. When, after some hours, the intoxicating vapor had quit her head and she had returned to a sober state, Kain did not delay in asking her who she was, what she was called, and what important matter she intended to report. "I am a merchant's wife," the woman replied to him. "My name is Fedosia Yakovleva, and I can report that I know of a vast number of heretics and schismatics who frequently assemble for the execution of their unlawful actions in a certain house and heretically worship a certain false Christ named Andriushka, who feigns to be mute and both summer and winter wanders the streets barefoot and in only his shirt. That is why many consider him holy, and they say owing to his feigned holiness, he has free entry into many noble houses."[137] In confirmation of this testimony the woman wrote a document in her own hand recounting this affair and yet several others, and after sealing it, she gave it to Kain with the intention that he would reveal it to the proper government office. Gathering several soldiers of his command, Kain went to the Secret Office and presented the aforementioned document to Councilor Kazarinov. Upon reading it, Kazarinov realized the gravity of the situation, and thinking that Kain would inform against him, ordered that he be placed under guard. Knowing his innocence in this matter, however, Kain did not permit himself to be put under guard, whereupon a fight almost arose between the men of his command and Kazarinov's servants. Finally, Kazarinov asked Kain where he had obtained the document and who had written it. "The person who has informed me of this," Kain responded, "and by whose hand this document was written is presently at my house." After such an answer from Kain, Kazarinov did not delay in the least and set off for the office of General Vasily Yakovlevich Levashev, who at the time was the chief administrator of the city of Moscow,[138] and reported everything to him. After discussing the matter with him, the general gave Kain leave to go home but ordered him to be in readiness whenever they might call on him and to maintain the aforementioned informer under firm guard at his house. When he returned home, Kain impressed upon his command that they maintain an even more vigilant guard. At nightfall the Secret Office sent one secretary, two senior officers, and one hundred and twenty soldiers under the command of Colonel Ushakov to Kain's residence, and when they arrived, they set about knocking on the gates. Kain, being exceedingly drunk since evening, was sleeping so deeply that his subordinates were barely able to rouse him. When he awakened to the sound of an uncommon knocking at his gates and the sight of a great number of armed soldiers beyond them, he didn't know what to think, so he alerted his entire command and, stationing them throughout the courtyard, ordered the gates to be opened. Upon entering the room, the colonel and the secretary inquired about the aforementioned woman, and Kain immediately presented her before them. Taking her into a special chamber, they asked her about the aforementioned document, and when she withheld nothing and affirmed everything with an oath, the colonel and the secretary seated her in a carriage and set off with the entire convoy for Pokrovskaia Street, where it was ordered that Kain should follow with his men. When they arrived at the house of the merchant Grigory Sapozhnikov, they put him under arrest and sent him to the Secret Office and then placed a guard at his house; from there they set off for various places, and in that one night they were in as many as twenty houses, at all of which they placed a substantial guard, which was ordered not to allow even one soul to leave them. The next day they seized the merchant Yakov Frolov in Taganka,[139] whom, with other people like him, they sent to the Secret Office, and Kain took Frolov's young son to his house and asked if he knew where the mute Andriushka lived and whether he had heard if he had spoken with anyone. "He speaks with all those people," the merchant's son responded, "who believe as he does, and he lives beyond the Sukharev Tower."[140] Upon receiving this information, the Secret

Office sent a military detachment, whose numbers included Kain, to capture the false Christ; Andriushka was not found at the house, but those who were there revealed that he had left for St. Petersburg. All those living in the house were taken away to the Secret Office, and as for Andriushka, General Levashev sent a special courier with a description of all the circumstances touching upon his case to St. Petersburg. Andriushka was eventually captured there and returned under guard to the Secret Office in Moscow, where, by the power of the knout, his falsely mute lips were opened and he was forced to acknowledge his guilt in all his vile and heretical actions. For the surest investigation, a special commission was appointed to pass judgment on the four hundred and sixteen persons who had been accused of this heresy, among which number there were people of various stations in life and of both the male and female sex. When the investigation was completed, the aforesaid Andriushka and his close confederates were flogged with the knout on Tsaritsyn Meadow[141] and exiled to hard labor in Rogervik,[*142] and others, after punishment with the lash, were conscripted as soldiers and sailors. Some of the female sex were designated for work in factories; two nuns were flogged with a whip and exiled to distant monasteries; and yet others who adhered to this heresy from simplicity and stupidity alone were freed to their former abodes, some after punishment with the lash and others without punishment. But one hundred and sixty-seven teachers and confederates of this heresy were not found. The aforementioned informer, the merchant's wife Fedosia Yakovleva, died during the time the commission for this case was in session, and the ringleader of the heresy was the merchant Grigory Sapozhnikov, mentioned above.[**143]

Were curious writers able to see the entire file that has been produced for this case, they would certainly be able to write a tolerably good history of it, which, although it would be another type of rogue's tale, would greatly surpass Kain's own. Such a history would clearly show how foolish superstition leads us astray and by what hypocritical sanctity this ignoramus Andriushka deceived even

---

*   Baltic Port. {See endnote 142.}

**   One can read about this heretical assembly in a decree published by the Holy Synod that was disseminated throughout the entire nation. {See endnote 143.}

judicious people, thus making those who had a mind incomparably superior to his so unhappy. But as this took place during our age and as all his fraudulent and repulsive actions are yet firmly lodged in the memory of many people even today, we shall leave these questions for a later time. Perhaps our descendants will someday turn their curiosity to Andriushka's history, but now we shall direct ourselves to the end of Kain's deeds: a just fate is preparing him a worthy retribution and his destiny is drawing nigh, for it is not possible to evade the hand of fate.

33.

Having become acquainted with a merchant's wife, one soldier of Kain's command called upon her quite frequently, most often in the absence of her husband. Noticing this (for no matter what precautions are taken, love between lovers cannot be concealed), the merchant looked upon his guest not without vexation and sought a favorable time to disassociate him from his house; consequently, one day in the morning, as he was leaving his house, the merchant told his wife that she should not expect him for the midday meal because he intended to dine with a friend and therefore would not return home before evening. Instead of visiting his friend, however, the merchant concealed himself in a secret place from where he could diligently view his gate, and after some hours caught sight of his rival walking up to his house. After lingering awhile, he stealthily entered his chambers and found the soldier in the embrace of his wife, whereupon he flew into an unspeakable rage, and because his head was full of intoxicating spirits, he laid hold of a knife and stabbed the soldier in the belly. Greatly afraid and not knowing what to do, the merchant's wife ran to Kain. Taking four of his soldiers, Kain immediately set off for their house, but by the time he arrived, the merchant was already gone, for after stabbing the soldier, he had fled his house. The soldier was still alive, and being at death's door and acknowledging himself as the reason for this misadventure, he begged Kain not to exact vengeance against his killer and then soon died. Seven days later Kain caught the merchant and took him to the

Department of Criminal Investigations, where, after surrendering a substantial part of his estate to pay for gifts for Kain and the secretaries, he was flogged with the knout and set free.

34.

After the passing of each winter, when the rivers are once again open to boats bringing grain and other goods from cities downstream, Kain would ride out several miles from Moscow to stop them and examine the passports of the barge haulers, in whose numbers he found many fugitives with false passports; however, he almost never took them where he was supposed to, but rather left them on their boats after taking gifts from both them and their masters. This is what gave rise to the composition about Kain in the first song given below.[144]

In just such a manner, practicing both good deeds and bad and seeing that everything he touched turned to gold, Kain continued to commit diverse affronts. One day he ventured to carry off and forcibly violate the wife of the police clerk Nikolai Budaev, who for this dishonor presented a petition against Kain to the police; consequently, Kain was summoned there, and General Aleksei Danilovich Tatishchev himself, the chief of the city police at that time, asked him why he had dared to commit such outrages.[145] As was his custom, Kain refused to admit anything, so His Excellency ordered that he be placed back under guard, and the next day, upon arriving at police headquarters, Tatishchev once more summoned Kain to appear before him and ordered him subjected to the cat-o'-nine-tails. Knowing full well that this severe general would eventually ascertain the truth and fearing the cruelest punishment, Kain shouted out a crime against the sovereign,[146] hoping through this to find a means for his deliverance. This scheme did not have the desired success it did earlier, however, for along with Budaev's written petition, Kain was immediately sent under armed guard from police headquarters to the Secret Office, where, in the presence of its chief member Count Alexander Ivanovich Shuvalov, he was interrogated under merciless torture. Not foreseeing any further means to his deliverance, Kain was forced to plead guilty to all the criminal deeds he had committed during the time he was a police spy. For the truest investigation of Kain's activities, a special commission was appointed for his case, just as had been done for Andriushka. The commission was in session a considerable time, and as a result of its evidence many investigations were carried out and many participants in Kain's criminal deeds were found. Finally, upon the completion of the investigation, Kain's back was flogged with the knout, the letters which are common for such people were placed on his forehead and both cheeks, and, after having both nostrils ripped out,[147] he was exiled to hard labor at Rogervik, which is now called Baltic Port.

N. M. KARAMZIN
"Poor Liza"

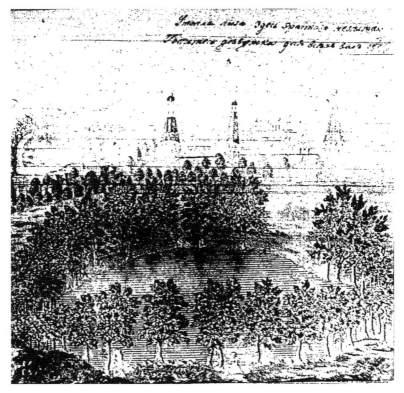

Frontispiece of the 1796 printing of *Poor Liza*. The pond that became a site of pilgrimage for many of the story's readers is in the foreground; the Simonov Monastery rises above it in the background. Drawing and engraving by N. I. Sokolov.

PERHAPS NO ONE LIVING IN MOSCOW knows the environs of the capital as well as I do, for no one is more often in the countryside than I, no one roams about on foot more than I, without a plan, without a goal—wherever my feet take me—over meadows and fields, through groves and thickets. Each summer I find pleasant new settings or discover new charms in familiar ones.

But for me most agreeable of all is the place where the gloomy Gothic towers of the Si*nov Monastery rise into the sky.[1] Standing on this hill, you see to the right almost the whole expanse of Moscow, this massive façade of buildings and churches which appears before your eyes in the image of a majestic amphitheater: what a magnificent picture, especially when the sun shines upon it, when its evening rays are ablaze on the innumerable golden cupolas, on the innumerable crosses ascending toward heaven! Below unfold fertile, lushly verdant meadows strewn with a variety of tiny white, red, and blue flowers, beyond which, along golden sands, flows a crystalline river agitated by the light oars of fishing boats or murmuring beneath the rudders of the heavily laden, flat-bottomed boats sailing from the most fruitful lands of the Russian Empire to provide covetous Moscow with grain. On the other side of the river, a copse of oaks is visible, alongside which graze numerous herds; there, young shepherds sitting under the shade of the trees sing their simple, melancholy songs and with them shorten their o-so-monotonous days of summer. A little farther on, in the dense verdure of ancient elms, shines the golden-domed Da*lov Monastery;[2] farther still, almost on the brink of the horizon, loom the Sparrow Hills, shaded in blue.[3] To the left are visible vast fields covered in crops, small forests, three or four modest villages, and, in the distance, the village of Kolomenskoe with its towering palace.[4]

I often come to this place and almost always greet spring here; I also come in the gloomy days of autumn to mourn along with Nature. The winds wail dreadfully within the walls of the desolate monastery, among the graves overgrown with tall grass, and in the dark passages of the cells. There, resting on the ruins of gravestones, I hearken to the dull moan of times now devoured by the abyss of the past—a moan which causes my heart to shudder and tremble. On occasion I enter the cells and imagine those who lived in them—what melancholy pictures! Here I see a gray-haired elder kneeling before the crucifixion, praying for swift delivery from his earthly fetters, for all pleasures in life have disappeared for him, all his feelings have perished, save for the feeling of illness and infirmity. There a young monk—with pale features and listless gaze—peers at the field through the grate of his window, sees merry little birds floating freely on a sea of air—sees them and sheds bitter tears. He languishes, withers, and wastes away—and the doleful peal of the bell heralds to me his untimely death.—On occasion at the gates of the church, I consider depictions of the miracles that have occurred in this monastery—there fish fall from heaven for the full relief of its inhabitants, besieged by a host of enemies; here the sacred image of the Mother of God puts enemies to flight. All this renews in my memory the history of our fatherland—the sad history of those times when fierce Tartars and Lithuanians ravaged the environs of the Russian capital with fire and sword and when unhappy Moscow, like a defenseless widow, placed its trust in God alone to deliver it from such cruel misfortunes.[5]

But what draws me to the walls of the Si*nov Monastery most frequently of all is the recollection of the lamentable fate of Liza—poor Liza![6] Oh! How I love those subjects that touch my heart and compel me to shed tears of tender sorrow!

Some seven score yards from the monastery wall, alongside a small birch grove in the middle of a green meadow, stands a desolate cottage, without doors, without windows, without a floor; the roof has long ago rotted through and caved in. In this cottage about thirty years earlier lived the beautiful, gentle Liza with her aged mother.

Liza's father was a rather successful peasant, for he loved work, tilled the earth with skill, and always led a sober life. But soon after his death his wife and daughter became impoverished. The lax hand of their hired laborer worked the field poorly, and the crops ceased to thrive. They were compelled to rent out their land, and for no great fee. Moreover, the poor widow, almost ceaselessly shedding tears over the death of her husband—for peasant women also know how to love!—became weaker by the day and was completely unable to work. Only Liza—who upon the death of her father had reached just her fifteenth year—only Liza, sparing neither her tender years nor her uncommon beauty, labored day and night—she wove linen, knitted stockings, picked flowers in the spring, and gathered berries in the summer—and sold all this in Moscow. The kind, sensitive[7] old woman, seeing the tireless laboring of her daughter, frequently pressed her to her faintly beating heart; proclaimed her divine mercy, provider, and the joy of her old age; and prayed to God that He would reward her for all she was doing for her mother. "God has given me hands that I may work," Liza would say. "You nourished me at your breast and watched over me when I was a child; now my turn has come to look after you. Only do not be forlorn, do not weep; our tears will not bring father back." But tender Liza was often not able to restrain her own tears—Oh! She recalled that she had a father and that he was no more! but to reassure her mother, she strove to conceal the sorrow in her heart and to appear tranquil and cheerful.—"In the next life, dear Liza," (the sad old woman responded), "in the next life, I will cease to cry. There, they say, everyone will be happy; I will be truly happy when I see your father. Only I do not want to die now—what would become of you without me? To whom could I leave you?[8] No, God grant that you be well settled before that happens! Perhaps a good man will soon be found. Then blessing you, my dear children, I will cross myself and peacefully lie down in the damp earth." —

About two years had passed since the death of Liza's father. The meadows were covered with flowers, and Liza had gone to Moscow with a bouquet of lilies of the valley. A handsome, well-dressed young man encountered her on the street. She showed him her bouquet of flowers—and blushed. "Are you selling it, miss?" he inquired with a smile. "I am," she answered.—"And what will you have for it?"—"Five kopecks."—"That is too little. Here is a ruble for you."—Liza was astonished, dared to cast a glance at the young man—blushed yet again, and, lowering her gaze to the ground, told him she could not accept a ruble.—"But why not?"—"I do not require more."—"I think a bouquet of beautiful lilies of the valley, picked by the hand of a beautiful young woman, is worth not less than a ruble. If you will not take it, here is 5 kopecks for you. I would always like to buy flowers from you; I would be pleased if you would pick them only for me."—Liza gave him the bouquet, took the five kopecks, bowed, and wished to go, but the stranger took her by the hand.—"But where are you going, miss?"—*Home.*"—"And where is your home?"—Liza told him where she lived, she told him and set off. The young man did not wish to detain her any longer, perhaps because passersby had begun to stop and, staring at them, were grinning mischievously.

When Liza arrived at home, she recounted to her mother what had happened to her. "You did well in not taking the ruble. Perhaps this was some sort of wicked person. . . ."—*Oh no, Mother! I do not think so. He has such a kind face, such a voice. . . .*"—"However, Liza, it is better to provide for yourself by your own labors and not to take anything for free. You still do not know, my friend, how wicked people may offend a poor maiden! My heart simply sinks each time you go to the city; I never fail to place a candle in front of the icon and to pray to the Lord God that He preserve you from any trouble and misfortune."—Tears welled up in Liza's eyes; she kissed her mother.

The next day Liza gathered some of the very best lilies of the valley and once again set off with them for the city. Her eyes secretly sought something. Many people wanted to buy her bouquet, but she answered that it was not for sale and gazed first to one side and then the other. Evening had arrived, and it was time to return home; the bouquet of flowers was cast into the Moscow River. "*Let no one possess you!*" Liza said, feeling a pang of melancholy in her heart.—The next evening she was sitting by the window, spinning and singing plaintive songs in a soft voice, when she suddenly leapt up and shouted "Oh! . . ." The young Moscow stranger was standing near the window.

"What has become of you?" inquired her startled mother, who was sitting beside her. "*Nothing, Mother*," Liza answered timidly. "*It is just that I have seen him.*"—"Whom?"—"*The gentleman who bought the flowers from me.*" The old woman glanced through the casement. The young man bowed to her so courteously, in such an agreeable manner, that she could think nothing but good of him. "*Hello, good woman!*" he said. "*I have become quite tired; would you not have some fresh milk?*" Complaisant Liza, not waiting for an answer from her mother—perhaps because she knew it beforehand—ran to the cellar—from where she brought a clean earthenware pot covered with a clean wooden top—then fetched a glass, washed it out, dried it with a white towel, filled it, and placed it on the window, though she kept her eyes on the ground. The stranger drank it down—and nectar from the hands of Hebe[9] herself would not have seemed sweeter to him. Anyone may guess that he then thanked Liza, and thanked her not so much in words as with his gaze. Meanwhile, the good-natured old woman succeeded in telling him of her sorrow and her consolation—about the death of her husband and the sweet virtues of her daughter, about her industry and tenderness, and so on, and so on. He listened to her attentively, but his eyes were—need I say where?[10] And Liza, timid Liza, looked at the young man from time to time, but each time upon meeting his gaze, her dark eyes darted to the ground more swiftly than a flash of lightning disappears into the clouds. "I would ask," he said to Liza's mother, "that your daughter sell her work to no one other than me. That way there will be no reason for her to journey so often into the city, and you will have no occasion to be separated from her. I myself, from time to time, shall begin to call on you."— — — At that moment a joy shone in Liza's eyes that she vainly tried to conceal: her cheeks were ablaze, like a sunset on an unobscured summer's night; she looked at her left sleeve and pinched it with her right hand.[11] The old woman accepted this proposition gladly, not suspecting any wicked intention in it, and assured the young stranger that the linen Liza wove and the stockings Liza knitted were uncommonly good and would wear longer than any others.—It was getting dark, and the young man wanted to be on his way. "And so how ought we to call you, good, gentle sir?" the old woman inquired.—"I am called Erast," he responded.—"*Erast!*" Liza said softly, "*Erast!*" She repeated this name five times, as though attempting to learn it by heart.—Erast took his leave from them till their next meeting and set off. Liza accompanied him with her eyes while her mother sat in thought and, having taken her daughter by the hand, said to her: "Oh, Liza! How good and kind he is! Were only your suitor such as he!" Liza's heart began to pound. "*Mother! Dearest Mother! How can that come to pass? He is a gentleman, and between peasants. . . .*" Liza did not finish her thought.

Now the reader should know that this young man, this Erast, was a rather wealthy nobleman who possessed a sound mind and kind heart, but although he was good by nature, he was also weak and capricious. He led a dissipated life, thought only of his pleasure, and sought it in the diversions of society, yet he rarely found it, was generally bored, and complained of his fate. Upon their first meeting, Liza's beauty had made an impression in his heart. He read novels and idylls, had a rather lively imagination, and in his mind frequently transported himself back to those times (real or imagined) when, according to the accounts of poets, everyone strolled lightheartedly through meadows, bathed in the waters of pure springs, kissed like turtledoves, reclined in the shade of rose and myrtle bushes, and spent all their days in happy idleness. It appeared to him that he had found in Liza what his heart had long sought. "Nature summons me into its embrace, to its unsullied joys"— he thought, and resolved—at least for a time—to withdraw from the *grand monde.*

Let us now turn our attention to Liza. Night had fallen—the mother had blessed her daughter and wished her a peaceful slumber, but on this occasion, her wish was not to be fulfilled:—Liza slept fitfully. The new guest of her soul, the image of Erast, appeared to her so vividly that she awoke almost every minute, awoke and sighed.—Before it was yet sunrise, Liza arose, went down to the bank of the Moscow River, sat down on the grass, and despondently gazed at the white clouds, which billowed in the air and, while rising aloft, left shining droplets on the verdant cover of nature. Silence reigned everywhere.

But soon the ascending daystar awoke all creation: groves and thickets came alive; small birds took wing and began to sing; and flowers raised their tiny heads that they might drink in their fill of the life-giving rays of the sun. But Liza sat there still, despondent. Oh, Liza, Liza! What has become of you? Until now, waking up together with the little birds, you rejoiced in the morning along with them, and a pure, joyful soul shone in your eyes, just as the sun shines in drops of heavenly dew, but now you are melancholy, and the mutual joy of nature is foreign to your heart.—Meanwhile, a young shepherd was driving his herd along the riverbank while playing his reed pipe. Liza fixed her gaze upon him and thought: "Had the one who now occupies my thoughts been born a simple peasant, a shepherd,—and were he now driving his herd past me, oh! I would bow to him with a smile and would say to him in a friendly way: '*Good morning, gentle swain, where do you take your herd? For here grows green grass for your sheep, and here bloom crimson flowers, which can be woven into a wreath for your hat.*' He would glance at me with a tender look—would perhaps take my hand. . . . Daydream! Daydream!" The shepherd, still playing his reed pipe, walked past and disappeared behind a close-by hill with his motley herd.

Suddenly, Liza heard the sound of oars—she looked to the river and caught sight of a boat, and in the boat—she saw Erast.

Every vein in her body throbbed, but of course not out of fear. She stood up, wanted to go, but could not. Erast jumped onto the bank, approached Liza, and—her reverie was in part fulfilled, for he *glanced at her with a tender look, took her by the hand.* . . . But Liza, Liza stood with downcast eyes, with burning cheeks, with trembling heart—she was not able to take her hand from him—or to turn away when he drew near to her with his rose-colored lips. . . . Oh! He kissed her, kissed her with such ardor that the entire universe appeared to her to be ablaze! "*Dear Liza!*" Erast said, "*Sweet Liza! I love you!*" and these words resounded in the depth of her soul like divine, ravishing music; she barely dared to believe her ears and. . . . But I put down my brush. I shall only say that, at this rapturous moment, Liza's timidity disappeared—Erast knew that he was loved, passionately loved, by a new, pure, and open heart.

They sat on the grass, and in such a way that no great distance remained between them—gazed into each other's eyes—repeated to each other *"Love me!"* and two hours seemed to them but an instant. Finally, Liza recalled that her mother might worry about her. It was time to part. *"Oh Erast!"* she said. *"Will you always love me?"*— "Always, dear Liza, always!" he answered.—*"And can you give me your oath?"*—"I can, dear Liza, I can!"—*"No! I require no oath. I believe you, I believe you, Erast. Is it possible you could deceive poor Liza? This could not be, could it?"*—"It is impossible, impossible, darling Liza!"—*"How happy I am, and how Mother will rejoice when she finds out that you love me!"*—"Oh no, Liza! Do not say a word to her."—*"But why?"*—"The old are suspicious. She will imagine something improper."—*"That could not happen."*—"However, I beg you not to say a word to her about this."—*"Very well: I must obey you, though I do not wish to conceal anything from her."*— —They took their leave of one another, kissed for the last time, and promised to see each other every day in the evening, either on the bank of the river, or in the birch grove, or somewhere near Liza's cottage, only faithfully, without fail, to see each other. Liza set off, but a hundred times her gaze returned to Erast, who continued standing on the bank of the river and followed after her with his eyes.

Liza returned to her cottage in a completely different mood than when she had left it. A sincere joy revealed itself on her face and in all her movements. *"He loves me!"* she thought and was carried away by the idea. "Oh Mother!" she said to her mother, who had just awakened. "Oh Mother! What a beautiful morning! How merry everything is in the field! Never have the larks sung so well; never has the sun shone so brightly; never have the flowers smelled so pleasantly."—Having propped herself up with her crutch, the old woman walked out into the meadow so that she might delight in the morning Liza had described in such charming hues. In reality, it did appear most pleasing to her; her sweet daughter brightened all of nature with her merriment. "Oh Liza!" she said. "How good is everything that comes from the Lord

God! I have lived to see three score years on this earth, and yet I never tire of looking at the Lord's works, never tire of looking at the clear sky rising like a high tent and at the earth, which each year is covered anew in grass and flowers. It must be so that the King of Heaven loves us very much, since He has adorned our world so well. Oh Liza! Who would want to die if at times we did not feel sorrow? . . . Evidently it must be so. Perhaps we would forget our soul if tears never flowed from our eyes." But Liza was thinking, "*Oh! I would sooner forget my soul than my dear friend!*"

After this, fearing to be untrue to their word, Erast and Liza saw each other every evening (when Liza's mother had already retired to her bed), sometimes on the bank of the river or in the birch grove but most frequently of all under the shade of hundred-year-old oak trees (which stood about one hundred and fifty yards from the cottage)— oak trees that shaded a deep, pure pond, which had been dug in times long past. There the silent moon, with its rays shining through the leafy branches, frequently silvered Liza's light-colored hair, which was gently lifted by the Zephyrs[12] and her dear friend's hand; frequently these rays illumined a shining tear of love in tender Liza's eyes, which was always dried by one of Erast's kisses. They embraced—but the chaste, modest Cynthia[13] did not conceal herself from them behind a cloud; their embraces were pure and innocent. "When you," Liza said to Erast, "when you tell me, '*I love you, my friend!*' when you press me to your heart and look at me with your sweet eyes, oh! at those times I feel so good, so good that I forget myself, forget everything—except Erast. It is strange, strange, my friend, that I could have lived peacefully and happily before I came to know you! This is incomprehensible to me now; now I think that without you, life is not life but rather melancholy and boredom. Without your eyes, the bright moon is dark; without your voice, the nightingale's song is tiresome; without your breathing, the gentle breeze is disagreeable." Erast was delighted by his shepherdess—so he called Liza—and seeing how much she loved him, he supposed himself to be worthier of esteem. All the glittering amusements of the *grand monde* seemed insignificant to him in comparison to those pleasures with which the *passionate friendship* of an innocent soul nourished his heart. He regarded the contemptuous voluptuousness in which his senses had previously reveled with revulsion. "I shall live with Liza as brother and sister" (he thought); "I shall not abuse her love and shall always be happy!"—Rash young man! Know you your heart? Can you always answer for the stirrings within you? Is reason always the master of your feelings?

Liza demanded that Erast visit her mother often. "I love her," she said, "and want only what is good for her, and I think to see you is a great happiness for anyone."—In reality, the old woman always did rejoice when she saw Erast. She loved to talk with him about her deceased husband and to recount for him the days of her youth, of how she had met her dear Ivan for the first time, of how he had loved her, and in what love and concord they had lived together. "Oh! We could never see enough of each other—up until the very hour when cruel death felled him. He died in my arms!"—Erast listened to her with unfeigned pleasure. He bought Liza's handiwork from her and always wanted to pay ten times more dearly than the price she had named, but the old woman never took anything extra.

And so passed several weeks. One evening Erast had been waiting for his Liza a great while. Finally she arrived, but she was so unhappy that he became startled; her eyes were red from weeping. *"Liza, Liza! What has come over you?"*—"Oh Erast! I have been crying!"—*"About what? What is it?"*—"I must tell you everything. A suitor is seeking my hand, the son of a rich peasant from a neighboring village; Mother would have me marry him."—*"And do you consent?"*—"Cruel one! Can you even ask? But I am sorry for Mother: she cries and says I am not thinking of her tranquility, that she will be tormented on her deathbed if she does not give me away before she dies. Oh! She does not know I have such a dear friend!"—Erast kissed Liza, said that her happiness was dearer to him than anything on earth, that upon her mother's death he would take her into his home and would live with her inseparably, in the countryside and in the dense forests, just as in paradise.—"However, it is forbidden for you to be my husband!" Liza said with a quiet sigh.—*"But why?"*—"I am a peasant girl."—*"You offend me. For your friend, your soul is most precious of all, your sensitive, innocent soul—and Liza will always be the closest to my heart."*

She fell into his arms—and at this moment her purity was destined to perish!—Erast felt an uncommon agitation in his blood—never had Liza appeared so charming to him—never had her caresses affected him so powerfully—never had her kisses been so passionate —she comprehended nothing, suspected nothing, feared nothing—the gloom of night nourished their desire—not one point of light shown in the sky—not a single ray was able to illumine their error—Erast feels a trembling within himself—Liza as well, not knowing why—not knowing what is happening to her. . . . Oh Liza, Liza! Where is your mother? Where is your guardian angel? Where is your innocence?

Their error was consummated in a moment. Liza did not understand her feelings, was astonished and questioning. Erast was silent— he searched for words but did not find them. "Oh, I fear" (Liza said), "I fear what has happened to us! It seemed to me that I was dying, that my soul. . . . No, I cannot say it! . . . You are silent, Erast? You are sighing? . . . My God! What is the matter?" Meanwhile, lightning flashed, and a peal of thunder rang out. Liza began to tremble all over. *"Erast, Erast!"* she said. *"I am terrified. I fear the thunder will slay me, criminal that I am!"* The storm roared menacingly, rain poured from black clouds—it appeared that nature was lamenting Liza's lost innocence—Erast tried to calm Liza and accompanied her to her cottage. Tears poured from her eyes as she was taking her leave of him. *"Oh Erast! Assure me that we will be as happy as before!"*—"We will, Liza, we will!" he replied.[14]—*"May God grant it be so! It is impossible for me not to believe your words, for you see, I love you! Only in my heart. . . . But enough! Forgive me! Tomorrow, tomorrow we will see each other."*

Their meetings continued, but how everything had changed! Erast was no longer satisfied by his Liza's innocent caresses alone—by just her gazes so full of love—by just the touch of her hand, or her kiss, or her pure embraces. He desired more, yet more, and finally was not able to desire anything—for whoever knows his heart, whoever has reflected upon the moral nature of man, will certainly agree with me that there can be no pleasure for us without desire.[15] For Erast, Liza was no longer the angel of innocence who had formerly inflamed his imagination and enraptured his soul. A Platonic love had ceded its place to feelings of which he could not be *proud*, and which for him were not new. And as concerns Liza, having surrendered herself to Erast completely, she lived and breathed for him alone, like a lamb obeyed his will in all things, and supposed her happiness to be in his pleasure. She noticed a change in him and often said: "*It used to be that you were happier! that we were happier and more at ease! and that I was not so afraid of losing your love!*" On some occasions, while taking leave of her, he told her: "*Tomorrow, Liza, I am not able to see you; an important matter has arisen*"—and every time upon hearing these words, Liza sighed.

Finally she did not see him for five days in a row and found herself in the greatest anxiety; on the sixth day he appeared with a sorrowful face and told her: "Dear Liza! I must say farewell to you for some time. You know that we are at war; I am an officer; my regiment is going into the field." Liza turned pale and almost fainted.

Erast caressed her, told her he would always love his dear Liza, and hoped upon his return never to be parted from her again. She was silent for some time, then dissolved into bitter tears, seized his hand, and, gazing at him with all the tenderness of her love, asked: "*Is it not possible for you to remain?*"—"I could," he rejoined, "but only in the greatest disgrace, with the greatest stain upon my honor. Everyone would despise me; everyone would shun me as a coward, as an unworthy son of the Fatherland."—"*Oh! If that be so,*" Liza said, "*then go, go where God commands! But you could be killed.*"—"Death for the sake of the Fatherland is not terrifying, dear Liza."—"*I will die the moment you are no longer on this earth.*"—"But why think of this? I hope to remain among the living, I hope to return to you, my friend."— "*May God grant it! May God grant it be so! I will pray for this every day, every hour. Oh! Why is it I can neither read nor write! You could inform me about everything that is happening to you, and I could write to you—about my tears!*"—"No, spare yourself, Liza, spare yourself for your friend. I would not have you cry when I am gone."—"*Cruel man! You wish to deprive me of even this comfort! No! After we have parted, I will cease to cry only when my heart has dried up."*—"Think of that pleasant moment when we will see each other again."—"*I will, I will think about it! Oh, would only it come soon! Dear, sweet Erast! Remember, remember your poor Liza, who loves you above herself!*"

But I am not able to describe everything they said on this occasion. Their last meeting was to be the next day.

Erast also wished to take his leave of Liza's mother, who could not restrain herself from tears hearing that her *dear, handsome gentleman* must go off to war. He compelled her to take some money from him, saying, "In my absence I do not want Liza to sell her handiwork, which, according to our compact, belongs to me."—The old woman showered him with blessings: "May the Lord grant," she said, "that you return safely to us and that I see you yet again in this life! Perhaps by that time my Liza will have found herself a suitor to her liking. How I would thank God if you came to the wedding! And when Liza has children, know, good sir, that you must stand as godfather to them! Oh! How I would like to live to that day!"—Liza stood alongside her mother and dared not look at her. The reader may easily imagine what she was feeling at this moment.

But exactly what was she feeling when Erast, having embraced her for the last time, for the last time having pressed her to his heart, said: "*Farewell, Liza . . .*"? What a touching picture! Daybreak, like a crimson sea, flooded the eastern sky. Erast stood under the branches of a towering oak, holding in his embrace his pale, languid, sorrowful friend, who, in bidding him farewell, was bidding farewell to her soul. All of nature attended in silence.

Liza sobbed—Erast wept—he left her—she collapsed—rose to her knees, raised her hands to the sky, and gazed at Erast, who was withdrawing—farther—farther—and finally was hidden from view—the sun had begun to light up the sky, and Liza, abandoned and wretched, fainted away.

Finally she revived—to find the world contained only melancholy and sorrow for her. All the charms of Nature were concealed from her along with the love of her heart. "Oh!" (she thought) "Why do I keep to this desert? What restrains me from flying after my dear Erast? War is not dreadful to me; the place that is dreadful is the one where my friend is not. I wish to live with him, to die with him, or to save his precious life with my death. Stop, stop, my dear one! I am flying to you!" She so wanted to run after Erast, but the thought "*I have a mother!*" stopped her. Liza sighed and, bowing her head, set off for her cottage with quiet tread.—From this moment on her days became days of melancholy and sorrow, sorrow which she needed to conceal from her delicate mother. And her heart suffered all the more for it! It found relief only when Liza secluded herself in the depths of the forest, where she could freely shed her tears and bemoan her separation from her dear one. Often, a melancholy turtledove united her plaintive voice with Liza's moaning. But sometimes—though quite rarely—a golden ray of hope, a sunbeam of consolation, illumined the darkness of her grief. "*When he returns to me, how happy I will be! How everything will change!*" With this thought her eyes brightened, her cheeks bloomed afresh, and Liza smiled like a morning in May after an evening storm.—In this manner passed some two months.

One day Liza was obliged to go to Moscow to purchase rose water, which her mother used to treat her eyes. On one of its grand streets she encountered a magnificent carriage, and in this carriage she caught sight of—Erast. "*Oh!*" Liza cried out and flew toward him, but the carriage passed by and turned into a courtyard. Erast alighted and was about to step onto the porch of a magnificent residence when he suddenly felt himself—in Liza's embrace. He turned pale—then without responding in any way to her exclamations, he took her by the hand, led her into his study, locked the door, and told her: "*Liza! Circumstances have changed; I am betrothed; you must leave me in peace and for your own tranquility forget me. I loved you and love you still, that is, I wish you well. Here is one hundred rubles—take them.*" (He put the coins into her pocket.)—"*Allow me to kiss you for the final time—and then go home.*"—Before Liza could collect herself, he had led her out of his study and said to his servant: "*Accompany this young woman to the door.*"

My heart is bleeding at this moment. I forget Erast's humanity—am prepared to curse him—but my tongue does not move—I gaze toward heaven, and a tear rolls down my face. Oh! Why did I not write a novel instead of this melancholy history?

And so, did Erast deceive Liza when he told her he was leaving for the army?—No. In reality, he had been in the army, but instead of battling the enemy, he played cards and lost almost his entire estate. Peace was soon concluded, and Erast returned to Moscow, burdened by his debts. Only one means of repairing his circumstances remained to him—marrying a rich, elderly widow who had been in love with him for a long time. He resolved to do this and took up residence in her home, having issued a sigh for his Liza. But is it possible all this can absolve him?

Liza found herself on the street and in a condition no pen has the power to describe. *"He, he turned me out? He loves another? I am lost!"* Such were her thoughts, her feelings! A cruel swoon interrupted them for a time. One good woman who was passing along the street came to a stop over Liza as she lay on the ground and tried to bring her back to consciousness. She opened her eyes—stood up with the aid of this good woman—thanked her, and set off, herself not knowing where. "It is not possible for me to live," thought Liza, "not possible! . . . Oh, if only the sky would fall on me! If only the earth would devour this wretched girl! . . . No! The sky is not falling; the earth is not moving! Woe is me!" She walked out of the city and suddenly found herself on the bank of a deep pond, under the shade of the ancient oaks which a few weeks earlier had been the silent witnesses of her joy. This recollection shook her soul; the dreadful torment in her heart was depicted on her face. But in a few minutes she had sunk into a certain melancholy reflection—then she looked around, caught sight of the fifteen-year-old daughter of her neighbor walking along the road— shouted to her, pulled ten imperials[16] out of her pocket, and, offering them to her, said: "Dear Aniuta, my dear, dear friend! Take this money to my mother—it is not stolen—tell her that Liza is guilty before her, that I hid from her my love for a certain cruel man—for E. . . . But why should she know his name? Tell her that he betrayed me—ask that she forgive me—God will be her comfort—kiss her hand just the way I now kiss yours—say that poor Liza ordered you to kiss it—tell her that I. . . ." Then she threw herself into the water. Aniuta shouted out, began to cry, but was not able to save her; she ran to the village—the people assembled and pulled Liza out, but she was already dead.

In such a manner this girl, beautiful in soul and body, ended her life. When we see each other *there*, in our new life, I will recognize you, dear Liza.

They buried her near the pond, under a somber oak, and erected a wooden cross on her grave. I frequently sit there, lost in reflection, leaning on the final resting place of Liza's ashes: the pond ripples before me; leaves rustle above.

Liza's mother heard of the dreadful death of her daughter, and her blood went cold from the horror—her eyes closed forever.—The cottage became deserted. Now the wind howls through it, and hearing this noise at night, superstitious villagers say: *"There moans the dead one; there moans poor Liza!"*

Erast was unhappy to the end of his life. Upon hearing of Liza's fate, he could not be consoled and considered himself her murderer. I became acquainted with him a year before his death. He recounted this history to me himself and led me to Liza's grave.—By now, perhaps, they have been reconciled!

APPENDIX A

Map of the Imperial Capital City of Moscow

Ivan Michurin, 1739

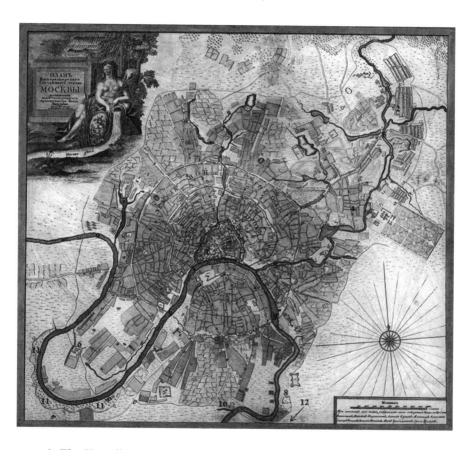

1. The Kremlin
2. The Village of Preobrazhenskoe
3. Kitai-gorod
4. The Foreign Suburb
5. The Yauza River
6. New Maidens' Convent
7. Tsaritsyn Meadow
8. The Simonov Monastery
9. The Moscow River
10. The Danilov Monastery
11. Sparrow Hills
12. The Village of Kolomenskoe

APPENDIX B
Monetary Values in Eighteenth-Century Russia

Money plays a prominent role in both *The Comely Cook*, which is set just after the Battle of Poltava in 1709, and *Vanka Kain*, where the action takes place in the 1730s and 1740s. The following information on wages and prices in eighteenth-century Russia is included to establish a frame of reference for understanding the relative value of the sums mentioned.

Late in the reign of Peter the Great, between about 1720 and 1725, a high-ranking official (councilor) in the College of Justice (one of twelve major departments of the Russian government) earned 800 rubles per year; clerks in the same institution received between 60 and 140 rubles every twelve months and porters just 21 rubles. On the low end of the socioeconomic scale, laborers on building sites were paid just 3 kopecks a day (one ruble = 100 kopecks), and peasant porters earned 5 kopecks per day, 10 if they had a horse (Hughes 144–45). In 1723 spinners in cloth factories received 6 kopecks per day, and weavers made 14. The comparable figures in 1741 dropped to 5½ and 8 kopecks, respectively (*Istoriia Moskvy* 262).

Examples of cheap goods of Russian manufacture that would have been within the price range of even the lowest layers of Russian society include copper crosses (1 kopeck), copper rings (10–30 kopecks per hundred), and needles (50 kopecks per thousand). A fox-fur hat selling for 60 kopecks, lambskin hats priced at 90 kopecks, and a cotton cloak costing 2–3 rubles would have been too expensive for people on the bottom of society and therefore purchased only by more well-to-do city-dwellers and the top layers of the peasantry (*Istoriia Moskvy* 290).

Given the lowly backgrounds of the three major characters (a destitute soldier's widow, an escaped serf, and a young peasant woman supporting her infirm mother in this collection), each of them would have considered the hundreds or even thousands of rubles that are frequently mentioned in their stories as virtually unimaginable riches. In "Poor Liza," for example, the title character sells her entire bouquet of hand-picked wildflowers on the streets of Moscow for 5 kopecks, a sum that may well represent her total income for the day.

NOTES

Introduction

1. In that year the descendants of Genghis Khan led by his grandson Batu invaded Russia, and for the next 150 to 250 years they subjugated and devastated large parts of the Russian lands. Riasanovsky and Steinberg survey the short-term effects of the Mongol "yoke" (the conquest and destruction of major cities such as Riazan, Vladimir, and Kiev and the massacre or enslavement of their populations) and its long-term consequences (the retardation of Russian culture by some 150 to 200 years) (63–71).

2. As Cracraft notes, Peter's reforms so fundamentally altered the shape of Russian society that they introduced not only new technology, devices, organizational schemes, and ways of doing things from the West but also the vocabulary to describe them. See Cracraft's Appendix II: Words in his *Petrine Revolution* for a list "of about 1,000 words . . . that were 'fixed' . . . in Russian during the Petrine era, as well as another 700 or so contemporary derivations" (377). Terms having to do with literature are given in the section spanning pages 430–71.

3. In particular, Levitt underscores the importance of the "large body of 'wandering tales' of chronologically diverse international sources that had proliferated in Western Europe during the late middle ages and the Renaissance and that thereupon had devolved into popular culture. The appearance and assimilation of these tales [in Russia], which came primarily via Polish intermediaries, marked something new: Russia's transition from a medieval, predominantly religious culture to an early modern secularized one" (6–7). The main focus of Levitt's article is in fact that one of these wandering tales, which was transformed into the *lubok* chapbook "The Story of the Merchant's Wife and the Shop Assistant," served as a model for Chulkov's *The Comely Cook*. Nikolaev adds that it was in the Petrine period that "literature learned to laugh, to laugh unrestrainedly, without worrying about morality" (51). Again, this is the sort of outlook Chulkov would exploit in his carnivalesque novel about a prostitute heroine. For a survey of how the proliferation of *lubok*, translated literature, and folklore influenced the rise of the Russian novel beginning roughly in the reign of Peter, see Gasperetti 39–48.

4. Contrary to the general paucity of original literary production during Peter's reign, oratorical prose flourished. The most famous practitioner of this form was the churchman Feofan Prokopovich, who became "the chief publicist in his time of the broader Petrine cause. In the last decade of Peter's reign, and for a decade thereafter, hardly a state occasion of any importance passed in St.

Petersburg or Moscow without a speech, prominently featured, by . . . Prokopovich" (Cracraft, *Petrine Revolution* 223; see also 222–25 for a survey of Prokopovich's efforts in the oration and sermon).

5. This is not to say that Peter did not help to create the preconditions for the development of a new literature. As Cracraft (*Petrine Revolution*) emphasizes, Peter's support for the establishment of printing houses (260), paper mills (260), a standardized civic alphabet (261–72), and a stylistically simplified form of Russian (293–95) laid the groundwork for the advances in Russian literature that would occur toward the middle of the century.

6. In some instances, the learning curve could be even much steeper than this. Concerning one of the figures in this collection, Garrard writes that "quite suddenly in the middle of the eighteenth century Russians had available to them in translation novels of almost every conceivable description. The rise of the native Russian novel is consequently chaotic and rapid. Chulkov provides us with an excellent example of the telescoped nature of literary developments at that time in Russia. In the space of four short years, from 1766 to 1770 when *The Comely Cook* appeared, it is almost as though Chulkov proceeded through several stages in the development of the novel which in France and England had lasted for more than a century" (*Čulkov* 142).

7. Adamant that he "had not taken more from Boileau than perhaps Boileau had taken from [his model] Horace" (Peskov 73), Sumarokov not only transferred much of *Art poétique* into his "Epistle on Poetry" but also partially blazed his own path. Peskov notes that, just like Boileau, Sumarokov emphasizes the process of literary creation, the emotional prerequisites for writing a particular type of work, and "the thematic range of each genre" (74). On the other hand, Sumarokov did at times deviate from Boileau's lead, for example when adding the song to the tragedy and elegy as genres of an essentially emotional coloring (74). There is no doubt, however, that Sumarokov saw himself as the "Russian Boileau" (and Racine, LaFontaine, and Molière as well [Peskov 75]), and his description of his French idol provides an insight into the role he intended to play in Russian letters. Referring to Boileau as "Confidant of the muses! Bearer of their statutes! / Connoisseur of poetry and scrupulous writer, / Who revealed to France the altar of the Muses / And served it himself by example in pure style!" ("On Poetry" 121), Sumarokov touches upon all those positions within Russian literary culture—inspired arbiter, aesthete, pioneering author—that he aspired to attain.

8. Sumarokov's advice on using the best writers of previous ages as models to be emulated is clearly summed up in the following lines: "If gazing upon the darkness of the passions in society causes you to burst forth, / Follow in the footsteps of Boileau and reform people. / If, however, you laugh while viewing human passions, present them to me as an example, / And in so doing, imitate Molière" ("On Poetry" 126).

9. In *The Paradise Myth* Baehr notes that the structure and philosophy of the last two novels, and, to a lesser extent, of *Numa* as well, are motivated by the ideology of Freemasonry, which itself influenced the thinking of many promi-

nent figures of the Russian Enlightenment (99–100). Baehr's comment that these works "reflect the general beliefs dominating much Masonic literature: that paradise is within the self; that only the virtuous person can achieve it; and that this achievement requires significant self-knowledge, self-improvement, and self-sacrifice" (100) underscores the principles of a deference to authority, an unstinting search for wisdom, and dedication to a life of virtue that also form the core of Russian Enlightenment thought. For a survey of the Masonic components in the plots, imagery, and themes of *Numa* (100), *Cadmus and Harmonia* (106–9), and *Polydorus* (109–11), see *The Paradise Myth*.

10. For an overview of the life and literary career of Fyodor Emin (the writer Budgen considers the first Russian novelist) and an explanation of why he merits the title of bastard, orphan, and outlaw, see Beshenkovskii.

11. It no doubt pained him to admit it, but in 1759 Sumarokov had already come to the conclusion that "novels have multiplied to such a degree that one can fill one half of the world's libraries with them" (350).

12. Ovsianikov describes how these broadsides were originally produced from carved wood boards (10–13), and Rovinskii explains the later process of using metal plates, which allowed a simple peasant operation to turn out almost five hundred pictures per day (338–39).

13. Ovsianikov 21–22. He adds that Sumarokov was the only author of high literature to have his work issued in *lubok* editions in the eighteenth century but that several others would experience the same fate starting in the 1830s, including Ivan Krylov, Alexander Pushkin, Mikhail Lermontov, and Aleksei Nekrasov.

14. The two sides of this argument are represented by Budgen (65), who does consider Emin to be Russia's first novelist, and LeBlanc, who writes that Emin's work contains "very little of what we might call 'Russianness'" in it (34).

15. Concerning the trajectory of Emin's popularity, Page writes that his "eclipse is understandable inasmuch as Emin's dated, often unwieldy prose style, his erudition and predilection for the 'huge' form of the novel were alien to the subsequent pre-romantic generations of Russian writers" ("Emin" 124). For a publication history of Emin's novels, see *Svodnyi katalog* 1: 247–48 (entry 1561), 2: 188 (entries 3849–53), and 3: 435–37.

16. Karamzin and his short story "Poor Liza" have always remained in the literary canon.

17. Unless otherwise noted, the information concerning Chulkov's biography in this paragraph and the next is taken from Garrard's *Čulkov* with only page numbers given.

18. For a complete list, see Garrard, *Čulkov* 155.

19. Chulkov's literary production is limited to just four years, 1766–70, with the exception of the third edition of *The Mocker* (1789), which included a new, fifth, part to go along with the four parts published between 1766 and 1768. *The Poets' Sad Downfall*, which appeared in 1775, consists of three burlesque poems, but they were originally published in *Both This and That* in 1769 (Garrard, *Čulkov* 70).

20. Zapadov notes that Chulkov was not an adherent of the type of humor Russians refer to as "*na litso*" ("personal" or "aimed at the person"), and that he considered his contemporary Novikov "an enemy of the human race" for adopting just such an approach in his satiric journals (102). Generally, Chulkov's barbs only hit individuals indirectly when he parodied what he considered the limitations in their literary production.

21. See, for example, Sumarokov's ecstatic praise of Boileau (202n7).

22. For Bakhtin's overview of the historical development of the carnival and other forms of folk humor, see his introduction 1–58.

23. For a lengthier survey of the history and development of the Russian carnival, see Gasperetti 32–39.

24. Chulkov, of course, also has his detractors. For a survey of modern critical reaction to his work, see LeBlanc 73–74.

25. Chulkov's design becomes even clearer when his novel is juxtaposed to the work that many see as one of its inspirations, Daniel Defoe's *Moll Flanders* (Gasperetti 215n24). Compared to Defoe's tale, *The Comely Cook* is far more lighthearted, and it is devoid of the numerous situations that threaten Moll's existence on a daily basis. For instance, "the shadow of the gallows never hangs over any of Martona's deeds, and the themes of incest, abortion, and child abandonment that so torment Moll never make an appearance in the world of Chulkov's free-spirited heroine" (Gasperetti 26). The more didactic basis of Defoe's work is also clear from its straightforward title, *The Fortunes and Misfortunes of the Famous Moll Flanders*, which does not try to pique reader interest with the implication of indecorous content, as does Chulkov's title. While the subtitle does refer to prostitution and Moll's life of crime, it ends by proclaiming that she *at last grew Rich, lived Honest, and died a Penitent* (27), thus serving as a clear blueprint of Defoe's fundamentally didactic approach to his subject. For an overview of the similarities and differences between the two works, see Gasperetti 24–28.

26. Levitsky adds that much of the parody in the prefaces may have been inspired by Sterne (114nn28, 29).

27. For a more linear interpretation of *The Comely Cook*, one in which Chulkov's heroine is called to account for her actions, see Morris 95–96.

28. Unless otherwise noted, citations given in Arabic numerals in this paragraph and the next refer to Shklovsky's monograph *Matvei Komarov*.

29. Marcia Morris is correct in concluding, however, that *one* of Komarov's goals is precisely to show the error of Kain's ways. The bandit's arrest, conviction, and exile to hard labor lead Morris to label him a "punished rogue," a type of character whose story reassures readers that "in all times and places, brigands are predestined to punishment" (116). Moreover, as Kain himself admits (145), his crimes call to mind the activities of other notorious outlaws in Russian history, such as the uprising of the rebel Stenka Razin. Morris argues that since Kain's actions eventually lead to his downfall, his story helps "readers to symbolically reexperience painful moments [in the past] and overcome them" (116). For more on the figure of the punished rogue in seventeenth- and eighteenth-century Russian prose fiction, see Morris 104–17.

30. Titunik enumerates Komarov's alterations, which include adding explanatory footnotes and regularizing the text with regard to language usage, formatting, and narrative style (*"Van'ka Kain"* 355–58).

31. The same cannot be said of some of the people Kain rounds up in his official capacity as police spy. See, for example, episodes 3 (152), 10 (154), and 19 (162).

32. In response to his petition, Karamzin received support for this project directly from Emperor Alexander I, who, on October 31, 1802, appointed him "historiographer with a stipend of 2,000 rubles a year" (Kochetkova, *Karamzin* 119). He died while at work on volume 12 (Anderson xvi).

33. Karamzin practiced short forms in prose and verse, but this did not stop him from advocating the reading of novels, even the type of adventure romances that were anathema to the leading literary figures of the previous generation, such as Lomonosov and Sumarokov. In "On the Book Trade and the Love for Reading in Russia," he encourages the reading of the lowbrow *Unfortunate Nikanor, or The Adventures of the Life of a Russian Nobleman* (1775), which was originally mistakenly attributed to Komarov, and he concludes his treatise with the statement that "in short, it is good that our public is reading novels!" (120).

34. Pumpianskii surveys the influence of key authors (Young, Thomson, Ossian/Macpherson [430–33], and Sterne [441–44]) on both European and Russian Sentimentalism, and LeBlanc emphasizes that the impact of European Sentimentalism on Russian writers of Karamzin's generation was so extensive that it reached even beyond the literary sphere: "The imitation syndrome that characterized much of Russian literature and literary culture during the late eighteenth century thus encroached, in the instance of the Russian Sentimentalists, upon the modes of human perception itself, influencing not merely their artistic representation of nature but also their emotional conduct in life" (42).

35. Although Sentimentalism departed from the principles of the Neoclassicist movement in many significant ways, there still was room for common ground regarding the issue of improving society. "The rationalistic view on the process of education ceded its place to new attitudes, which found favorable soil in the literature of Sentimentalism with its cult of feeling and attention to the 'inner person.' A moral education ('an education of the heart') came to be considered the top priority, more essential than the instruction itself, than the enlightenment of the mind. But while changing the accent, Russian Sentimentalist writers did not break with the preceding tradition. A concern for the upbringing of worthy members of society, of people who value and develop their national culture was preserved. There also was preserved a respectful attitude toward knowledge, a conviction that . . . 'learning is beneficial for Morality'" (Kochetkova, *Sentimentalizm* 42).

36. Kochetkova (*Sentimentalizm*) surveys Kheraskov's role as one of the initiators of Sentimentalism in Russia (8) and outlines the difficulty of clearly defining the boundaries of this movement (8–15).

37. Titunik analyzes Emin's often ironic appropriation of Rousseau's novel in "Èmin's *Pis'ma Èrnesta i Doravry*."

38. LeBlanc summarizes the plot of Lvov's novel and also explains the author's predicament, as he strove not only to imitate Richardson's model but also to outdo it by depicting the superior virtues inherent in Russian culture (37–39).

39. Kahn describes the content and conception behind what he calls Karamzin's "most artistically ambitious and original work" (15): "Written by a man steeped in the values and theories of sensibility, they [*Letters of a Russian Traveler*] have a literary and philosophical awareness and sophistication worthy of European models that are unprecedented in the eighteenth-century Russian canon. . . . The sum total is a work in which fiction, philosophy, literary criticism, art criticism, historical writing and biographical writing coalesce, producing nothing less than an anthropology of the Enlightenment movement" (1).

40. Tosi places this idea in historical context, writing that "the term [sentimentalism], defined in its turn by Richardson in his Postscript to *Clarissa* as 'a delicacy of feeling, swiftness of response to the emotions of love and pity,' became a *topos* of sentimental literature indicating a kind of responsiveness that is both aesthetic and moral, the capacity to feel both for others' sorrows and for beauty" (193). She adds that *Clarissa* was first translated into Russian in 1791–92.

41. This view has been affirmed by various generations of readers. For example, the Soviet critic Dmitry Blagoi called "Poor Liza" "the single most important piece of sentimental prose in Russia" (Anderson 73), and the contemporary Russian scholar V. N. Toporov considers Liza the most convincing heroine of her type (168) and the entire tale itself the first perfectly balanced literary work in all of Russian literature (47).

42. Orwin sums up the historical importance of Karamzin's choice of locale and heroine: "By setting his tale in a concrete location outside Moscow, Karamzin planted the foreign seeds of sentimentalism in Russian soil, which henceforth is associated in the minds of the readers of 'Poor Liza' with the new myths that Karamzin wants them to adopt" (16).

43. What Kochetkova calls the "classless valuation of a person" was one of the defining traits of Sentimentalism. Although the roots of this concept can be traced as far back as the Petrine Tales of the early eighteenth century, such as "Vasily Koriotsky" (*Sentimentalizm* 59–61), the Sentimentalists modified it by emphasizing a person's moral worth rather than his capabilities. Thus peasants, and also serfs (which Liza and her mother are not), could be seen as having the same good heart as some members of the gentry.

44. Toporov notes at least seven distinct functions of the dash in "Poor Liza," including separating characters' speech in dialogues; heightening the intensity of what has been said or done; explaining the consequences of a thought or action; clarifying, expanding, or supplementing an idea; conveying a warning; revealing an intimate detail; and providing psychological insight (58–63).

45. More information about Karamzin's contributions to the formation of the modern Russian literary language can be found in Zhivov 356–68, 376–78 and Kochetkova, *Karamzin* 97, 112–14. Kahn sums up the situation

this way: "As late as the 1810s and 1820s schools of writers continued to debate Karamzin's ideas [regarding language], which in fact had taken hold very quickly" (6).

46. The *Cheti minei* were "a collection of religious texts to be read on the feast day of each saint and arranged chronologically for the twelve months of the year" (Picchio 282), and Korobeinikov's *Journey* was an account of the two pilgrimages the title character made to Mount Athos, Constantinople, and Palestine in the sixteenth century (Terras, *History* 63–64). "Eruslan Lazarevich" and "Frantsyl Ventsian" are tales of chivalric romance containing many often improbable adventures and frequent flights of fantasy (Brown, *Seventeenth-Century* 47–49).

47. Kahn summarizes both sides of Karamzin's career, writing that "by the time of his death in 1826 Karamzin had become Russia's great and authoritative historian, and a legendary personal figure to the generation of Pushkin. His literary and linguistic legacy remained an enormous active influence even if his increasingly conservative political views were out of step with the calls of the younger post-Napoleonic generation for governmental reforms. Pushkin, perhaps more than most of his generation, held Karamzin personally in great reverence, seeing his work as a literary and historical touchstone" (8).

48. This is not to say that Karamzin was not popular with the lower classes as well. For example, Orwin recounts Iurii Lotman's analysis of the reactions of a workman and a peasant to the story of "Poor Liza" (15).

49. Toporov surveys Karamzin's approach to punctuation, including, in addition to italics and ellipses, the dash, question mark, exclamation point, and parentheses (52–68). He notes, however, that not all of Karamzin's innovations were always well received. For example, for readers from Karamzin's day and even up to our own, his frequent recourse to the exclamation point can seem too heavy-handed and redundant: "'Exclamatoriness' either becomes ineffective because it is only partially comprehended, or, what is worse, calls forth a reaction of conscious annoyance, of distancing, and even of irritation. Such 'over-emotionalism,' 'oh' sentimentality, and exaggerated exaltation quickly became the subject of parody, with the parodists themselves losing a sense of measure and falling into their own sort of exaggeration" (66–67).

The Comely Cook

1. Gaius Cilnius Maecenas, a confidant of the Roman emperor Augustus, was famous for his patronage of the arts, in particular literature. Among the recipients of his largesse were Horace, Virgil, and Propertius (Bunson 252–53). In eighteenth-century Russia, Maecenas was synonymous with "patron," but I have retained the proper name here because it is the first in a long line of burlesque references to Classical culture in *The Comely Cook*.

2. Chulkov's appeal to an anonymous benefactor is infused with both satire and parody. On the one hand, Chulkov's social origins (he was of non-noble birth, most likely the son of a priest or merchant) made it difficult for him

to gain the attention, much less the protection, of the upper reaches of society. In short, he is far from the sort of person to whom the tsar would give his portrait, and his highborn benefactor not only is, but will almost certainly always remain, unknown because no such person is likely to come forward to support his work. Chulkov's implied critique is that the nobility would take little notice of someone like him, whose previous occupations included barber and court actor. On the other hand, Chulkov's commentary on the mutability of life and his insistence that both he and his novel are fated to be completely forgotten are a parody of both Enlightenment philosophizing and the inflated sense of self-importance expressed in the works of his contemporaries.

3. Chulkov's verse preface is written in iambs with most lines containing six feet, although a few have four, three, or even just one. The six-stress lines all contain a caesura after the third foot, and virtually all lines rhyme in pairs. The six-stress lines would appear to be modeled on the French Alexandrine, which entered Russian verse "through the intermediary of German poetry, from which it was borrowed by Lomonosov." Given that "throughout the eighteenth century the longer and more serious genres—including dramatic works, narrative poems, and long epistles—tended to be written in the iambic hexameter" (Scherr 61), Chulkov is most likely using this meter to parody the elevated sentiments that it normally conveyed. It is worth noting that Sumarokov's epistle "On Poetry," which set out to define the parameters of a new Russian literature, was written in Alexandrines. See my introduction 7–8.

The following translation is in prose and aims to capture the playful, parodic emphasis of Chulkov's doggerel. The term used to label this section—*preduvedomlenie*—can be translated not only as "preface" but also as "advance notice" or even "forewarning." Given the jesting nature of the material that precedes the novel—a mock preface in prose relegated to the status of a footnote, a facetious dedication, and a burlesque preface in verse—readers have been more than warned to expect, at the very least, a tongue-in-cheek treatment of the story of the comely cook Martona.

4. On July 9 (NS), 1709, Russian forces under the command of Peter the Great engaged the Swedish army of King Charles XII outside the Ukrainian village of Poltava, located 190 miles east-southeast of Kiev. The battle resulted in a stunning victory for the Russians and marked a turning point in the Great Northern War (1700–1721) Russia and Sweden were waging for control of the Baltic (Paxton 320–21, Wieczynski 29: 24–25). Ultimately victorious, Russia acquired the Baltic coastline from Vyborg to Riga, which was instrumental in establishing it as a major European state (Wieczynski 13: 106, 113). In keeping with the carnivalesque nature of Martona's tale, her story begins with a victory for official culture that deals her a temporary defeat when her husband's death on the field of battle leaves her destitute.

5. Chulkov is playing with two definitions of the adjective *vol'nyi*, which most often means "free," in the sense of being at liberty, but which can also mean, with regard to one's conduct, "free and easy" and "unduly familiar." Martona is free in an ironic sense because she is poor and homeless and therefore can

do whatever she likes. The reason why she would describe herself as loose will soon become apparent. In addition, Martona's comment that "people like us" are never given anything contains a double-edged barb that is both satiric, when interpreted to mean women or anyone of non-noble birth, and carnivalesque, as this appellation implies the type of loose woman Martona will soon become. For background on the carnivalesque mentality in Chulkov's work, see the introduction 21–25.

6. In just this one brief paragraph, there are at least two references generated by the mocking spirit of the carnival. In the proverb Martona recites to describe her situation, the word I have translated as "scandalous" (*nebyl'nye*) also has the meanings of "false," "lying," and "gossipy," which are all concepts that fit nicely within the carnivalesque mentality. Her statement that the world "fell on top of me" is also the first, though far from the last, image she evokes that is based on the carnivalesque penchant for inversions.

7. The word Martona uses for "pledge"—*zalog*—also has the meanings of "guarantee" or "deposit," both of which not only seem appropriate in this context but also initiate the intertwining themes of commerce and sex that run throughout the novel.

8. Martona's frequent expeditions to the Merchants' Arcade, or central shopping district, underscore the commercial motif in the novel and also help to define her character, which is guided by the twin pursuits of wealth and pleasure.

9. In the spirit of carnivalesque mockery, Chulkov has the lowborn prostitute Martona compare herself to Helen of Troy, "'the face that launched a thousand ships' and the most beautiful woman who ever lived." She was the daughter of Zeus, the supreme deity in the Greek pantheon of gods, and Leda, a Spartan queen (March 183). Paris, a prince of Troy, seduced Helen with the aid of the goddess Venus (see endnotes 11 and 12).

10. In Greek mythology Adonis was so beautiful that several goddesses, including Aphrodite (Venus in Roman mythology), vied for his affection (March 19).

11. Venus was the "goddess of erotic love, the giver of beauty and sexual attraction" (March 55). Her betrayal of her crippled husband through an affair with Mars, the god of war (March 55–56), serves as the vehicle for Chulkov's burlesque humor later in the story when Martona abandons a decrepit "protector" for a young and handsome lover.

12. The goddess Eris (Strife) threw a golden apple inscribed with the words "to the fairest" into a gathering attended by the goddesses Hera, Athena, and Aphrodite (Venus). When each of them claimed the apple, Zeus called upon Paris, the son of King Priam of Troy, to settle the dispute. Paris awarded the apple to Aphrodite after she promised him the love of the most beautiful woman in the world, Helen of Troy, the wife of King Menelaus of Sparta. Although Martona rejoices over her snuffbox, she should be mindful that trouble could be on the horizon: in Greek mythology Paris's decision to give the golden apple to Aphrodite was the event that eventually led to the Trojan War (March 225).

13. Mertvago 188; more literally the proverb reads: "Whoever hasn't seen the new version is happy with the old one."

14. Levitt (4–6) outlines the plot of this eight-page *lubok* picture book, in which the wife of an elderly merchant uses her feminine charms to deceive her husband and seduce a young and handsome shop assistant. Moreover, he builds a strong case (9–19) for the proposition that *"The Comely Cook* might be thought of as a further verbal dramatization and extension-adaptation of *Women's Wiles"* (9).

15. In other words, Martona has gone to bed a pauper but awakened a princess. As happens so often in *The Comely Cook,* this is an example of how Martona uses proverbs to sidestep the moral consequences of her actions, in this case "the fact that she has summarily discarded an unattached bachelor lover for a wealthy married one" (Morris 94). But, then, such concerns rarely register with Chulkov's carnivalesque heroine.

16. Judging by this gift, Sveton certainly is a gentleman "not of the lowest rank." Five hundred rubles were roughly the equivalent of half a year's salary for a high-ranking government official (see Appendix B).

17. A colloquial, English-language equivalent would be "You can't hide a guilty conscience" (Mertvago 157).

18. Chulkov is exploiting multiple meanings of the word *sozhitel'*, which in addition to "husband" and "spouse" also means "a man who lives with another person in the same room," "roommate" (*Slovar' sovremennogo iazyka* 14: 146). In other words, Sveton's spouse is a wife in name only and more like a roommate, someone with whom he lives but is not intimate.

19. This ambiguous proverb is a good example of Martona's inverted, carnivalesque logic. In it, she apportions blame equally to all parties concerned but does not necessarily denounce her conduct. Whether she sees herself as the cow (the feminine noun *korova*) and Sveton as the bear (the masculine noun *medved'*) or associates Sveton and herself with the cow and Sveton's wife with the bear, the whole incident is chalked up to human nature. Although it is true that bears devour cows, the cow is not guilty of doing anything immoral but only of succumbing to the quite common impulse of looking for greener pastures. Morris notes that Martona's philosophy of "natural inevitability" also underpins her earlier statement that "the bee always flies to a pretty flower" (94).

20. Martona may be a simple woman from the country, but her words and wit reveal a high degree of sophistication. This phrase represents just one of many instances when she expresses herself using Classical rhetoric, in this case syllepsis, which is "a grammatically correct construction in which one word is placed in the same grammatical relationship to two words but in quite different senses, as *stain* is linked in different senses to *honor* and *brocade* in Pope's line 'Or stain her honor, or her new brocade'" (Harmon 466).

21. Martona's comment plays with the French word for Wednesday, "*mercredi*" or "Mercury's day" (Artem'eva and Zamaleev 279). Why the god of roguery would facilitate her employment in the home of a civil servant will soon become apparent.

22. In addition to Easter, the feast of feasts, the Russian Orthodox Church celebrates twelve major holidays: the Nativity of Mary, her Presentation in the

Temple, the Annunciation, the Nativity of Christ (Christmas), the Baptism of Christ (Epiphany), Mary's Purification, the Transfiguration of Christ, the Entry of Christ into Jerusalem (Palm Sunday), Christ's Ascension, the Descent of the Holy Spirit on the Apostles (Pentecost), the Dormition of Mary, and the Raising of the Cross (celebrating the finding of Christ's cross) (Wieczynski 32: 130).

23. Once again, and this time even more clearly, Chulkov exploits the multiple meanings of *sozhitel'nitsa*—the feminine form of *sozhitel'* (see endnote 18). As Martona makes clear in the next paragraph, the secretary's wife sleeps with many men and therefore is more of a roommate, and business partner, to her husband than a wife.

24. An approximation in English would be "Birds of a feather flock together" (Margulis and Kholodnaya 194).

25. Mikhail Vasilievich Lomonosov (1711–65) was something like the Russian Ben Franklin, his achievements spanning the fields of art, the humanities, and the social sciences. Within the discipline of letters, his accomplishments include a guide to rhetoric, a study of Russian grammar, and a work laying down the principles of Russian versification that have served as the foundation for Russian poetry to this day. As the clerk's comment suggests, Lomonosov was also a writer of verse, his most successful efforts belonging to the genre of the ode, which he used to celebrate state occasions (military victories and dates important to Russia's rulers) and also to express contemplative themes (see, for example, "Evening Meditation on the Greatness of God") (Silbajoris 264–65). Certainly the clerk's inability to appreciate Lomonosov's ode and, even more so, to be able to identify him is a satiric gibe at the ignorance and obscurantism that was so widespread in eighteenth-century Russian society. In addition, the incomprehensibility of Lomonosov's writing and his virtual anonymity among the scribes in the secretary's office also make him a target of Chulkov's humor. Lomonosov would have condescendingly dismissed a prose adventure narrative like *The Comely Cook*, but in this passage Chulkov seems to be saying the snub is returned in kind by the reading public, which does not know what to make of Lomonosov's elevated themes and bombastic style. Last of all, Chulkov sidesteps the issue of making a direct attack on Lomonosov through the chronology of the story. Martona's adventures begin just after the Battle of Poltava in 1709, but Lomonosov was not born until 1711. He wrote his first ode in 1739, and his first literary work appeared in 1741 (Stepanov 500).

26. Beginning in the reign of Peter the Great, Russian hussar (light cavalry) regiments were made up of Serbs (Stepanov 500), hence the colonel's remark below that he is a foreigner.

27. Here is another example of Martona's use of syllepsis.

28. The word Martona uses for "good times"—*gulian'e*—has several layers of meaning in Russian. Among others, they include "merriment," "mirth," "amusement," "fun," "feast," and "banquet." It is also the word for the ultimate period of "good times" in eighteenth-century Russian society, "carnival." In common parlance, the verb derived from the same root—*guliat'*—means "to enter into amorous relationships," "to lead a dissolute life" (*Slovar' XVIII veka* 6: 12).

29. Nicholas was a popular saint in Russia, and in the eighteenth century Moscow had many churches named after him. To distinguish them, residents frequently associated each one with a colorful nickname. "Chicken legs" most likely refers to the church's elevated foundation, since it was not uncommon at the time to erect buildings on top of the stumps of trees cleared at the site ("V Moskve," "Pouchitel'naia"). The church of St. Nicholas mentioned by Martona is located beyond the Smolensk Gates in Moscow, on Bolshaia Molchanovka Street (Stepanov 500).

30. Russian Orthodox churches do not contain pews, and the congregation stands throughout what tend to be quite long services (Wieczynski 32: 129).

31. With these words the colonel unwittingly continues Chulkov's burlesque of Classical mythology. If the comely Martona is compared to the beautiful Helen of Troy, the colonel will indeed play the role of Menelaus, the husband Helen betrayed when she sailed to Troy with Paris. In a close parallel to Homer's description of events (March 251–52), the colonel will open his house to Martona's Paris, thus providing him the opportunity to win her heart and also, of course, her body and then run off with her. In addition, as Menelaus did with Helen, the colonel will end up forgiving Martona when she once again seeks his protection.

32. In a bit of carnivalesque humor, Martona's reference to the grave is playfully ambiguous. If she is referring to the colonel's death, her sentiments are far less magnanimous than if she is referring to her own.

33. The word "reference" is used to translate the Russian *attestat*, which was "a document certifying the identity, social class, and employment [of the bearer]. It was issued to officials upon retirement and served as a permanent identity card (a passport)" (Belovinskii 21). *Attestat* also referred to testimonials of the bearer's professional accomplishments (*Slovar' XVIII veka* 1: 113).

34. The ancient Greek philosophers known as Stoics believed that "moral virtue is the only good" and that satisfying material and bodily needs was not important in our quest to "do what is right" (Honderich 896). Obviously, Martona's self-characterization is an understatement.

35. The word Martona uses—*blagopoluchie*—can be defined as "happiness" and "prosperity" in addition to "well-being." While her aged lover interprets the word as it is rendered in the text, Martona knows her suitor Akhal will understand that she is talking about the road to his "happiness," which he will secure through a sexual liaison with her. In addition, the implication of "prosperity" foreshadows the get-rich-quick scheme Martona and Akhal will soon devise and reinforces the commercial motif in the novel.

36. An English-language equivalent would be "If you have a tongue in your head, you can travel the world over" (Margulis and Kholodnaya 247).

37. The Coachmen's Suburb (Yamskaia sloboda) is where coachmen (*yamshchiki*) lived and worked. This suburb was located on the way out of Moscow on the road to Tver, not far from the Church of St. Nicholas (Stepanov 500).

38. Jupiter was "the supreme divinity of the Romans . . . with supreme power over gods and men" (March 226); Mercury was, among other things, the

god of eloquence, trading, and thieving as well as messenger to the gods (Dixon-Kennedy 205).

39. Apparently Akhal and Martona's pseudo-marriage has not only turned the colonel into a jilted lover but also reduced him in rank: from this point forward in the story, he is referred to as a lieutenant colonel.

40. Classical mythology connects Phyllis, a Thracian princess, with the brothers Acamus and Demophon, sons of Theseus and Phaedra (March 9–10). In these stories she marries one or the other of the brothers, who then deserts her shortly after the wedding. Instead of seeking revenge, as Martona declares she would like to do in the following paragraph, Phyllis takes her own life, an idea that would never cross the mind of Chulkov's carnivalesque heroine. In addition to Classical mythology, the more proximate target of Chulkov's parody is the Russian literary aesthetic of the 1750s and 1760s and, more specifically, Lomonosov (see footnote 25), who published a tragedy entitled *Demophon* in 1752 (Brown, *18ᵗʰ Century* 85, 104). Through Martona's heated response to Akhal's treachery, Chulkov strongly implies that the flesh-and-blood woman his heroine represents would have a completely different response to being betrayed than does a model taken from Classical mythology.

41. Here is yet another example of Martona's use of syllepsis.

42. Originating in Spain in the sixteenth century, ombre (in Spanish *hombre* or "man") became the most popular card game in the Western world between the seventeenth and nineteenth centuries. By the time of Martona's story, it had developed into a three-player game using a deck of forty cards. In this version one player would declare himself the "man" in order to choose the trump suit and then would compete against the other two players to take the majority of tricks (Parlett 197–99). In other words, ombre serves as a perfect metaphor for the Akhal-Martona-Svidal love triangle.

43. This grove (Marina roshcha) is located in the northeast region of Moscow on the Kopytovka River, a right tributary of the Yauza (see Appendix A). At the time this story takes place, it was sparsely populated by artisans working for the hereditary noble family of the Cherkasskys (Aver'ianov 386–87).

44. The word Svidal uses—*sovokupliat'sia*—provides an example of mocking double entendre. In addition to the meaning given in the text, this verb can also be translated as "to copulate," "to consummate a sex act."

45. For Martona, whose daily income would have been calculated in kopecks rather than rubles had she remained a sergeant's wife, this is a queen's ransom. See Appendix B.

46. True to the tenets of the carnivalesque, Chulkov appears to be making not only the merchant's wife the target of his laughter here but himself as well: after all, *The Comely Cook* is a novel that contains a verse preface.

47. Chulkov's choice of words—*khoroshikh ikh nauk i khudozhestv*—is difficult to translate. More literally it means "sciences and arts" or "lessons and tricks."

48. The three Graces of Classical mythology were "the personifications of beauty, charm, and grace, and also of favour and gratitude for favour. . . .

They were fond of poetry, song and dance, . . . and they are often associated with Aphrodite and Eros as creators of the love bond between men and women" (March 173). In his description of the crone as a toothless Grace, Chulkov is both parodying the bombast of Russian Neoclassicism and satirizing the mores of polite society.

49. Once again, Chulkov uses the word *sozhitel'nitsa*, which can mean "wife," "spouse," or "a woman living with another person in the same room," "roommate" (*Slovar' sovremennogo iazyka* 14: 146). One of the last two meanings seems more appropriate here, since the woman is wiping the officer's brow rather than her husband's. See also endnotes 18 and 23.

50. In the eighteenth century the word *medik* had the meaning of "a barber who also performs some of the responsibilities of a doctor; a physician" (*Slovar' XVIII veka* 12: 107).

51. If the uncle of the merchant's wife has the same lack of ethics that she does, the "business" he is attending to may well be serving out a criminal sentence in exile.

52. Here is another quite appropriate use of *sozhitel'*, which carries the additional meaning of "a man living with another person in the same place." See endnote 18.

53. The word Martona uses (*petimetry*, from the French *petits-maîtres*) has shades of meaning that are difficult to translate into a one-word English equivalent. In the *Slovar' sovremennogo iazyka*, it is defined as "a young society dandy, a fop who slavishly imitates French fashions, tastes, and manners" (9: 1103).

54. Even in what is the most serious part of the novel, Martona maintains a carnivalesque sense of humor in the midst of tragedy. Her comment about pitying a brother can be taken two ways. On the one hand, in keeping with the gravity of the situation, it could be seen as an expression of intense gratitude for a person who has done everything possible for her. On the other, given that one of Martona's highest priorities in life is to acquire wealth, her statement could be a mocking dismissal of someone who has nothing more to give her.

55. Although the closing words and title page of *The Comely Cook* claim that it is the first part of a larger work, Chulkov never wrote a part two. Morris notes that Chulkov's familiarity with the picaresque tradition, in which a "lack of closure is a perfectly appropriate outcome" (89), would have justified the misdirection implied in the term "part one." Levitsky takes this reasoning even further and considers the implication of a second part to the novel as nothing more than a well-conceived hoax (107). More specifically, previous clues in the text imply that Chulkov has indeed created the sort of open-ended finale he had in mind, one that is consistent with his carnivalesque view of the world. In the tale of the merchant's wife that immediately precedes the last scenes with Akhal, a fake poison is used to bring about a happy result, and the descriptions of Akhal behaving like a "madman" (107) call to mind the actions of the merchant (98–99), which also earn him the same epithet (100). Although Chulkov never states anything directly, it is possible that Akhal is only feigning suicide and that he is

in fact about to take his revenge on the now repentant Martona, which in turn would set her up for a whole new round of adventures. For in-depth discussions of how the apparent tragedy of Akhal's looming death may in fact be a comedy, see Gasperetti 80 and Morris 94–96.

Vanka Kain

1. Komarov is referring to *An Authentic Account of the French Rogue Cartouche and His Accomplices.* . . . St. Petersburg, 1771, a work that was translated from the original French into German and then into Russian (Rak 346–47). The Russian translation of this text, which recounts the life of the notorious French criminal Louis Dominique Cartouche (1693–1721) (Artem'eva and Zamaleev 286), was appended to the second printing of Komarov's life of Vanka Kain, which, like the first one, was issued in 1779.

2. The Department of Criminal Investigations (Sysknoi prikaz) was re-established in Moscow on July 22, 1730, and given authority over criminal investigations in the areas of theft, robbery, and murder. The clerks in this office served as investigators (Rak 347).

3. Komarov is referring to one of the first-person accounts of Kain's life, which were most likely dictated by the brigand himself (Kain claimed to be illiterate). Generally circulated by hand, some of these tales were later published, such as *On Vanka Kain, The Famous Thief and Rogue, A Brief Story* (St. Petersburg, 1775) and *The Life and Adventures of the Russian Cartouche, by Name Kain, a Notorious Thief and Informer on People of That Trade, Who for His Repentance for His Villainy Received a Reprieve from a Death Sentence but Who for His Return to His Former Trade Was Exiled for Life to Hard Labor, First in Rogervik and Then in Siberia, Written by Him Himself at Baltic Port in 1764* (St. Petersburg, 1777). (Artem'eva and Zamaleev 285, Rak 335–36).

4. See the Gospel of Matthew 25:14–30.

5. The Moscow police oversaw cases having to do with, among other things: drunkenness; fighting; assaults; the illegal trading in vodka; the capture of fugitives, beggars, and wanderers; and the enforcement of the decree against carrying a torch in the city at night (Rak 347). The Secret Office (in full The Office of Secret Investigations [Kantseliariia tainykh rozysknykh del]) was a type of political police established by Peter the Great to investigate major political crimes. Its first case involved the charge of treason against Peter's son Aleksei. Catherine the Great abolished the Secret Office in 1762 (Wieczynski 38: 159).

Komarov's comment on Zadeka refers to the fictitious author of *The Prognostications Worthy of Note of the Celebrated Martyn Zadeka, Who Revealed Them in the 106th Year from the Day of His Birth to His Friends, on December 20, 1769, in Zoloturn, Switzerland* (St. Petersburg, 1770). Topics in this work include predictions of natural disasters, the destruction of America, and the fall of the Turkish Empire. After the publication of *Prognostications Worthy of Note* in Russia, Zadeka's name was appropriated to sell books on fortune-telling and dream interpretation. Tatiana Larina, Pushkin's heroine in the novel in verse

Evgeny Onegin, kept a copy of a work attributed to Zadeka under her pillow (Rak 347–48).

6. Rak notes that the year of Kain's birth given in the first-person account Komarov used as the basis of his narrative differs from the record in his criminal case, which states he was born in 1718 (348). Artem'eva and Zamaleev add that "the historical Ivan Osipov was born . . . into the family of a peasant from the village of Ivanov in the Rostov district" (285).

7. This phrase is an allusion to the French philosopher and mathematician Blaise Pascal's (1623–62) well-known metaphor that man is "a thinking reed" (66) (Artem'eva and Zamaleev 285).

8. In the 1779 version used for this translation, this phrase reads "all sorts of burdens" ("*vo vsiakikh tiagostiakh*"). The 1794 version published by Reshetnikov replaces "burdens" (*tiagosti*) with "pranks" (*shalosti*). In the context of this passage, the wording in the later edition seems more appropriate.

9. The saying "habit is our second nature" was popularized in the work of ancient writers such as Aristotle and Cicero (Rak 348). The use of this phrase, like the earlier reference to Pascal, underscores that despite Komarov's humble background, he was familiar with authors whose ideas had been filtered through the Russian Enlightenment.

10. The word used to describe Filatiev—*gost'*—more commonly means "guest" or "visitor," but here, as was common in the first half of the eighteenth century, it is used to designate a merchant who traveled on business. The *Slovar' XVIII veka* gives one meaning of this word as "a rich merchant who conducted inter-city trade or trade with other countries; a foreign merchant" (5: 196). Wieczynski adds that *gosti* were "distinguished from rank and file traders by the larger dimensions of their business, the greater distances over which it was conducted and their superior prestige" (13: 74). Baranov notes that the Filatievs were a family of merchants and businessmen in seventeenth- and eighteenth-century Russia whose trading relationships extended to Siberia and the East (607).

11. Hunters' Row (Okhotnyi riad) was a collection of shops near the Kremlin (see Appendix A) trading in domestic and wild game, both live and slaughtered (Baranov 607).

12. Kamchatka was not a retired sailor but rather a fugitive from the Sail Factory (Parusnaia fabrika or Khamovnyi dvor). Located in the village of Preobrazhenskoe (see Appendix A) on the bank of the Yauza River, the Sail Factory was a state enterprise that manufactured sailcloth, and its workers were listed as sailors (Rak 348–49). As befits this character's former occupation, the word Kamchatka means "a linen, patterned fabric" (*Slovar' XVIII veka* 9: 229).

13. Kain's saying is an example of a type of doggerel known as a *raek* or *raeshnyi stikh*. Humorous and often satirical, *raeshnyi stikh* is structured around lines of unequal length that rhyme in pairs. It is thought to derive from the folkloric tradition, specifically proverbs and popular sayings (Brown, *Seventeenth-Century* 75–76). In Russian, Kain's saying reads: "Pei vodu kak gus', esh' khleb kak svin'ia, / A rabotai u tebia chort, a ne ia." Throughout the novel, Kain's speech contains many examples of this type of discourse.

14. After dark only the police and clergy had the right to be on the streets of Moscow (Rak 349).

15. A caftan is a man's traditional long-sleeved outer garment. It fits closely at the waist and has wide cuffs, large flaps over two front pockets, and pleats on the side. In the full caftan, the skirt of the garment falls below the knee; Kamchatka is wearing a shorter version that ends above the knees (Belovinskii 190, 348).

16. Built at the end of the seventeenth century, the Stone Bridge (Kamennyi most) was the first stone bridge over the Moscow River from the west side of the Kremlin. It was a gathering place and haven for many of Moscow's vagrants, including thieves and robbers (Rak 349).

17. This is another example of *raeshnyi stikh*. The original reads "'Nogoty, bosoty naveshany shesty, / A golodu i xolodu polnye anbary stoiat; / My, zhivuchi zdes', pokoi svoi v naem otdaem, / A prokhodiashchim po semu mostu noch'iu tikhuiu milostyniu podaem, / A pravdu tebe skazat', / Tak u nas tol'ko pyl' da kopot', / A inogda nichego i lopat'.'" The phrase "we rent out our rooms and give silent alms" is thieves' cant for thieving and robbery.

18. Located near the Kremlin and surrounded by a brick wall (Rak 349), Kitai-gorod (see Appendix A) was the commercial center of eighteenth-century Moscow and also held the Moscow Magistrate's Office (Wieczynski 17: 54). It occupied the area from the Corner Arsenal Tower (Uglovaia Arsenal'naia bashnia) to the banks of the Moscow River, including the present-day sites of Revolution Square, Hunters' Row, and the Lubianka (Rak 349). The Merchants' Arcade (Gostinyi dvor) is where outside and foreign merchants (*gosti*) congregated and displayed their goods. It was organized in rows, "in which goods of similar nature were sold in adjacent shops" (Wieczynski 13: 78). Customs House (Mytnyi dvor) "administered the collection of custom duties imposed in Moscow on commerce in forest products, hay, cattle, edibles (except grain) and various other commodities" (Wieczynski 24: 30), and Ambassadors' Court (Posolskii dvor) served as quarters for ambassadors in Moscow (Rak 349).

19. Like the Merchants' Arcade, other mercantile areas of Kitai-gorod were organized along rows, each one offering a particular type of goods, such as boots, candles, icons, fish, and gingerbread, or, as in the case of Pansky Row, high-quality manufactured fabrics (Rak 349, 350).

20. The Border Militia (*Landmilitsiia*) consisted of soldier-settlers who primarily defended the borders of Russia in the eighteenth century. Regiments were formed in Ukraine and Siberia (Belovinskii 239). In the first-person account of his life, Kain hints that he had a hand in the soldier's death (Rak 350).

21. The words Kain uses here—literally, "the sovereign's word and deed" (*slovo i delo gosudarevo*)—are the Russian equivalent of the French *lèse majesté*, which translates as (the crime of) "injured majesty." In eighteenth-century Russia, this phrase was used to report a threat against the sovereign's person or reputation. A government edict of 1713 states that "'anyone who writes or utters the accusation of a crime against the sovereign by word or deed, such persons are ordered to write and testify only in such matters as concern the health of his

tsarist majesty or the lofty monarchical honour or know of some rebellion or treason'" (Hughes 126). For a description of the Secret Office, see endnote 5.

22. Located near Moscow on the Yauza River, the village of Preobrazhenskoe (see Appendix A) was closely associated with the Russian court in the seventeenth and eighteenth centuries. Peter the Great spent time there as a child (Paxton 325), and his father Aleksei Mikhailovich Romanov resided in Preobrazhenskoe with his family in the summer (Wieczynski 29: 194).

23. This is another example of rhyming doggerel from Kain: "'Ia ni punktov ni funtov, ni vesu, ni pokhodu ne znaiu.'"

24. In 1732 Saltykov (1672–1742) was named the chief administrator in Moscow and at the same time headed the Secret Office (Rak 350, Wieczynski 49).

25. The Foreign Suburb (see Appendix A) was an outlying district of Moscow located on the right bank of the Yauza River. In 1652 Tsar Aleksei Mikhailovich, Peter the Great's father, designated the area for the habitation of foreigners (Rak 350). The literal translation of the Russian term is "German Suburb." The root of the Russian word for German—*nem*—means "mute," an epithet often applied to all foreigners in the eighteenth century who did not speak Russian.

26. The Yauza River (see Appendix A) is a tributary of the Moscow River that joins it in the center of the city not far from the Kremlin. Lefortovo Palace was a gift of Peter the Great to one of his closest associates, the Genevan Franz LeFort (1656–99) (Baranov 607). Located on the right bank of the Yauza River in the Foreign Suburb (Rak 350), it would later become notorious in Soviet times as the harshest prison in Moscow (Wieczynski 19: 122–24).

27. The Danilov Monastery (see Appendix A) was founded by Prince Daniil Aleksandrovich of Moscow in 1282 (Wieczynski 8: 179). It is located on the right bank of the Moscow River at the corner of present-day Danilov Embankment and Dubinsk Street (Rak 350–51).

28. Such an amount of money would have represented a fortune for men like Kain. If he had remained Filatiev's serf, he would have earned just kopecks per day. See Appendix B.

29. New Savior (Novospassky) Monastery was located on the left bank of the Moscow River (on present-day Novospassky Street), just downstream from where the Yauza River joins it (Rak 351).

30. In contemporary Moscow this area is called the Square of the Ilinsky Gates (Rak 351).

31. This was the factory of Peter the Great's former stoker. One of the largest enterprises in Moscow (Baranov 607), it manufactured silk cloth and braid (Rak 351).

32. Literally meaning "Clean Pond," Chistyi prud was located in Kitaigorod. Until the early eighteenth century it was called Stinking Pond because butchers, who were common in the area, dumped carcasses and offal into it. With the stench too much to bear, it was cleaned up in 1703 and renamed Chistyi prud. Today it lies between the lanes of Chistoprudny Boulevard and is called Chistye prudy (Clear Ponds) (Rice and Rice 112).

33. The Mint (Denezhnyi dvor) was located near the Voskresenky Gates of Kitai-gorod (see Appendix A).

34. The Life Guards (*Leibgvardiia*) consisted of either special units that served as the tsar or tsarina's personal bodyguard, like the Preobrazhensky Regiment, or units in the army that were under the monarch's patronage (*Encyclopedia* 14: 488).

35. Kain's explanation contains the jingling cadence of the verse form known as *raeshnyi stikh*. In Russian the first part of this passage reads: "'Ia ne vor, ni tat', / Tol'ko na tu zhe stat'.'"

36. A looser translation might be "Don't look a gift horse in the mouth." The Russian text reads: "'Vot tebe lukovka popova, / Obluplena gotova. / Znai pochitai, / A umru pominai.'"

37. Founded in the early thirteenth century on the Volga River, Nizhny Novgorod became famous in the medieval period for its annual trade fairs, which lasted until 1816 (Raymond and Duffy 213). Renamed Gorky in Soviet times, Nizhny Novgorod reverted to its earlier appellation after the collapse of the Soviet Union. St. Peter's Day was June 29 OS (July 12 NS) (Rak 351, Baranov 607).

38. Situated approximately 75 miles to the east of Vladimir on the right bank of the Kliazma River, Viazniki was at the time of Kain's adventures a village known for its handicrafts, trade, and the cultivation of flax. Moreover, it is yet one more location that underscores Kain's carnivalesque penchant for bringing his lawless band to holy places: beginning in 1622, Viazniki was a destination for pilgrims wishing to see the miracle-working icon of the Kazan Mother of God (*Geografiia* 136).

39. The Russian word used here—*lub'ia*—refers to layers of bark, usually from the linden tree, used for roofing material (Artem'eva and Zamaleev 286).

40. Archival material identifies this person as Lieutenant Colonel Retkin, whose detachment was based in Nizhny Novgorod, at least between the years of 1732–36 (Rak 352).

41. A *kalach* is a fancy wheat bread baked in the shape of a lock with a hasp. Kamchatka's choice of this item to smuggle in keys for Kain's escape is a touch of lighthearted mockery consistent with the carnivalesque mentality running throughout *Vanka Kain*.

42. This small chest (*podgolovok*) is a type of slanted headrest meant to be placed under a pillow (Rak 352).

43. This village on the right bank of the Volga is located across from the Makariev Monastery less than two miles from the river (Rak 352).

44. Kain's bribe is another instance of his use of *raeshnyi stikh*. In Russian, it reads: "'Tebe ot menia budet muki funta tri s pokhodom, / To est' kaftan s kamzolom.'" For a description of a caftan, see endnote 15.

45. Located on the right bank of the Moscow River, Horse Square (Konnaia ploshchad') was the horse market in Moscow. The area is currently known as the Square of the Barbarian Gates. The suburb of Nizhniaia Sadovnicheskaia,

situated in the area of present-day Sadovnicheskaia Street, was where the gardeners (*sadovniki*) who tended the royal gardens lived (Rak 352).

46. The Paupers' Home (Ubogii dom) was a morgue for unidentified corpses, which were then buried in a common grave. It was located on present-day Durova Street (Rak 353).

47. The Nikolsky Greek Monastery, located on present-day Nikolsky Street in Moscow, was mentioned in the chronicles as early as 1390. "In 1556 the monastery was granted by Tsar Ivan the Terrible, at the request of the monks of the Hilandar Serbian Monastery on Mount Athos, as a town church for the temporary residence of monks who came to Moscow from Athos for the collection of charity and alms" (*Russkie monastyri* 375).

48. Archival materials identify Kuvai as Ivan Kuvaev, an apprentice in the Cloth Market (Sukonnyi dvor), a Moscow factory that produced cloth, and Zhulza (or Zhuzla) as a fugitive soldier (Rak 353).

49. Kashin, a city located on the Kashinka River roughly 95 miles northeast of Tver, was a center of commerce and various trades (*Geografiia* 249–50).

50. This name (Yamskaia sloboda) designated the place in a city or town where coachmen lived (Artem'eva and Zamaleev 286).

51. The Frolishchev Hermitage was a monastery located not far from Nizhny Novgorod in the village of Gorokhovets, which stands on the right bank of the Kliazma River (Baranov 607, Rak 353, *Geografiia* 147). In Russia the term "hermitage" (*pustyn'* or *pustynia*) designated "a monastery of not large size that arose in a deserted, uninhabited area" (*Slovar' sovremennogo iazyka* 11: 1732).

52. A. N. Radishchev (1749–1802), the author of the landmark work *Journey from St. Petersburg to Moscow* (1790), explains the motivation for this place name: "'Many people were robbed at Silk Cove, and it has this soubriquet because both the inhabitants as well as the criminals of a single settlement on this cove had such an abundance of everything as a result of their plundering that they wore silk foot wrappings with their bast-shoes'" (qtd. in *Slovar' XVIII veka* 8: 120).

53. In the eighteenth century the word "ataman" meant both "an elected leader among the Cossacks" and "the leader of a robber gang" (*Slovar' XVIII veka* 1: 110). Although the description of the group Kain meets in the tavern reflects some traits of Cossack organization—for example, Kamchatka is made an esaul (see the following endnote)—Zaria is the head of a gang of outlaws. In addition, his name is most likely a nickname: in Russian, *zaria* means "daybreak," "dawning." The literal translation of the proverb Komarov uses here is "one fisherman can recognize another from far away in the stream" (Margulis and Kholodnaya 194).

54. The term *esaul* designates both the assistant (lieutenant) of the leader of a gang of robbers and the rank of captain in Cossack detachments (*Slovar' XVIII veka* 7: 81).

55. The Tsarevich (Grand Prince) Bakar Bakhtanovich (1700–1750) fled his native Georgia to seek sanctuary in Russia after losing a struggle for the Georgian throne. He eventually became a Russian citizen and was appointed

the head of the Office of Artillery in Moscow with the rank of lieutenant general (Rak 353–54).

56. This is a dense pine and spruce forest located along the Kerzhenets River, which empties into the Volga above the Makariev Monastery in Nizhny Novgorod Province. Zaria's choice of a temporary hideout is a good one: from the seventeenth through the nineteenth centuries, Old Believers—a sect of religious dissenters often persecuted by the government—used the forest as a place of refuge, where they established communities and covert monasteries (*Encyclopedia* 12: 425).

57. This village is located on the Volga, about 35 miles southeast of Nizhny Novgorod ("Rabotki, Russia").

58. The Kalmyks are a Mongol people who migrated in the seventeenth century from western China to the Nogay Steppe, which is located primarily in the present-day Republic of Dagestan between the rivers Terek and Kuma (Paxton 191, *Geografiia* 412).

Shubin was a favorite of the princess and later tsarina (1741–62) Elizabeth, who promoted him to the rank of major general and granted him various hereditary estates, among which was the village of Rabotki (Rak 354). As Kain's banter with the Kalmyk in the following lines indicates, he is making a joke at the expense of the general's last name: Shubin is derived from the Russian word for "fur coat."

59. The sash (*sharf*) was an obligatory part of an officer's field and dress uniforms. Made of woven fabric, it had red, blue, and gray stripes running through it with a tassel at the end (Belovinskii 505). It was worn at the waist and tied on the left side. An officer's medal was a silver or gilded disk worn around the neck, and the word used here for hat (*shliapa*) was "the official name for the headwear worn by officers and soldiers in the 18th century" (Artem'eva and Zamaleev 286).

60. From the Pereslavskaia Coachmen's Suburb (which was located in the area of the present-day metro station Ryzhskaia), coachmen took passengers and freight to cities north of Moscow; from Rogozhskaia, the road ran toward the village of Rogozh (present-day Noginsk) and on toward Vladimir and Nizhny Novgorod (Rak 354–55).

61. The menagerie was located in Izmailovo, one of the tsar's ancestral estates in the environs of Moscow (Rak 355).

62. This is an area of Moscow on the left bank of the Yauza River that is located in the vicinity of present-day Lefortovo Park (Rak 355).

63. Located on the Oka River about 85 miles southeast of Vladimir, Murom is an ancient Russian city first mentioned in one Russian chronicle under the year 862. By the seventeenth century it was an important center of various trades and contained several famous churches dating back as far as the eleventh century (*Geografiia* 382).

64. See endnote 51.

65. Yazykovo was located in the district of Simbirsk in Kazan Province (Rak 355); the Sura is a right-bank tributary of the Volga that enters it at Vasilrusk, a

small city about 95 miles east of Nizhny Novgorod (*Geografiia* 98, 561).

66. The chief bargeman (*vodoliv*) looked after the safety of the cargo and also served as the ship's carpenter and treasurer (Artem'eva and Zamaleev 286).

67. Boriatina was located just upriver from Yazykovo on the Sura (Rak 355).

68. A left tributary of the Sura (Rak 355).

69. This term designates a member of the Islamic clergy (*Slovar' XVIII veka* 1: 12).

70. The Bogoliubov Monastery is located in the settlement of the same name on the banks of the Kliazma River, about six miles southwest of Vladimir (*Geografiia* 77, 111). The settlement was founded as a castle-residence by Andrei Bogoliubsky, "the most powerful prince of Rus from 1158 to 1175 and the seminal 'Great Russian' ruler" (Wieczynski 218).

71. Razin was the "Cossack leader of the great peasant rebellion of 1670–71 in the southwestern area of the Volga [in which] many members of the upper classes were massacred." By the time Razin reached Simbirsk, his ranks had swelled to 200,000, but he was defeated by a Muscovite army, eventually captured, and executed (Paxton 383). Gavriushka may refer to the bandit Gavrila Starchenok, whose criminal activities around Kostroma are recorded in archival materials (Rak 355–56). I have not been able to identify Sennoi.

72. The Senate (or Governing or Ruling Senate) was created by Peter the Great in 1711 to serve as the supreme legislative and administrative institution in the land. During the time recounted in Kain's story, some of its powers had been limited by other branches of government (Wieczynski 34: 6–7).

73. In the 1740s Kropotkin was also the chief judge in the Department of Criminal Investigations (Rak 356).

74. According to archival documents relating to Kain's case, this occurred on December 27, 1741 (Rak 356).

75. Upon his arrival at the Department of Criminal Investigations, Kain made a rather articulate, if somewhat disingenuous petition, in which he claimed to be moved by the "'fear of God'" and the "'fatal hour'" to amend his ways. Rak reproduces Kain's petition on 356–57. The detachment given to Kain mentioned in the following line consisted of fourteen soldiers and a clerk from the department named Peter Donskoi (Rak 357).

76. Zariadie was a district "located in the southern section of Kitai-gorod [see Appendix A], to the east of the Kremlin, between present-day Varvarka Street, Kitaigorod Street, the Moscow River, and Red Square" (Rak 357).

77. Syromiatniki, or the imperial suburb of Syromiatnaia, was the area of the city where master tanners lived and worked. It was located in the present-day region of the Syromiatnicheskaia Embankment as well as along various streets and lanes bearing this name. The Office of Deeds registered documents recording the transfer of property (Rak 357).

78. The archives for Kain's criminal case report that on the night of December 27–28, 1741, a total of thirty-two persons were arrested on his instructions (Rak 357).

79. The Military Collegium (or College) was one of nine such bodies created by Peter the Great in the second decade of the eighteenth century as part of his reform of the Russian government (Wieczynski 7: 172). During the time recounted in Kain's story, it supervised "all persons and institutions of the higher military administration" and concentrated on "complex and controversial problems" (*Encyclopedia* 5: 255).

80. The author of this epigram, published in 1760, was the poet, dramatist, and prose writer Mikhail Kheraskov (1733–1807) (Rak 358).

81. This translation of the Russian original is based on Margulis and Kholodnaya 178.

82. See endnote 18.

83. The Russian term used here—*volost'*, or "rural district"—designated the smallest administrative division in tsarist Russia. A court district belonged to the system of court lands, which were the personal property of the royal family. The peasants who worked these lands—court peasants—were also the personal property of the tsar and his family, for whom they labored to provide provisions and income (Wieczynski 8: 91–93). The district mentioned here is actually Gzhel (Rak 358, Baranov 608).

84. A chancery (*kantseliariia*) was "an office attached to an official or an institution where clerical work was performed; a state institution with independent functions" (*Slovar' XVIII veka* 9: 238). This is most likely the Main Court Chancery, which had jurisdiction over court lands and peasants (Wieczynski 8: 93).

85. The Monastery of the Intercession (Pokrovsky Monastery), which was located in Moscow at the Pokrovsky Gate (presently Taganska Street building 58), was founded in 1635 (*Russkie monastyri* 376, Rak 358).

86. For a description of the city of Kashin, see endnote 49.

87. This area of Moscow was located in the eastern part of the city on the left bank of the Moscow River, between present-day Solianka Street, the embankment of the Moscow River, and the wall of Kitai-gorod (Baranov 608, Rak 358). Either Skorobogaty is a nickname, or this criminal was born into the right family: his name means "get rich quick."

88. This suburb was in northwest Moscow in the neighborhood of present-day Tver and Coachman Streets (Rak 358).

89. In the eighteenth century, Staritsa, which is on the Volga River 48 miles southwest of Tver, was well established as a major landing place on the water route to St. Petersburg (*Geografiia* 555). (In the novel, this city is called Staritsy, but given the geographic area that serves as the main locus of Kain's activities, the city of Staritsa is more likely the setting for the crime mentioned here.)

90. This office supervised the administration of Siberia from 1637 to 1727 and again from 1730 to 1763 (Wieczynski 29: 226).

91. The Monastery of the Holy Trinity and Saint Sergius (Troitsa-Sergeeva Lavra), located 44 miles north of Moscow, was established in 1337 by Saint Sergius of Radonezh, "the greatest spiritual leader of Russia during the fourteenth

century" (Wieczynski 39: 213). The monastery is connected with several prominent events in Russian history, including Dmitry Donskoi's defeat of the Mongols at Kulikovo Field in 1380 and its valiant refusal to surrender to two separate sieges laid by Polish invaders during the Time of Troubles (1598–1613) (Wieczynski 39: 214–15). The theft referred to in this account took place in a *podvor'e*, which is the term for a church established in a town (in this case Moscow) that belongs to a monastery located somewhere else.

92. "One of the most important monasteries in the Moscow region," New Maidens' (Novodevichy) Convent (see Appendix A) "was founded in 1524 by Grand Prince Vasily III of Moscow to commemorate the taking of Smolensk" (Wieczynski 25: 107).

93. This area was located in the western outskirts of the city, on the right bank of the bend in the Moscow River (Rak 359).

94. In the eighteenth century, *kompaneishchik* designated a person belonging to one of any number of groups or fields, ranging from business and the military to the theater and even robber gangs. Given the sum of money involved, Demidov was most likely a member of a trading or industrial association or perhaps a tax-farmer; that is, someone who had purchased the right to sell alcohol from the government (*Slovar' XVIII veka* 10: 123–24).

95. In his depiction of Kain's courtship and wedding, Komarov follows his source material, which does not accord with historical fact. Before he became a spy, Kain proposed to a soldier's widow, who, owing to his criminal occupation, coarsely refused him. In retribution, Kain denounced her to the authorities in his initial sweep of criminals on the night of December 27–28, 1741. She stubbornly remained in prison until 1743 when, fearing she would be tortured, she finally consented to marry Kain. After she became his wife, she took part in his criminal activities (Rak 359).

96. In the body of the text Komarov uses the recent (1698 [*Slovar' XVIII veka* 1: 74]) loanword *antipatiia*; he defines it in his footnote with the more established word *otvrashchenie*.

97. Rak identifies the persons Komarov mentions in his footnote: Dnski is Peter Donskoi, the clerk who accompanied Kain on his first sweep for criminals in the city of Moscow (see endnote 75), and Bgmlv is Ivan Bogomolov (359).

98. Margulis and Kholodnaya 22, 237–38; literally, "Repaired dishes live two lifetimes."

99. In contemporary Moscow this street is known as Varvarka (Rak 360).

100. Amvrosy (1708–71) was named Archbishop of Moscow in 1768 (Rak 359–60). A consistory is a church office in a diocese. "It consisted of religious and lay officials, . . . exercised control after the bishop, implemented the issuance of documents to the laity (certificates of marriage and others), and [served as] the court for parish clergy" (Belovinskii 213).

101. Traditionally, the day after a wedding the bride treated guests to vegetables (Rak 360).

102. Cheese Week (*syrnaia nedelia*) and *maslenitsa* denote the week

before the start of Lent in the Russian Orthodox calendar. The rough equivalent of Shrovetide in the Western church, it marks a time when meat is already prohibited, but dairy products can still be consumed before they are proscribed during Lent, hence the common Russian name for this period of *maslenitsa* (*maslo* means "butter" or "oil"). As Kain's creation of a snow mountain implies, during *maslenitsa* the faithful could still indulge in certain entertainments that would be inappropriate during Lent, and therefore it was a popular time to stage carnivals. In this regard *maslenitsa* is similar to carnival season in the West, which culminates in Mardi Gras (Fat Tuesday) on the day before Ash Wednesday. A snow or ice mountain of the type Kain had constructed was similar to a toboggan run. A tall wooden tower served as the upper anchor for a steeply sloping, curved ramp that could extend as far as two hundred feet. The ramp was covered with chunks of ice and then flooded with water to create a smooth gliding surface. Riders slid down the slope on small sleds or toboggans, and with the momentum they had gained on their downward run, they could glide as far as four hundred feet. The snow mountain was such an essential part of Russian winter carnivals that they were known among the masses as "under (or 'by') the mountains" (Kuznetsov, *Russkie narodnye gulian'ia* 25), and it was such a common form of entertainment that it crops up even in monuments of high culture, such as Tolstoy's *War and Peace* (592). Following the original text, the numbering of this episode repeats the number given to the previous section devoted to Kain's wedding.

103. *About King Solomon* was a popular dramatic parody on the subject of the wise and merciful justice of the biblical King Solomon. In keeping with the type of carnivalesque entertainment that would have appealed to a character like Kain, the roles of Solomon and his adversary were traditionally portrayed by two fools (Rak 360).

104. The carnivalesque penchant for denigrating official culture (see the introduction 21–25) permeates this episode, with the military being derided for the amusement of the crowd. The actor wears the white kerchief of a soldier or officer; he is punished according to the military-criminal code enacted by Peter the Great, an iconic figure of authority in eighteenth-century Russia; and the "major" overseeing the mockery of military order is the criminal Peter Wolf, who was eventually captured by the police and transported to the Department of Criminal Investigations along with Kain (Rak 360–61).

105. The Petrovsky Monastery was located north of the Kremlin and inside the present-day Boulevard Ring Road, at what is now Petrovka Street, 28 (Rak 361). Mantle Row, where merchants dealt in clothing (Baranov 608), must refer to one of the many rows of goods for sale in Kitai-gorod (see endnote 18).

106. Kain's sarcastic comment makes use of a play on two Russian words that share the same root: ***chernyi***, which is the word for "black" (the color of tar), and ***chernets***, which means "monk," or, more literally, "a person in black."

107. The Feast of St. Nicholas is celebrated twice during the year, on May 9 (May 22 NS) and December 6 (December 19 NS) (Baranov 608).

108. The Secret Imperial Office was the personal office of the Empress Elizabeth (reigned 1741–62). Ivan Antonovich (not Ivanovich) Cherkasov was

the empress's personal secret-office secretary. Ivan *Ivanovich* Cherkasov (1732–1811), the secretary's son, was still a boy at the time of the event depicted in this story. Later in life he served in high-ranking military positions (Rak 361).

109. The Russian word *luchina*, here rendered as "torch," is difficult to translate in one word. It designates a sliver of wood used to produce light or to ignite something (*Slovar' XVIII veka* 11: 249).

110. A city roughly 81 miles southeast of Tver (*Geografiia* 64).

111. See endnote 79.

112. A 364-man company of grenadiers belonging to the Preobrazhensky Life Guards Regiment (see endnote 34) (*Encyclopedia* 14: 488–89).

113. This was a Life Guards regiment formed by Peter the Great in 1687, the oldest in the Russian guards (*Encyclopedia* 23: 347, Baranov 609).

114. Founded at the beginning of the eleventh century by Yaroslav the Wise, Yaroslavl has a long and storied position in the annals of Russian history. Located on the land route from Moscow to Arkhangelsk, by the mid-eighteenth century it had already become a major center of manufacturing and commerce (*Geografiia* 696–97).

115. The Donskoi Monastery was founded in 1593 to commemorate Muscovy's defeat of the Crimean Tartar khan Kazi Girei. Located in the Russian capital of present-day Gagarin Square (Rak 361), this monastery enjoyed the protection of grand princes and tsars, which helped it to become one of the wealthiest monasteries in Russia. With its founding it also became the home of the revered icon of Our Lady of the Don, the icon Russians believed contributed to Dmitry Donskoi's victory over the Mongols at Kulikovo Field in 1380 (Wieczynski 9: 224).

116. See endnote 94.

117. The Office of Contraband Alcohol (Korchemnaia kontora) combated the illegal manufacture, transporting, and sale of alcohol, which was regulated by a state monopoly. In order to stop this activity, the authorities established checkpoints with military detachments at the entrances to cities, and cities were sometimes surrounded with ditches and ramparts. Illegal traders in alcohol were conscripted into the army or exiled to work in mines. If they were nobles, they were stripped of their rank, and for a repeat offense their estates were confiscated in favor of their heirs and they were deported to Siberia (Belovinskii 219–20).

118. Tsaritsyn Meadow (see Appendix A) was located on the right bank of the Moscow River across from the Kremlin, in the area that is now known as Bolotnaia (Swamp) Square (Rak 361–62).

119. The Maidens' Convent of the Passion (Strastnoi devichii monastyr') was located in Moscow near the Tver Gates, on the sight of present-day Pushkin Square (*Russkie monastyri* 378–79, Rak 362).

120. In his roundabout way, Kain is saying that, like the woman who gave birth to her, the nun would rather enjoy all the pleasures of life instead of being locked away in a convent.

121. See endnote 22 and Appendix A.

122. The Ascension (Voznesensky) Convent was located in the Kremlin near Spassky Tower (Rak 362).

123. For a description of a caftan, see endnote 15. In addition, the skirts of the military version could be pulled up and buttoned on the sides to aid in horseback riding and wearing a sword (Belovinskii 190).

124. Count Shuvalov (1710–62) was a senator and lieutenant general (Rak 362).

125. Kain recites the first part of a Russian proverb. In its entirety it reads: "The kite has flown beyond the sea and has not come back a swan" (Mertvago 99, Margulis and Kholodnaya 181). In other words, the lesson Kain draws from the relationship between Sovetov and the nun is that there is no changing who you are, since the nun, no matter how she is dressed, is first of all a woman.

126. The Wolf (Peter Wolf) is the same figure who played the mocking role of major in the carnivalesque beating of the character of the "thief" after the performance of the parodic play *King Solomon* (see endnotes 103 and 104). Like the Wolf, the Monk and the Hat were also arrested sometime later and transported along with Kain from the Moscow police to the Department of Criminal Investigations (Rak 362).

127. Shinkarko was yet another member of Kain's gang who is listed as having been transported with him in fetters from the Moscow police to the Department of Criminal Investigations (Rak 363).

128. These gates were located in the Zariadie section of Moscow. See endnote 76.

129. Lace Row was most likely one of the rows of shops and stalls located in Kitai-gorod. At the time of Kain's tale, Kaluga was a well-established trading post on the Oka River situated approximately 120 miles southwest of Moscow. In 1606–7 "it was the center of the peasant uprising under the leadership of Ivan Bolotnikov" (*Geografiia* 228).

130. See endnote 25.

131. The proceedings of Kain's criminal case state that this underground enterprise was located in three houses under Kain's protection and that he exacted tribute from the ringleaders in the form of money, silver ingots, and goods made from gold (Rak 363).

132. Gorokhovo (Pea) Field is an outlying district of Moscow located to the east beyond the embankment of Zemlianyi gorod (present-day Zemliany Embankment Street) in the neighborhood of present-day Kazakov Street (Rak 363).

133. The St. John the Baptist (Ivanovsky-Predtechensky) Convent, located in Moscow to the east of Kitai-gorod near Solianka Street (contemporary address: 2 Ivanovsky Monastery Lane), has existed from at least the sixteenth century. It is the repository of the wonder-working icon of St. John the Baptist (*Russkie monastyri* 378, Rak 363, Baranov 609).

134. The holy day mentioned here, which corresponds to Pentecost in the West, is celebrated on the fiftieth day after Easter and commemorates the descent of the Holy Spirit upon the disciples (Wieczynski 32: 130, *Historical*

Dictionary 128). The Zhivoi Bridge was a wooden pontoon bridge located where the Bolshoi Moskvoretsky Bridge is today (Rak 363).

135. Kain is more grasping than his humble words imply. The first part of his response paraphrases a proverb that more literally means: "Once you've become a priest, you need to officiate at funerals." In other words, Kain is prompting the grateful merchant to follow through on his responsibility to pay him a reward. An English-language equivalent of the Russian proverb might be "Once you pledge, don't hedge" (Margulis and Kholodnaya 186).

136. See endnote 92.

137. The merchant's wife is referring to a sect of flagellants connected with the St. John the Baptist Convent who were led by the serf and False Christ Andrei Petrov (Rak 364). They preached a life of asceticism, self-inflicted bodily pain, and ecstatic forms of worship and did not recognize a distinction between clergy and laity. For the most part, the sect comprised peasants who labored under the quitrent system of Russian serfdom (Artem'eva and Zamaleev 287). By referring to Petrov as Andriushka (the suffix –úshka is pejorative), Komarov is expressing his disdain for him and strongly implying that he is an impostor, a charge the narrator will make explicitly later in the section.

Andriushka is leading the life of what the Russians call a holy fool or fool in Christ (*iurodivyi*), a term that designates "a class of saints and a type of asceticism." Holy foolishness began in the Greek church and is known in the West but was most widespread in Russia (*Historical Dictionary* 133). Holy fools "often employed shockingly unconventional behavior or imitation of insanity to challenge complacently accepted values, to deliver unpalatable prophecies or other teaching and to cloak their own sanctity, so deflecting worldly honor. St. Basil's cathedral in Red Square is named for a holy fool, Basil of Mangazeia (d. 1552)" (*Blackwell Dictionary* 233). Thompson notes that prior to the Bolshevik Revolution, "the inhabitants of practically every sizable Russian town or village included a strange-looking person called . . . a *iurodivy* (holy fool)" (1). In real life, the "mad monk" Grigory Rasputin, who was notorious for ingratiating himself into the household of Tsar Nicholas II and his wife Alexandra, is perhaps the most well known of all Russian holy fools (Thompson 3–5); in literature, prominent examples of this type include Grisha in Tolstoy's first published work, the novella *Childhood*, and Stinking Liza in Dostoevsky's *The Brothers Karamazov*.

138. Levashev (1667–1751) was a general-in-chief, senator, and, in the late 1740s, the top-ranking official in the city of Moscow (Rak 364, Baranov 609).

139. In the eighteenth century the Tagansky region, which is a central district of contemporary Moscow located between the Boulevard and Sadovaia Ring Roads, consisted of numerous neighborhoods where various artisans lived and worked (Aver'ianov 101–2).

140. This tower, which was constructed at the initiative of Peter the Great and located at the site of present-day Sukharev Square, housed the Schools of Mathematics and Navigation. It was taken down in 1934 (Baranov 609, Rak 364).

141. See endnote 118.

142. Rogervik is a bay in the western reaches of the south shore of the Gulf

of Finland, where in 1723 Peter the Great founded the city of Baltic (Baltiisky) Port. Located in present-day Estonia, the city is now called Paldiski (Rak 364).

143. The function of the Holy Synod, which was created at the behest of Peter the Great, was "both to rule and reform the church." It was "the central administrative organ of the Russian Orthodox Church from 1721 to 1917" (Wieczynski 14: 75).

144. Despite the statement made in this sentence, the so-called Kain songs were not included in the first printing of Komarov's version of *Vanka Kain*, which serves as the model for this translation. These songs were included in the second printing of the tale, which came out later the same year.

145. The historical record of Kain's downfall differs in some details from the account given here. "According to the investigation into his case, Kain was arrested on the complaint of Fyodor Tarasov Zevakhin, a soldier of the Kolomensky Regiment, whose fifteen-year-old daughter he had enticed from her home through deceitful means and raped on January 17, 1749" (Rak 365). As a young man, General Tatishchev (1697–1760) had been an orderly to Peter the Great (Rak 366).

146. For a definition of what constituted a crime against the sovereign, see endnote 21. This event occurred on February 1, 1749 (Rak 366).

147. Branding and the slashing of nostrils were common punishments in the eighteenth century for any number of crimes and usually preceded a sentence of hard labor. The intent was to leave the criminal with an indelible mark of shame that would also serve as a warning to others (Hughes 130, 171).

"Poor Liza"

1. The narrator is referring to the Simonov Monastery of the Assumption (see Appendix A), which was founded about 1379 and, like many Russian monasteries, also served as a line of defense against invaders, in this case guarding "the Russian capital from the side along the Moscow River and the Brashevskaia Road" (Wieczynski 35: 132). Pumpianskii notes that the phrase "gloomy Gothic towers" shows Karamzin's indebtedness to European Sentimentalism in that such an image "would be more appropriate for the description of a Catholic abbey than an Orthodox monastery" (435).

2. "Founded in 1282 on the right bank of the Moscow River," the Danilov Monastery (see Appendix A) "played an important role in the defense of Moscow from incursions by the forces of the Crimean Tatars," and it was here that the rebellion of Ivan Bolotnikov and his peasant army was defeated in 1607 (Wieczynski 8: 179, 5: 64–68). Before he begins to tell Liza's story, the narrator calls to mind several places, events, and eras associated with the darker pages of Russian history in order to establish an atmosphere of foreboding. Note his reflection on Russia's struggles against the Tartars (Mongols) and Lithuanians in the next paragraph.

3. Divided by deep ravines and home to deciduous forests, the Sparrow Hills (see Appendix A) form the steep right bank of the Moscow River, rising over two hundred feet above the surface of the water in what is present-day southwestern Moscow (*Geografiia* 127).

4. The village of Kolomenskoe (see Appendix A), now part of the city of Moscow, was "the site of one of the palaces used by the princes of Moscow, a wooden structure that was the eminent accomplishment of Russian architecture during the seventeenth century. Peter the Great was often at this palace during his childhood years. When the palace fell into decay, it was ordered torn down by Catherine II in 1767" (Wieczynski 17: 130), roughly five years after the time established in this story.

5. The Tartars, or Mongols, invaded Russia in 1237 and devastated Russian society for the next 150 to 250 years (Riasanovsky and Steinberg 63–71). Lithuania had been an enemy of Russia as early as the eleventh century. Conflict intensified in the fifteenth and sixteenth centuries when the Russians vied first with Lithuania and then after 1569 with a united Polish-Lithuanian state for influence in Ukraine, Belo-Russia, and Western Russia (Riasanovsky and Steinberg 123–28). Toporov notes that by immediately preceding the beginning of Liza's story with the narrator's contemplation of the scenes painted on the monastery walls, Karamzin associates the tale of his heroine with real events taking place in real time. In essence, the two stories are juxtaposed "like two variants of the reflection of 'the historical': the old and the new, the strictly 'historical' and 'the novelistic,' the collective and the personal-individual" (166). As Kahn emphasizes, Karamzin had already explored such a narrative perspective in detail in his earlier work *Letters of a Russian Traveler* (460–61).

6. The epithet used here—*bednaia*—had several meanings in eighteenth-century Russian, all of which apply to Karamzin's heroine. In addition to "poor" they include "modest," "frail," "unhappy," "unfortunate," "wretched," and "miserable" (*Slovar' XVIII veka* 1: 157–58).

7. Karamzin's selection of this adjective (in Russian, *chuvstvitel'naia*) underscores that Liza's mother is just as much an archetype of Sentimentalism as is her daughter. It is based on the root meaning "feeling" or "emotion" and can also be translated as "sentimental." In the *Dictionary of the Russian Academy* (1794), the noun form of this concept was defined as "'Compassion, the quality of a person who is moved by the unhappiness of another. Compassion of the heart'" (Kochetkova, *Sentimentalizm* 18), which is one of the cornerstones of Karamzin's Sentimentalist philosophy.

8. Although Liza's mother has only her daughter's best interests at heart, the verb she uses (*pokinut'*), translated here as "leave," also contains the darker shadings of "to abandon or forsake," which hint at Liza's vulnerable position in life and foreshadow further twists in the plot.

9. Daughter of Zeus and Hera, Hebe was the goddess of youth and spring and the cupbearer who brought nectar and ambrosia to the gods of Olympus (Gushchina et al. 123).

10. Even though the narrator says that Erast listens "attentively" to Liza's mother, Toporov already detects a faint note of insincerity in the young man's character. He contends that "Erast listens to the mother's story with, so to speak, just one ear open (the author's 'and so on, and so on' [in the previous line] hints at a certain indifference and lack of interest in this information, a distancing of

himself from it) although he preserves a sense of propriety and attentiveness, or, rather, the semblance of it" (174–75).

11. Toporov considers the subtle description of Liza's pinching her sleeve in reaction to Erast's attentions as one of those flourishes that made Karamzin such a groundbreaking author: "And right here . . . is something that is unprecedented for the 18th century, that takes one's breath away with its laconism and psychological insight, . . . [it is] a sign of confusion, delight, [and] inner rapture which is being suppressed only with great difficulty" (175). Toporov adds that this description anticipates two famous lines of verse from one of the greatest Russian poets of the twentieth century. In "The Song of Our Last Meeting," Anna Akhmatova alludes to the disturbed state of mind of the poem's persona by writing, "Onto my right hand / I placed the glove for my left."

12. Zephyrus, the West wind and its god in Greek mythology, often rages in Homer, as it does in the poem "Ode to the West Wind" by one of Karamzin's contemporaries, Percy Bysshe Shelley. By the eighteenth century, however, this god was also depicted "as warm and gentle, with his name surviving in our word 'zephyr,' meaning a soft and pleasant breeze. It was with this nature that he was seen as the lover of *Flora*, goddess of spring and flowers, who was transformed from the nymph Chloris at his touch, just as the cold earth is transformed in spring at the warm touch of the West Wind" (March 399). Karamzin is no doubt alluding to the gentler, procreative nature of the zephyrs, as Liza is deeply affected by Erast's attentions (she falls in love, conceals this liaison from her mother, and strives to overcome the social taboo of desiring a nobleman) and will eventually surrender to his blandishments.

13. With this reference to Cynthia, Karamzin again emphasizes the innocence of the present encounter between Erast and Liza while also presaging the sexual element that is yet to surface. Cynthia is one of the names of the Roman goddess Diana (Greek, Artemis), who "was considered the goddess of both virgin purity and chastity as well as vegetation and fruitfulness" (Gushchina et al. 51). "The daughter of Jupiter and the twin of Apollo, she had strong associations as a fertility deity and was invoked by women to aid both conception and childbirth" (Dixon-Kennedy 110). Diana/Artemis is also associated with the moon, which the narrator links to Liza in the preceding sentence.

14. Toporov contrasts Erast's echo of the phrase "we will" with Liza's repetition of such important concepts as "believe," "assure," "remember," and "love." While Liza's words have deep significance for the couple, Erast's use of repetitions "at times reveals the hero's unconscious intention to escape from the heart of the matter, to reduce it to a formal device, to something like 'yes, yes, certainly,' which means incomparably less than an unadorned 'yes'" (56).

15. Karamzin expresses this thought more directly in a later version of the story, stating that "fulfillment of *all* desires is the most dangerous trial of love" (*Sochineniia* 1: 515).

16. "A Russian gold coin introduced in 1755 which was worth ten rubles" (*Slovar' XVIII veka* 9: 85).

WORKS CITED

Texts Used as the Sources for the Translations in this Collection

Chulkov, Mikhail Dmitrievich. *Prigozhaia povarikha, ili Pokhozhdenie razvratnoi zhenshchiny* [*The Comely Cook, or The Adventures of a Debauched Woman*]. Part 1. St. Petersburg: Morskoi kadetskii korpus, 1770. Print.

Karamzin, Nikolai Mikhailovich. "Bednaia Liza" ["Poor Liza"]. *Moskovskii zhurnal* Book 3 (June 1792): 239–77. Print.

Komarov, Matvei. *Obstoiatel'nyia i vernyia istorii dvukh moshennikov: pervago rossiiskago slavnago vora, razboinika i byvshago moskovskago syshchika Van'ki Kaina so vsemi ego syskami, rozyskami sumozbrodnoiu svad'boiu i zabavnymi raznymi ego pesniami, i portretom ego . . .* [*The True and Detailed Histories of Two Scoundrels: The First Being the Famous Russian Thief, Robber, and Former Moscow Police Spy Vanka Kain with All of His Investigations, Inquests, Madcap Wedding, and Various Humorous Songs and with His Portrait . . .*]. St. Petersburg: Senatskaia tipografiia, 1779. Print.

Other Primary Texts by Chulkov, Komarov, and Karamzin

Chulkov, Mikhail Dmitrievich. *Peresmeshnik, ili Slavenskiia skazki* [*The Mocker, or Slavic Tales*]. Part 1. Moscow: Ponomarev, 1789. Print.

Karamzin, Nikolai Mikhailovich. "Bednaia Liza" ["Poor Liza"]. *Sochineniia* 1: 506–19. Print.

———. "Chto nuzhno avtoru?" ["What Does an Author Need?"]. *Sochineniia* 2: 60–62. Print.

———. "O knizhnoi torgovle i liubvi k chteniiu v Rossii" ["On the Book Trade and the Love for Reading in Russia"]. *Sochineniia* 2: 117–20. Print.

———. *Sochineniia v dvukh tomakh.* 2 vols. Leningrad: Khudozhestvennaia literatura, 1984. Print.

Komarov, Matvei. *Nevidimka. Istoriia o fetsskom koroleviche Aridese i o brate ego Polumedese s raznymi liubopytnymi povestiami* [*Nevidimka. The History of the Fetsskian Prince Arides and His Brother Polumedes with Various Curious Stories*]. Moscow: Reshetnikov, 1789. Print.

———. *Povest' o prikliuchenii aglinskago milorda Georga i o brandeburgskoi markgrafine Friderike Luize* [*The Tale of the Adventures of the English Milord George and the Brandenburg Margravine Friderika Louisa*]. St. Petersburg: Shnor, 1782. Print.

Modern Russian Editions of Source Texts with Notes and Commentaries

Artem'eva, T. V., and A. F. Zamaleev, ed. *Prigozhaia povarikha, ili Pokhozhdenie razvratnoi zhenshchiny*. By Mikhail Chulkov. St. Petersburg: Lenizdat, 1992. Print.

Baranov, Sergei, ed. *Van'ka Kain*. By Matvei Komarov. Moscow: Èksmo, 2008. Print.

Rak, V. D., ed. *Istoriia moshennika Van'ki Kaina; Milord Georg*. By Matvei Komarov. St. Petersburg: Zhurnal "Neva"/Letnii sad, 2000. Print.

Stepanov, V., comp. *Mikhail Chulkov. Prigozhaia povarikha, ili Pokhozhdenie razvratnoi zhenshchiny*. Moscow: Èksmo, 2008. Print.

Secondary Sources and Supporting Material

Anderson, Roger B. *The Teller in the Tale: A Study in Narrative Technique*. Houston: Cordovan Press, 1974. Print.

Aver'ianov, K. A., ed. *Istoriia moskovskikh raionov: èntsiklopediia*. Moscow: Astrel', 2005. Print.

Baehr, Stephen L. "Kheraskov, Mikhail Matveevich." Terras 222. Print.

———. *The Paradise Myth in Eighteenth-Century Russian Culture*. Stanford: Stanford University Press, 1991. Print.

Bakhtin, Mikhail. *Rabelais and His World*. Trans. Hélène Iswolsky. Cambridge, MA: M.I.T. Press, 1968. Print.

Becker, Christopher. "*Raznochintsy*: The Development of the Word and the Concept." *American Slavic and East European Review* 18 (1959): 63–74. Print.

Belovinskii, L. V., comp. *Rossiiskii istoriko-bytovoi slovar'*. Moscow: Studiia "TRITÈ" Nikity Mikhalkova, "Rossiiskii arkhiv," 1999. Print.

Beshenkovskii, E. B. "Zhizn' Fedora Èmina." *N. I. Novikov i obshchestvenno-literaturnoe dvizhenie ego vremeni*. Vol. 11 of *XVIII Vek*. Leningrad: Nauka, 1976. 186–203. Print.

The Blackwell Dictionary of Eastern Christianity. Ed. Ken Parry, David J. Melling, Dimitri Brady, Sidney H. Griffith and John F. Healy. Oxford: Blackwell Publishers, 1999. Print.

Brown, William Edward. *A History of 18th Century Russian Literature*. Ann Arbor, MI: Ardis, 1980. Print.

———. *A History of Seventeenth-Century Russian Literature*. Ann Arbor, MI: Ardis, 1980. Print.

Budgen, D. E. "The Concept of Fiction in Eighteenth-Century Russian Letters." *Great Britain and Russia in the Eighteenth Century: Contacts and Comparisons*. Ed. A. G. Cross. Newtonville, MA: Oriental Research Partners, 1979. 65–74. Print.

Bunson, Matthew. *Encyclopedia of the Roman Empire*. New York: Facts on File, 1994. Print.

Collins, Samuel. *The Present State of Russia. In a Letter to a Friend at London;
Written by an Eminent Person Residing at the Great Tzar's Court at
Moscow for the Space of Nine Years.* London: John Winter, 1671. Print.

Cracraft, James. *The Petrine Revolution in Russian Culture.* Cambridge, MA:
Belknap Press of Harvard University Press, 2004. Print.

———. *The Revolution of Peter the Great.* Cambridge, MA: Harvard University Press, 2003. Print.

Cross, A. G. *N. M. Karamzin: A Study of His Literary Career, 1783–1803.* Carbondale, IL: Southern Illinois University Press, 1971. Print.

Defoe, Daniel. *The Fortunes and Misfortunes of the Famous Moll Flanders.*
Harmondsworth, England: Penguin Books, 1985. Print.

Dixon-Kennedy, Mike. *Encyclopedia of Greco-Roman Mythology.* Santa Barbara, CA: ABC-CLIO, 1998. Print.

Garrard, J. G. *Mixail Čulkov: An Introduction to His Prose and Verse.* The Hague: Mouton, 1970. Print.

———. "Narrative Technique in Chulkov's *Prigozhaia povarikha.*" *Slavic Review* 27.4 (December 1968): 554–63. Print.

Gasperetti, David. *The Rise of the Russian Novel: Imitation, Stylization, and
Mockery of the West.* DeKalb, IL: Northern Illinois University Press, 1998. Print.

Geografiia Rossii: èntsiklopediia. Ed. A. P. Gorkin. Moscow: Nauchnoe izdatel'stvo "Bol'shaia rossiiskaia èntsiklopediia," 1998. Print.

Goodliffe, J. D. "Some Comments on Narrative Prose Fiction in Eighteenth Century Russian Literature with Special Reference to Chulkov." *Melbourne Slavonic Studies* 5–6 (1971): 124–36. Print.

Great Soviet Encyclopedia. 32 vols. New York: Macmillan, 1973–83. Print.

Gushchina, E. V., and I. V. Kolosova, S. V. Koshevarova, A. K. Lukina, N. E.
Medvedeva, N. F. Petriakova, N. S. Rokotian, M. S. Sitkina, and S. G.
Kholod, ed. *Slovar' antichnosti.* Transl. from German by V. I. Gorbushin,
L. I. Gratsianskaia, I. I. Kovaleva, O. L. Levinskaia, G. A. Nikolaev, I. V.
Rozanov, A. A. Rossius, V. K. Starikov, A. R. Shaverdian, and A. Ia. Iarin.
Moscow: Progress, 1989. Print.

Hammarberg, Gitta. *From the Idyll to the Novel: Karamzin's Sentimentalist
prose.* Cambridge: Cambridge University Press, 1991. Print.

Harmon, William. *A Handbook to Literature.* 12th ed. Boston: Longman, 2012. Print.

Historical Dictionary of the Orthodox Church. Ed. Michael Prokurat, Alexander Golitsin, and Michael D. Peterson. Lanham, MD: Scarecrow Press, 1996. Print.

Honderich, Ted, ed. *The Oxford Companion to Philosophy.* Oxford: Oxford University Press, 1995. Print.

Hughes, Lindsey. *Russia in the Age of Peter the Great.* New Haven: Yale University Press, 1998. Print.

Istoriia Moskvy: period feodalizma XVIII veka. Ed. S. V. Bakhrushin, B. B. Kafengauz, P. K. Alefirenko, and E. N. Kusheva. Vol. 2. Moscow: Akademiia nauk, 1953. Print.

Kahn, Andrew, trans. and ed. *Letters of a Russian Traveler.* By Nikolai Karamzin. Oxford: Voltaire Foundation, 2003. Print.

Kochetkova, Natalya (N. D.) *Literatura russkogo sentimentalizma (Èsteticheskie i khudozhestvennye iskaniia).* St. Petersburg: Nauka, 1994. Print.

——. *Nikolay Karamzin.* Boston: Twayne, 1975. Print.

Kukushkina, E. D. "Perevodnaia novella v rukopisnykh sbornikakh XVIII veka." *Russkaia literatura XVIII veka-nachala XIX veka v obshchest-venno-kul'turnom kontekste.* Ed. A. M. Panchenko. Leningrad: Nauka, 1983. 180–92. Print.

Kuznetsov, Evgenii. *Iz proshlogo russkoi èstrady: istoricheskie ocherki.* Moscow: Iskusstvo, 1958. Print.

——, comp. *Russkie narodnye gulian'ia po rasskazam A. Ia. Alekseeva-Iakovleva.* Leningrad: Iskusstvo, 1948. Print.

LeBlanc, Ronald D. *The Russianization of "Gil Blas": A Study in Literary Appropriation.* Columbus, OH: Slavica, 1986. Print.

Levitsky, Alexander. "Mikhail Chulkov's *The Comely Cook*: The Symmetry of a Hoax." *Russian Literature Triquarterly* 21.2 (1988): 97–115. Print.

Levitt, Marcus C. "'Women's Wiles' in Chulkov's *The Comely Cook.*" To be published in *Seeing Satire,* ed. Kelly Malone and Elizabeth Mansfield. Studies on Voltaire and the Eighteenth Century. Oxford: Voltaire Foundation. Print.

Lomonosov, M. V. *Kratkoe rukovodstvo k krasnorechii [A Brief Introduction to Rhetoric].* Vol. 7 of *Polnoe sobranie sochinenii.* Moscow: Akademiia nauk, 1952. 89–378. Print.

March, Jenny. *Cassell Dictionary of Classical Mythology.* London: Cassell, 1998. Print.

Marker, Gary. *Publishing, Printing, and the Origins of Intellectual Life in Russia, 1700–1800.* Princeton: Princeton University Press, 1985. Print.

Margulis, Alexander, and Asya Kholodnaya. *Russian-English Dictionary of Proverbs and Sayings.* Jefferson, NC: McFarland & Company, 2000. Print.

Mertvago, Peter. *The Comparative Russian-English Dictionary of Russian Proverbs and Sayings.* New York: Hippocrene Books, 1995. Print.

Michurin, Ivan. *Plan imperatorskago stolichnago goroda Moskvy sochinennoi pod smotreniem arkhitektora Ivana Michurina v 1739 godu [Map of the Imperial City of Moscow Composed under the Supervision of the Architect Ivan Michurin in 1739].* Library of Congress, Geography and Map Division. Library of Congress. n.d. Web. 03 June 2010.

Moiseeva, G. N., and I. Z. Serman. "Zarozhdenie romana v russkoi literature XVIII veka." *Istoriia russkogo romana.* Vol. 1. Ed. G. M. Fridlender. Moscow: Akademiia nauk, 1962. Print.

Morris, Marcia A. *The Literature of Roguery in Seventeenth- and Eighteenth-Century Russia.* Evanston, IL: Northwestern University Press, 2000. Print.

Nebel, Henry M., Jr. *N. M. Karamzin: A Russian Sentimentalist.* The Hague: Mouton, 1967. Print.

Nikolaev, S. I. *Literaturnaia kul'tura Petrovskoi èpokhi*. Studiorum Slavicorum Monumenta. St. Petersburg: Dmitrii Bulanin, 1996. Print.

Orwin, Donna Tussing. *Consequences of Consciousness: Turgenev, Dostoevsky, and Tolstoy*. Stanford: Stanford University Press, 2007. Print.

Ovsianikov, Iurii. *Lubok: russkie narodnye kartinki XVII–XVIII vv.* Moscow: Sovetskii khudozhnik, n.d. Print.

Page, Tanya. "Emin, Fyodor Aleksandrovich." Terras 124. Print.

———. "Karamzin, Nikolai Mikhailovich." Terras 215–17. Print.

———. "Sentimentalism." Terras 395–97. Print.

Parlett, David. *The Oxford Guide to Card Games*. Oxford: Oxford University Press, 1990. Print.

Pascal, Blaise. *Pensées*. Trans. A. J. Krailsheimer. London: Penguin Books, 1966. Print.

Paxton, John. *Encyclopedia of Russian History*. Santa Barbara, CA: ABC-CLIO, Inc., 1993. Print.

Peskov, A. M. "Sumarokov i Bualo." *Nauchnye doklady vysshei shkoly: filologicheskie nauki* 2 (1982): 73–77. Print.

Picchio, Riccardo. "Minei Chet'i." Terras 282. Print.

"Pouchitel'naia vsiakaia vsiachina." *Literaturnaia gazeta*. Literaturnaia gazeta, n.d. Web. 19 March 2010.

Pumpianskii, L. V. "Sentimentalizm." *Istoriia russkoi literatury*. Vol. 4. Moscow: Akademiia nauk, 1947. 430–45. Print.

"Rabotki, Russia." *MSN Encarta Atlas*. MSN Encarta, n.d. Web. 06 August 2009.

Raeff, Marc. "The Enlightenment in Russia and Russian Thought in the Enlightenment." *The Eighteenth Century in Russia*. Ed. J. G. Garrard. Oxford: The Clarendon Press, 1973. 25–47. Print.

Raymond, Boris, and Paul Duffy. *Historical Dictionary of Russia*. Lanhan, MD: The Scarecrow Press, Inc., 1998. Print.

Riasanovsky, Nicholas V., and Mark D. Steinberg. *A History of Russia*. 7th ed. New York: Oxford University Press, 2005. Print.

Rice, Christopher, and Melanie Rice. *Eyewitness Moscow*. New York: DK Publishing, Inc., 1998. Print.

Rovinskii, D. *Russkiia narodnyia kartinki*. Vol. 5. St. Petersburg: Akademiia nauk, 1881. Print.

Russkie monastyri: tsentral'naia chast' Rossii. Ed. Anatolii Feoktistov. n.c.: Ocharovannyi strannik, 1995. Print.

Schaarschmidt, Gunter. "The Lubok Novels: Russia's Immortal Best Sellers." *Canadian Review of Comparative Literature* 9.3 (Sept. 1982): 424–36. Print.

Scherr, Barry P. *Russian Poetry: Meter, Rhythm, and Rhyme*. Berkeley, CA: University of California Press, 1986. Print.

Segel, Harold B. "Classicism and Classical Antiquity in Eighteenth- and Nineteenth-Century Russian Literature." *The Eighteenth Century in Russia*. Ed. J. G. Garrard. Oxford: The Clarendon Press, 1973. 48–71. Print.

————, ed. *The Literature of Eighteenth-Century Russia: An Anthology of Russian Literary Materials of the Age of Classicism and the Enlightenment....* Vol. 1. New York: Dutton, 1967. Print.

Shklovskii, Viktor. *Matvei Komarov: zhitel' goroda Moskvy.* Leningrad: Priboi, 1929. Print.

Silbajoris, Frank R. "Lomonosov, Mikhailo Vasilievich." Terras 264–65. Print.

Slovar' russkogo iazyka XVIII veka. Ed. Iu. S. Sorokin. 17 vols. Leningrad/St. Petersburg: Nauka, 1984–2007. Print.

Slovar' sovremennogo russkogo literaturnogo iazyka. 17 vols. Moscow: Nauka, 1950–65. Print.

Sumarokov, A. P. "Èpistola o stikhotvorstve" ["Epistle on Poetry"]. *A. P. Sumarokov: izbrannye proizvedeniia.* Ed. P. N. Berkov. Leningrad: Sovetskii pisatel', 1957. 115–25. Print.

————. "Pis'mo o chtenii romanov" ["Letter on the Reading of Novels"]. *Polnoe sobranie vsekh sochinenii.* Vol. 6. Moscow: Universitetskaia tipografiia u N. Novikova, 1787. 350–51. Print.

Svodnyi katalog russkoi knigi grazhdanskoi pechati XVIII veka, 1725–1800. 5 vols. Moscow: Kniga, 1963–67. Print.

Terras, Victor. *Handbook of Russian Literature.* New Haven, CT: Yale University Press, 1985. Print.

Thompson, Ewa M. *Understanding Russian Culture: The Holy Fool in Russian Culture.* Lanham, MD: University Press of America, 1987. Print.

Titunik, I. R. "Fedor Èmin's *Pis'ma Èrnesta i Doravry* and Jean-Jacques Rousseau's *Julie, ou La Nouvelle Héloïse." Russian Literature* 34 (1993): 333–50. Print.

————. "Matvei Komarov's *Van'ka Kain* and 18th-Century Russian Prose Fiction." *Slavic and East European Journal* 18.4 (1974): 341–56. Print.

Tolstoy, Leo. *L. N. Tolstoi: polnoe sobranie sochinenii.* Vol. 8. Moscow: Khudozhestvennaia literatura, 1936. Print.

————. *War and Peace.* Trans. Richard Pevear and Larissa Volokhonsky. New York: Knopf, 2007. Print.

Toporov, V. N. *"Bednaia Liza" Karamzina. Opyt prochteniia.* Moscow: Rossiiskii gosudarstvennyi gumanitarnyi universitet, 1995. Print.

Tosi, Alessandra. *Waiting for Pushkin: Russian Fiction in the Reign of Alexander I (1801–1825).* Amsterdam: Rodopi, 2006. Print.

"V Moskve na Bol'shoi Molchanovke eshche v nachale XX veka stoiala tserkov'. . . ." Otvety@mail.ru. Mail.Ru, n.d. Web. 19 March 2010.

Wieczynski, Joseph L., ed. *The Modern Encyclopedia of Russian and Soviet History.* 60 vols. Gulf Breeze, FL: Academic International Press, 1976–94. Print.

Zapadov, A. V. "Zhurnal M. D. Chulkova *I to i s'o* i ego literaturnoe okruzhenie." *XVIII vek.* Vol. 2. Moscow: Nauka, 1940. 95–141. Print.

Zhivov, Viktor. *Language and Culture in Eighteenth-Century Russia.* Trans. Marcus Levitt. Boston: Academic Studies Press, 2009. Print.